THE
50
GREATEST
FOOTBALL
MATCHES

THE TIMES

50 GREATEST FOOTBALL MATCHES

EDITED BY RICHARD WHITEHEAD

The History Press

*Cover Illustration:*based off an original photograph by Gerry Cranham/Offside Photography.

First published 2019
This paperback edition first published 2023

The History Press
97 St George's Place
Cheltenham Gloucestershire, GL 50 3QB
www.thehistorypress.co.uk

British Library Cataloguing in Publication Data.
A catalogue record for this book is available from the British Library.

ISBN 978 1 80399 557 1

Typesetting and origination by The History Press
Printed and bound by TJ Books Limited, Padstow, Cornwall

CONTENTS

FOREWORD

BY HENRY WINTER
CHIEF FOOTBALL WRITER, *THE TIMES*

GEOFFREY GREEN'S CLASSIC account of England's humiliation by Hungary in 1953 still stands as one of the most important, agenda-setting pieces of writing on football. This was the match that changed the game forever, and Green immediately realised its significance and captured it perfectly.

He understood that English football now needed to change direction to keep pace with the new game played by the likes of the Magical Magyars. The headline on Green's piece, "A New Conception of Football", was a challenge to the cradle of the sport to modernise or risk sliding towards the grave. It was such a momentous day that Green begins his epic piece with, effectively, a dateline. "Yesterday by 4 o'clock on a grey winter's afternoon within the bowl of Wembley Stadium…" He builds and builds like a grand lawyer, presenting the case for the prosecution with portents and ceremony. And then it comes, the sledgehammer conclusion to the sentence swinging down: "the inevitable had happened." I defy anybody not to read on. We knew the scene of the crime, and the time. But what had happened? And why was it inevitable?

It is gripping reporting, compelling in leading the reader into a piece that will alter history. The byline was simply "From Our Association Football Correspondent", but this was vintage Green, with the subtle reminder of his authority as one of the great voices of the game: "To those who had seen the shadows of the recent years creeping closer and closer there was perhaps no real surprise." What had happened? Again the suspense, and then came the answer:

"England were at last beaten by the foreign invader on English soil." And then it flowed, tributes to the quality of Ferenc Puskas and Nandor Hidegkuti. The sublime, informing opening paragraph – the shop window to lure the reader in – climaxes with a sentence that felt carved from finest marble: "Here, indeed, did we attend, all 100,000 of us, the twilight of the gods."

Green captured history unfolding, not with the benefit of hindsight, but instantly. He conjured up beautiful imagery, describing England as "strangers in a strange world, a world of flitting red spirits", which eloquently emphasised his central point. "English football can be proud of its past but it must awake to a new future," he concluded.

The best match reports balance passion and perspective, revelling in the moment and the sport, yet also able to take a step back and understand the ramifications, just as Green did in 1953. With Alf Ramsey on the pitch and Ron Greenwood and Bobby Robson looking on, a swathe of future England coaches were given insight into this "new conception of football".

One of Green's most famous lines, describing Billy Wright as resembling "a fire engine going to the wrong fire" after being wrongfooted by Puskas, is frequently attributed to his match report when on the day he wrote about Puskas "evading a tackle" with "sheer jugglery". The fire engines don't arrive on the scene for nineteen years and Green's book *Great Moments in Sport: Soccer*.

That book was required reading at school. I grew up devouring Green's work in *The Times* just before he retired in 1976. Rereading some of his reports in the book made it seem like the perfect life, watching football and exploring the world. He is still a legend to match reporters, not least for his extrovert approach to his time on earth. Green was as fearless in life as in prose, once playing *Moon River* on the harmonica in front of prime minister Harold Wilson and Ramsey. On another occasion, while needing a crutch after a leg injury, he turned up to matches with a stuffed parrot on his shoulder. We'd get trolled on social media for that now, and certainly have the parrot confiscated by stadium security.

Green's words ring throughout the decades, still wonderful to read. He famously began a despatch of a match scarred by fisticuffs at Southampton with "Ding Dong bell, trouble at The Dell". The poet in him frequently shaped his match reporting.

One of many reasons to marvel at these fifty match reports is that, certainly the first thirty up – until Italia 90 – would often have been filed under trying circumstances with a scramble for phone lines. Only in the past ten years has WiFi been widely available. Technology has transformed the ease of match reporting, removing concerns of getting a telephone line out from far-flung places. It is a world away from the feats of those capturing Blackburn Olympic 2 Old Etonians 1 in the 1883 FA Cup final. The sheer effort involved – of finding a connection to London, then dictating copy, as well as keeping an eye on the game – was astonishing from the likes of Green. To conjure up such epic prose while juggling erratic phone lines required supreme patience.

They certainly had plenty of good material to go at. To write "England 4 West Germany 2" must have felt a joy and a privilege, so many twists and turns to reflect and one huge party to celebrate. Rereading that *Times* report, every word is perfect, every theme considered, the flow majestic. Amid all the emotion, Green gave a clear-eyed view of the performances with his appraisal that "if England, perhaps, did not possess the greatest flair, they were the best prepared in the field, with the best temperament based on a functional plan." That said it all.

I started out in 1985 plugging phones in for the great and the garrulous of southern press boxes, crawling over polished brogues and scruffy trainers to reach plug points under the desk, and then sitting back to admire the masters at work. A particular joy was listening to Brian Glanville ad-lib his eloquent, authoritative reports to a copy-taker while ticking off spaces in a notepad so he knew how many words he had filed.

Increasingly, reporting became as much about the circus and personalities surrounding the game as it was about the sport. Yet many of those who chronicle the nation's favourite pastime will settle back in the press box before a game and say, "it's time to get the ball out", to focus on the sport, the unscripted drama of 90 fluctuating minutes, just to remember that everything in football reporting has to start with the 90 minutes as embodied in these fifty reports.

Green helped change the game with his writing, certainly with that defining piece on the Hungarians. Match reports still carry weight, and clubs often ask for copies, but there are so many voices in football reporting now, including the expansion in broadcast commentary and explosion in social media, that there really isn't a modern-day Green.

But the thrill remains, the adrenalin of the first edition "runner" with the report filed in three chunks: at half-time, on 60 minutes and then an introduction on the final whistle. I used to file more at half-time but then began to delay briefly into the second half after long experience covering Manchester United under Sir Alex Ferguson, when his players would frequently storm into second halves following interval talk from The Boss.

A match report can be tidied up or completely rewritten for the second edition. Any call from home between 10 p.m. and 11 p.m. is invariably dealt with in perfunctory fashion. Every second counts between the first and second edition. It is not simply about the press conference, or checking on any gems from flash TV interviews such as Ferguson's famous "Football, bloody hell!" It is about quickly acquiring a greater understanding of the significance of a result. I spend five minutes flying through Twitter, dodging the trolls, looking for further insight and weighing up reactions from fans. I spend another five minutes on the main fans' forums of both sides, again assessing the major talking points.

Social media has changed the art of match reporting. We were never the first draft of history, due to the immediate and mellifluous strains of radio, and then television commentators. Now we are not even compilers of the second draft of match history, as that debate rages more quickly on Twitter. It's about reporting on the emotion, the occasion, the tactics and the significance.

There are some matches when I just try to imagine how a fan there would describe it – so the frustration and fury of an England supporter witnessing the Euro 2016 defeat to Iceland was simple to put down in toxic print, as well as immediate calls for Roy Hodgson's resignation. Sometimes it is good to write angry.

Or happy. It was easy to relay the emotions of Liverpool fans celebrating the compelling 5–2 defeat of Roma at Anfield in 2018. What the real greats like Green achieved was chronicling historic events as they happened. Genius always passes the test of time. Enjoy this marvellous compendium of *Times* classics.

INTRODUCTION

BY RICHARD WHITEHEAD

AT 9.30 ON the night of 26 May 1999, the atmosphere on *The Times* sports desk in Wapping, east London was one of controlled tension. The Champions League final – which the paper doggedly still insisted on calling the European Cup – was proceeding towards a deflating but manageable conclusion with Bayern Munich successfully protecting a 1-0 lead over Manchester United.

The pages containing pieces from several journalists at the game in Barcelona's Nou Camp stadium were all ready to go the moment that referee Pierluigi Collina blew the final whistle. Those words reflected United's lack-lustre performance, the failure at the final hurdle of their attempt to win an unprecedented league, FA Cup and Champions League Treble and yet another triumph for Germany over England.

Then, one minute into added time, United equalised. Now surely there would be extra time. Copy would need to be rewritten, deadlines renegotiated. But two minutes later, they scored again. On the pitch and in the stands there was pandemonium, in the press box a moment of panic followed by a burst of activity, in Wapping a few seconds of disbelief followed by a frantic re-editing of the words waiting on the pages and a rapid changing of headlines. Just a few minutes after the deadline, the pages for the first edition of the following day's *Times* were finished and electronically despatched to the printing presses.

More remarkably still, 45 minutes later, a second edition had been assembled with new words, new pictures and new page layouts with a completely different tone and emphasis: United's glorious failure had become United's glorious victory.

You will be relieved to learn that this is not a book about newspaper production (a subject of interest to only a few), but the story of how United's remarkable 1999 triumph came to appear in print offers an insight into the relationship between football and journalism. In particular it demonstrates the extraordinary ability of writers, photographers and editors to produce work of lasting authority and impact at breathtaking speed. No one re-reading Oliver Holt's report of that United–Bayern epic in this book would gain any clue as to the hugely challenging circumstances in which it was compiled.

The reports in this book fall into two categories: some are of midweek games and are filed directly from press boxes, sometimes in the breathless aftermath of the matches, sometimes as the action was unfolding before the reporter. Others are Monday morning accounts of weekend matches and are therefore written with pause for due consideration and with time to include the post-match thoughts of managers and players.

It is a diverse and – I hope – diverting collection. Many of the obvious candidates are here: Stanley Matthews's Wembley star-turn in 1953, the Hungarians' apocalyptic thrashing of England later that year, England's 1966 World Cup final victory over West Germany, Sunderland's FA Cup final giant-killing of Leeds United in 1973 and the title-grabbing late winners of Michael Thomas in 1989 and Sergio Aguero in 2012.

You will become reacquainted with Gordon Banks's save from Pele, with Ronnie Radford's right foot, with the Hand of God, with tears in Turin and with the Miracle of Istanbul.

And along the way – and across 135 years – you will be able to trace the history of a national obsession through the pages of *The Times*.

FOOTBALL CORRESPONDENTS OF *THE TIMES*

IT IS LIKELY that Dudley Carew was the first man to have the title 'Association Football Correspondent' (although he continued to cover other sports, contribute book, film and theatre reviews and write third leaders). The four men listed before him were general sports writers who included football in their portfolios.

George West: *c.* 1870s–1896
Ernest Ward: 1897–1907
Edward Osborn: 1910–*c.* 1914
Frederick Wilson: *c.* 1919–1930
Dudley Carew: 1930–*c.* 1939
Geoffrey Green: 1946–1976
Norman Fox: 1976–1981
Stuart Jones: 1981–1993
Rob Hughes: 1993–1997
Oliver Holt: 1997–2000
Matt Dickinson: 2000–2007
Martin Samuel: 2007–2008
Oliver Kay: 2009–2019
Henry Winter (as Chief Football Writer): 2015–

Other writers featured

Peter Ball, James Ducker, James Fairlie, David Miller, Owen Slot, Clive White, John Woodcock.

Photographic credits

Marc Aspland
Arsenal v Manchester United, 1999
Bayern Munich v Manchester United, 1999
Germany v England, 2001
Tottenham Hotspur v Arsenal, 2004
AC Milan v Liverpool, 2005
Barcelona v Manchester United, 2011
Manchester City v Queens Park Rangers, 2012
England v Iceland, 2016

Stanley Devon and Horace Tonge
Blackpool v Bolton Wanderers, 1953

Tom Dixon and David Jones
England v Poland, 1973

Fred Harris and Neil Libbert
England v West Germany, 1966

Bradley Ormesher
Manchester City v Queens Park Rangers, 2012

Fred Shepherd
TSV 1860 Munich v West Ham United, 1965

NOTES ON STYLE

THE MATCH REPORTS in this book for the most part appear exactly as they were published at the time. Some small alterations have been made where the style would otherwise look outdated – for instance, it was once common to put a full point after the word 'Mr' – and obvious printing errors and literals have been corrected. The 'Match Facts' boxes at the end of each report have been newly compiled and in some cases the goal times and attendances will differ from what was reported at the time.

The biggest change is to put the names of writers at the top of the articles that were not bylined at the time. Bylines were not introduced in the newspaper until January 1967, but thanks to the magnificent *Times* archive we are now able to credit those writers.

50
GREATEST
FOOTBALL
MATCHES

1

BLACKBURN OLYMPIC v OLD ETONIANS

FA CUP FINAL, 1883

The twelfth FA Cup final – all but one held at Kennington Oval – was the most significant yet. Until then the trophy had been in the grip of southern amateur teams mostly comprising former public-school boys. Old Etonians had defeated Blackburn Rovers in 1882, but the following year Blackburn Olympic (who were clearly paying at least two of their players) took the Cup north for the first time – and changed the game forever.

"The weather was charming and the attendance very large"

BLACKBURN OLYMPIC 2
OLD ETONIANS 1

AFTER EXTRA TIME

FA CUP FINAL
31 MARCH 1883
KENNINGTON OVAL

....

2 April

Many interesting encounters have been furnished by the ties for this, the most important of the challenge cups, but probably none more so than the final match played at Kennington Oval between these clubs on Saturday. The weather was charming, and the attendance very large. The Etonians, who won the cup last year and in 1879, were successful in the toss, and at the outset defended the Harleyford Road goal. Hunter kicked off within a few minutes of half-past 3. The play at once became fast, the northerners being the first to act on the aggressive, and had it not been for Eton's back play they would speedily have scored. As it was, Gibson kicked the ball against the bar and it went behind. The Etonians now played up in a most determined style, and having run the ball down the ground Goodheart attempted to send the ball between the posts but failed. Even play followed, the forwards on either side making alternate attacks on the others' goal, but being well repulsed by the backs. Now came a most determined onslaught by the Lancashire team, and the downfall of the Etonian goal seemed inevitable. The ball was worked away, however, and a fine run down the ground by the light blue forwards ended in Goodheart sending the ball underneath the bar. The utmost enthusiasm greeted this achievement, and was continued when Eton very nearly repeated it. Nothing further of a distinct advantage was secured during the remainder of the first portion of the game. The Etonians, however, soon after ends were changed, sustained a great loss, as Dunn in running the ball down the left side of the ground was cannoned against and thrown, he being unable to take further part in the match. Still the light blues had a slight advantage for a little while, but the northerners were not long before they assumed the aggressive and Matthews kicked a goal for them. Although both teams strove hard to gain some decisive score neither were able to do so during the customary hour and a half's play. The game was therefore prolonged for another half-hour. It seemed at one time probable that even this extension would not be sufficient to admit of the match being brought to a definite issue. During the first quarter of an hour nothing transpired, but subsequently Astley who had the ball well passed to him by Dewhurst, gained the decisive point. Blackburn Olympic, the first Northern club that has yet gained the cup, were thus successful by two goals to one.

MATCH FACTS

Blackburn Olympic 2   `After extra time`   **Old Etonians 1**
Matthews, Crossley   *Goodheart 30*

Blackburn Olympic: T. Hacking, J.T. Ward, S.A. Warburton, T. Gibson, W. Astley, J. Hunter, T. Dewhurst, A. Matthews, G. Wilson, J. Crossley, J. Yates
Old Etonians: J.F.P. Rawlinson, T.H. French, P.J. De Paravicini, The Hon. A.F. Kinnaird, C.W. Foley, A.T.B. Dunn, H.W. Bainbridge, J.B.T. Chevallier, W.J. Anderson, H.C. Goodhart, R.H. Macauley
Referee: Major Marindin
Attendance: 8,000

2

ASTON VILLA v EVERTON

FA CUP FINAL, 1897

Such was football's rapid growth that the landscape of the game had been transformed 14 years after Blackburn Olympic's victory at Kennington Oval. The legalisation of professionalism in 1885 and the arrival of regular league competition three years later helped to establish the super-clubs, two of whom – Aston Villa and Everton – met in a classic FA Cup final in 1897.

"There is no half-heartedness in the enthusiasm of those who follow football in the North and Midlands"

**ASTON VILLA 3
EVERTON 2**

**FA CUP FINAL
10 APRIL 1897
THE CRYSTAL PALACE**

....

BY ERNEST WARD

12 April

To those who remembered the thin ring at the final stages of the National Cup competition in the '70s and early '80s on the Oval the crowd and scene at the Crystal Palace on Saturday were most striking. The official return of those passing the Palace turnstiles was 65,024, a number which exceeds anything in the way of football attendances previously recorded.

There were over 50,000 people at the Glasgow international last year, and 40,000 has been passed both at the Palace in the final tie and at Liverpool three seasons ago. One fact which accounted for the large increase in the "gate" was that the clubs engaged came from the two great professional centres of football – Birmingham and Lancashire – and the excursion trains on all the railways from the North were very heavily laden, for there is no half-heartedness in the enthusiasm of those who follow football in the North and Midlands. The Crystal Palace is the only place in England where such a crowd could all get a view of some sort of the game. Quite half of Saturday's huge crowd were gathered on the turf slopes on the eastern side of the field, and this mass of people presented a wonderful sight from the pavilion. The afternoon was bright, and the keen wind was not much felt in the hollow in which the ground is situated. The arrangements for dealing with the company were efficiently carried out under the direction of Mr Henry Gillman, the manager of the Crystal Palace.

Aston Villa won the match, beating Everton by three goals to two after a contest in which the excitement continued to the end. The enthusiasm was raised to a high pitch by the variations of fortune and the rapidity of the scoring. All the scoring occurred in a period of 25 minutes in the first half. That Aston Villa deserved their victory was unquestionable, for they played the better football, and were consistent to the end, whereas the Everton men were rather uneven. It was certainly one of the best finals which has been seen for some years, and the sides thoroughly merited the praise bestowed on them by Lord Rosebery when he was presenting the cup to Devey, the captain of the Aston Villa eleven. The game was remarkable for the superb defence at both ends, and for the high standard of the half-back play. It was the Villa half-back play which enabled the forwards to do so well and which time after time broke up the Everton attack. Everton, too, were not lacking in this respect, although they demonstrated it in a less degree. The halves placed the

ball for the forwards with wonderful accuracy, and Reynolds and Holt, who are approaching the veteran stage, were particularly clever in this respect. As for the full-backs, Spencer and Storrier distinguished themselves amid the general excellence; while of the goalkeepers Whitehouse carried off the chief honours largely through the shots which he saved in the closing quarter of an hour. Athersmith, Devey, and Bell were the pick of the ten forwards, and it was a wonder that the forward work was so good as it was in view of the fine defence by which it was opposed.

Aston Villa have thus won their third final tie, and, as their first position in the League is now assured, they have achieved a feat only once before accomplished in football – the winning of the Association Cup and the championship of the League in the same year. Preston North End performed the feat some years ago. The Aston Villa Club has been popular since the early days of football, and the result of Saturday, gained as it was by so much excellent play, was very well received.

The game began at 4 o'clock, Everton kicking towards the north goal, which meant that they had to face a fresh breeze. Aston Villa seemed at once to settle down, and their football was more regular than that of Everton, whose full backs had a good deal to do at the outset of the match. Storrier's kicking was very good; but the Villa halves seemed too clever for their opponents, and their constant feeding of the forwards made the Villa look much the better team. This state of things lasted for some time, and it was only the stout defence of Everton which prevented any score. Athersmith, with his great pace and his cleverness in dribbling, was dangerous. Twice he got up, but being pressed he had to shoot at difficult angles, and the ball in each case went behind. It seemed quite a long while before Aston were at all pressed. But there was one sharp attack by Everton, caused by one of the Birmingham men "fouling" Hartley. The scrimmage in front of goal passed away without any definite result but it immediately preceded the scoring of the first goal for Aston Villa. The ball went up the field in a direct line from Spencer to Reynolds, and then on to Athersmith, who reached a distance of 20 yards from the posts, and then passed to Campbell, who made a long shot, and the ball swerved owing to the wind and passed into the net. Menham, of Everton, had allowed, apparently, neither for the wind nor the screw on the ball, and had crossed too far to intercept the shot. Some 18 minutes had elapsed from the start when this occurred. Aston were not long in possession of their advantage, for after a spell of even play Bell broke away and went between the two full-backs. Whitehouse's only policy was to go out and meet Bell, but the

Everton forward got in his kick before he was charged, and the ball went into the net. Thus were the scores even. The pace then seemed to increase, and both ends were visited, but inside the first half-hour Everton took the lead. They had a free kick not far from goal, and Hartley scored out of a scrimmage. For a moment the Everton men again strongly attacked, and seemed likely to get through. But in the course of five minutes Aston Villa got two more goals. The first was put through out of a scrimmage, and following a free kick, by Wheldon, and the second was cleverly headed by Devey. Menham had just previously saved a couple of swift shots from the right wing. Aston Villa, having drawn ahead, steadied themselves, and for the rest of the first half, of which only a few minutes remained, remained for the most part on the defensive. Whitehouse saved twice, and at the interval Aston Villa led by three goals to two.

In the early moments of the second half the Everton team forced the game, giving Spencer and Whitehouse much work; but the Villa came out successfully and were able to take the game to the other end. Their half-backs again did well, and very soon the game became more even, for the full-backs of both teams were difficult to pass. The most noticeable incident for some time was a free kick to Everton within 20 yards of the Villa posts. This was executed well enough, but from a scrimmage the ball was headed high over the bar. Several fine pieces of work by the Aston right wing and centre were warmly cheered, and a fine shot by Devey went across the mouth of the Everton goal and passed just outside, as Menham had thrown himself full length on the ground to guard the corner. Sundry free kicks benefited neither side. The football continued fast and even, but the Aston Villa forwards seemed decidedly the better. When the last 20 minutes were reached the teams were still playing at a wonderful pace. Aston Villa attacked for a long time without gaining anything, and then the enthusiasm of the spectators was aroused by several brilliant efforts on the part of Everton to get level. Bell, Milward, and Hartley each got up and shot low, swift, and straight but Whitehouse, the goalkeeper, came off with flying colours and each was saved. Twice the ball, too, passed just outside the posts. These were anxious moments for the Villa but the time at last ran out, and the victory remained with Aston Villa by three goals to two. The crowd swarmed into the enclosure and the players were heartily cheered. Mr Lewis, of Blackburn, was referee.

The Earl of Rosebery, who had seen the whole of the game with Lord Kinnaird and Major Marindin, from the pavilion, presented the cup to the Aston Villa captain, Devey. Before doing this he briefly addressed the company from the pavilion steps. He spoke of the excellence of the football seen that afternoon, and was sure that the development of the game served to bring out those splendid characteristics of the British race – stamina and indomitable pluck. Lord Rosebery was heartily cheered both on his arrival and departure.

MATCH FACTS

Aston Villa 3	Everton 2
Campbell 18, Wheldon 35, Crabtree 44	Bell 23, Boyle 28

Aston Villa: J. Whitehouse, H. Spencer, A. Evans, J. Reynolds, James Cowan, J. Crabtree, C. Athersmith, J. Devey, J. Campbell, F. Wheldon, John Cowan
Everton: R. Menham, P. Meecham, D. Storrier, R. Boyle, J. Holt, W. Stewart, J. Taylor, J. Bell, A. Hartley, E. Chadwick, A. Milward
Referee: J. Lewis (Blackburn)
Attendance: 65,891

3

BOLTON WANDERERS v WEST HAM UNITED

FA CUP FINAL, 1923

Before the First World War, the Crystal Palace had provided a grand stage for the FA Cup final, even if spectator facilities were rudimentary. For three years after the war the final was held at Stamford Bridge, but in 1923 it moved to the newest and most remarkable sports ground in the world – Wembley Stadium, in North London, built at a cost of £750,000. Unfortunately, no one thought it necessary to make the match all-ticket.

"Others got to their seats in plenty of time and were pushed out of them; whirled away like straws on a stream by the sheer weight of numbers sweeping irresistibly forward from behind"

BOLTON WANDERERS 2
WEST HAM UNITED 0

FA CUP FINAL
28 APRIL 1923
WEMBLEY STADIUM

BY FREDERICK WILSON
30 April

The Bolton Wanderers beat West Ham United in the Cup Final at the Wembley Stadium on Saturday by 2 goals to 0.

This bald statement represents the result of the football side of a matter which has been discussed from many points of view for months. The fact that the Wembley Stadium has been advertised as the greatest of its kind had much to do with the enormous crowd which came from all sorts and conditions of places to see the first Cup Final to be played there. The claims made for the Stadium were not in the slightest degree extravagant. It was built to hold 125,000 people in comfort and to give to each and every one of that huge total a fair view of the football ground and track. The Stadium can hold even more than that number, and yet give to all the spectators a fair view; but no building and ground could accommodate 300,000 people, and at least that number must have turned up on Saturday at Wembley.

SCENES AT THE FIRST CUP FINAL AT WEMBLEY.

THE KING AT WEMBLEY.—His Majesty acknowledging the cheers of the vast crowd at the Stadium. The Duke of Devonshire is behind him.

STORMING THE STADIUM.—A section of the crowd swarming over the turnstiles. It is estimated that some eighty thousand people were outside the ground when the gates were officially closed.

THE AMAZING SCENE AT THE WEMBLEY CUP FINAL.—Extraordinary incidents marked the final tie of the Football Association Cup competition played for the first time at the Imperial Stadium, Wembley. The estimated accommodation for over 125,000 persons proved insufficient, and thousands of those excluded forced their way into the ground. This striking aerial photograph, taken when the match should have been in progress, shows how completely the crowd dominated the situation before police reinforcements arrived. The match, which was begun three quarters of an hour late and was interrupted for ten minutes by the crowd swarming over the touch-line again, was won by Bolton Wanderers, who beat West Ham United by two goals to none.

The reasons for the mammoth congregation were many. The opening of the Stadium for the first Cup Final might become — as in fact it has become — an historic occasion. There was the fact that a London club were in the Final Tie; the day was perfect; and, by the irony of fate, the superb organisation of the many railway lines converging on the stations round the Stadium was the crowning factor in producing such a crowd that it was impossible for any arrangements there to be carried out according to plan.

Except on two important points — the spirit of the people and of the police, and the absolute loyalty of a very mixed congregation to the King — the day was an ugly one. Many ticket-holders never reached their seats; others got to their seats in plenty of time and were pushed out of them; whirled away like straws on a stream by the sheer weight of numbers sweeping irresistibly forward from behind. The crowd was out of hand, very often most unwillingly. By 2.30pm many people were attempting to get back the way they had come, the one more difficult thing than pushing on as indeterminate atoms of the throng. The playing-ground on Saturday morning was a beautiful picture. Later on, there must have been tens of thousands of people on it at one time. It was defiled with orange peel and papers and refuse, but the surface "stood" the trampling of the mob, the police, and the hoofs of the horses of the mounted police most astonishingly well. Many of the thousands on the field of play were not there of their own volition – they were whirled away from seats and places of vantage secured by patient waiting. By the help of large reinforcements of police, mounted and unmounted, and the players, who appealed right and left for fair play, the ground was gradually cleared, the people being pushed back to the touchlines. That play could ever be begun and continue seemed, at one time, quite impossible. That the seemingly impossible, could and did happen was, one must believe, owing to the presence of the King, whose reception when he reached the ground was an event to remember. It was after "God Save the King" had been sung with boundless enthusiasm that the people began, slowly enough it is true, to help rather than to hinder in the clearing of the ground.

At 3.41 it was possible to kick off. Some 11 minutes later, a part of the crowd were squeezed on to the ground, but play was again possible after 10 minutes' patient work on the part of the police. The Bolton Wanderers were leading at the time by one goal to none, having scored in the first two minutes; but, five minutes before the second interruption, West Ham United had nearly equalised, Watson missing a chance which he would have taken with absolute certainty on an ordinary occasion.

Taken merely as an Association football match, the play at Wembley on Saturday was rather disappointing. No doubt, the long wait and the doubt as to the possibility of the game being finished, even if begun, had an effect on players already keyed up to a high state of tension. To win a Cup-tie medal is preferred by quite a many to winning an international cap. West Ham United had not only been preparing to win the Cup, they had also, if possible, to force their way into the League Championship next season. The double event has proved beyond their powers, but they certainly deserve promotion on the season's play; particularly on the latter part of the season's play. They were a good side for the first ten minutes of the great final, but afterwards, they were never convincing. When the sun was against them in the first half both the backs and the half-backs kicked too high and too hard. In the second half, when the sun was shining in the faces of the Bolton Wanderers' defence the high kicking, followed by a rush, with all the forwards in something like a line, might have proved extremely good tactics. The Bolton Wanderers' backs and half-backs, however, seldom had to use their heads for safety in the second ball. The game was started at a great pace, and the Bolton Wanderers scored after just two minutes' play. Nuttall dribbled up the field, half drew a man, and passed perfectly to Jack. Jack took the ball along slowly and feinted to pass out to Butler; when the pass looked as good as made, he dribbled inside to the left, went through the West Ham United defence at a great pace, and scored from close in with a hard, high shot into the right-hand corner of the net. Hufton could strike only at the direction in which he hoped the ball would take, and he cannot be blamed for letting the ball pass him. Three minutes later came the great chance for West Ham United to equalise. Pym, misjudging a perfectly taken corner by Ruffell, came out of goal and missed the ball. The ball came to Watson, who had an open goal yawning only a few yards in front of him. How he managed to kick the ball over the crossbar instead of into the net one cannot imagine; if a player tried to do it the odds against him would be generous. Watson, however, did fail to score.

West Ham United were every bit as good as their opponents until the second stoppage of play occurred. Even when the match was continued the crowd were actually on the touchline and sometimes over it. The West Ham United outsides never showed confidence near to the crowd; one was reminded constantly of the speech of the Maltese cat on the subject of crowding in Rudyard Kipling's wonderful polo story, called after the great pony. Now Vizard seemed to enjoy the human wall which marked or obliterated the touchline. On an ordinary day Bishop might have held him; in the circumstances his mentality was at fault, for which he is scarcely to blame. Richards made one brilliant dribble and breakthrough for West Ham United and Pym fumbled a clever shot, though he eventually cleared comfortably. A little later a beautiful centre by Vizard was headed just wide by J.R. Smith; Bolton Wanderers continued to attack, and J.R. Smith scored from a clever centre from Butler. J.R. Smith was ruled offside, although he appeared to be well behind the ball when it was kicked. The Press Stand, however, is some distance in mere yards from the field of play, and the angle was not easy to judge. Until half-time Bolton Wanderers were always the more dangerous combination, and, but for the magnificent game which Henderson played at right full back, they would probably have scored again on at least one occasion.

The teams did not leave the field at half-time; if they had done so the match would not have been finished on Saturday, but crossed over and resumed play after a five-minutes interval. West Ham United began the second half well and Watson had a good chance from a centre of Kay's, the centre half-back having worked out on to the wing with a clever individual effort. Watson, however, misjudged the flight and direction of the ball and did not start for it in time. Pym saved two shots quietly and confidently and then came the movement that settled the result of the match. Vizard niggled the ball down the wing, very close to the touchline. Suddenly he kicked and ran, passed Bishop, and centred right across the goal mouth. J.R. Smith got to the ball and shot immediately. The ball hit the inside of the crossbar and bounced out again into play. It was, however, a goal and the referee had not the slightest hesitation in ruling it as such. Even before this goal was scored a rivulet of spectators were leaving the ground; now this rivulet swelled to a steady stream. The match, to all intents and purposes, was over.

Bolton Wanderers, on the day's play, were always the better side after the first 10 minutes. They did not realise the hopes of the big contingent of their supporters, whose Saga, after the second goal was scored, "One, Two, Three, Four, Five," was repeated mechanically and at brief intervals until the finish. Seddon, the Bolton Wanderers' centre half-back, carried off the honours of the match. He called the tune to his side, and generously they piped. All of them could be picked out for good work, at times for brilliant work; but the other 10 would be the first to award merit where merit was due, and would fasten on Seddon as the ultimate winner of the FA Cup.

At the finish of the match the King presented the Cup to J. Smith, the captain of the Bolton Wanderers, and the medals to the different players. He drove away amidst a scene of heartfelt enthusiasm.

MATCH FACTS

Bolton Wanderers 2
Jack 2, J.R. Smith 53

West Ham United 0

Bolton Wanderers: R. Pym, R. Haworth, A. Finney, H. Nuttall, J. Seddon, W. Jennings, W. Butler, D. Jack, J.R. Smith, J. Smith, E. Vizard
West Ham United: E. Hufton, W. Henderson, J. Young, S. Bishop, G. Kay, J. Tresardern, R. Richards, W. Brown, V. Watson, W. Moore, J. Ruffell
Referee: D.H. Asson (West Bromwich)
Attendance: 126,047

4

ENGLAND v SCOTLAND

BRITISH CHAMPIONSHIP, 1928

There was dismay in the crowd outside the Scottish FA offices when the team to face England at Wembley in 1928 was announced. Most believed the forward line – Alex Jackson, James Dunn, Hughie Gallacher, Alex James and Alan Morton – lacked the stature to prosper against the physical England defenders. But in his team talk the night before the game, Scotland captain Jimmy McMullan said: "Go to bed and pray for rain." The next day it poured – and the legend of the Wembley Wizards was born.

"There were moments when the Scottish players seemed to be indulging in the artistic pleasure of playing with the mouse rather than killing it outright."

ENGLAND 1
SCOTLAND 5

BRITISH CHAMPIONSHIP
31 MARCH 1928
WEMBLEY STADIUM

BY DUDLEY CAREW
2 April

Scotland beat England at Wembley on Saturday by five goals to one, and so England finished the season at the bottom of the Championship table.

It was not so much defeat that England suffered as humiliation. There was a period in the second half when the football verged on the ludicrous; the Scottish players were taking and giving their passes at a walking pace, underlining with rather cruel emphasis the ease with which they could draw the English defence out of position. Indeed, paradoxical as it may sound, Scotland would probably have scored more goals had England put up a stronger fight, for the temptation to weave intricate patterns in front of goal for the sake of weaving them was occasionally too strong to be resisted, and there were moments when the Scottish players seemed to be indulging in the artistic pleasure of playing with the mouse rather than killing it outright.

While their forwards deserve all the praise that can be given them for an entrancing exhibition of football, it was the strength of their half-back line, coupled with the weakness of England's that gave them so overwhelming a victory. Gibson, Bradshaw, and McMullan were everything that a line of half-backs should be. They kept in perpetual touch both with their backs and their forwards, tackled strongly, and never parted with the ball until they had some constructive purpose in doing so.

The contrast with the English half-backs was pathetic. All of them tried desperately hard, but from the beginning of the game to the end they looked lost and bewildered. The speed and cleverness of the Scottish forwards prevented them from being of any use to their own attack, and they were given little time to think of anything but the bare necessity of getting the ball away, anywhere, anyhow. The forwards never got together as a line, and Hulme and Smith on the wings were, not to put too fine a point on it, failures. Dean spent most of his time in waiting for passes that never came, but, as in every match in which he plays, he proved what great power he can get into his shots taken on the run. Kelly, with one or two characteristic dribbles, was the only man on the side who looked capable

of playing the Scots at their own game. For a long time rain fell with positively tropical violence, and the ball and the turf became very treacherous, but it was significant to see how much more easily the Scottish players succeeded in keeping their feet and controlling the ball. King Amanullah[*] was present at the match, and before the start of play the players were presented to the Duke of York. Bishop, the English captain, was unable to play, Goodall captaining the side and Healless coming in at left-half.

The 80,000 spectators had not to wait long for their first thrills, as within three minutes England came literally within an inch of scoring, whereas Scotland actually scored. Dean gave Smith a beautifully judged pass and Smith, beating Wilson, converged on goal and sent in a shot that passed out of J.D. Harkness's reach and hit the far post, to rebound into play. No English forward was up, and a great chance of establishing a moral advantage was lost. A moment later, however, James, whose dribbling and passing must have delighted even the most fervent English supporter, passed up the centre to Gallacher, who, in his turn, pushed the ball out to Morton. Throughout the game Morton's centres were models of accuracy, and this one was no exception, and, with the English defence spread-eagled, it was

[*] King of Afghanistan, 1926–1929

easy for Jackson to get his head to the ball and steer it out of Hufton's reach. For some time after this England had as much of the play as their opponents, but even with the ball in the Scottish half of the field the impression that the English side was a collection of rather desperate individuals opposed to a team that, secure in the knowledge of superiority, could afford to take its time was difficult to shake off. Dean, however, got in a tremendous drive from a distance of 35 yards which Harkness stopped but could not hold. The ball came back, and it looked as though Bradford would get to it first and score, but Harkness won a ten-yard race by a foot and the danger was averted.

Goodall twice fouled Gallacher just outside the penalty area, and Hufton saved two hard shots, the first from Jackson and the second from Gibson. Hulme gave Dean another chance of showing what a fine shot he is, and it was bad luck that a good run should finish with a tremendous left-foot drive that shaved the bar. Scotland's half-backs, however, were taking a firmer and firmer control of the game, and just before half-time the second goal came, James, from the inside-right position, beating Hufton with a drive that curled deceptively away.

If in the first half England had succeeded in throwing a decent disguise over the real difference between the two teams, the second exposed it in all its nakedness. Gibson, Jackson and Dunn did very much what they liked with Healless and Jones, and again and again they took the ball through the English defence, but a certain finicalness on the part of the Scottish insides in front of goal and, it must in fairness be added, the unwearying way in which Wilson shadowed Gallacher prevented Scotland from increasing their lead. Once during this period of Scottish pressure England succeeded in breaking away, and from a centre by Smith Bradford headed over the bar. From a neat pass by Jackson, James drove in a terrific shot, which glanced off the cross-bar, but after 17 minutes Scotland got their third goal. Goodall made a flagrant mistake and let in Morton, who dropped in a centre for Jackson to head into the goal. From this point to the end one's memory of the game resolves itself into a picture of the Scots playing a leisurely and elaborate game of passing among themselves, and of the Englishmen running about aimlessly and every now and again touching the ball.

James scored the fourth goal for Scotland after Gibson had taken a free kick from near the touchline and Gallacher had a shot saved by Hufton, while the fifth came from another perfect movement started by Dunn, carried on by Morton, and once again neatly finished off by Jackson. Scotland, by overindulgence in the pleasant pastime of making the

English defence look supremely silly, cheated themselves out of a sixth, and, possibly seventh, goal, and just on time England scored in the only way that looked possible for them – direct from a free kick.

MATCH FACTS

England 1	Scotland 5
Kelly 89	*Jackson 3 65 85, James 44 74*

England: E. Hufton, R. Goodall, H. Jones, W. Edwards, T. Wilson, H. Healless, J. Hulme, R. Kelly, W. Dean, J. Bradford, W. Smith
Scotland: J.D. Harkness, J. Nelson, T. Law, J. Gibson, T. Bradshaw, J. McMullan, A. Jackson, J. Dunn, H. Gallacher, A. James, A. Morton
Referee: W. Bell (Scotland)
Attendance: 80,868

5

ARSENAL v HUDDERSFIELD TOWN

FA CUP FINAL, 1930

Apart from two isolated FA Cup wins by Tottenham Hotspur, the game in England was still dominated by the great clubs of the North and Midlands. All that began to change in 1925, when Arsenal lured Huddersfield Town's innovative manager Herbert Chapman south. But the club – called 'The Arsenal' by *The Times* – had still not won a first trophy when they met his former employers in the 1930 FA Cup final.

"It was the skill and bold tactics of James that turned the scale in favour of his side. To his remarkable control of the ball he added the craft that both sees and makes an opening"

ARSENAL 2
HUDDERSFIELD TOWN 0

FA CUP FINAL
26 APRIL 1930
WEMBLEY STADIUM
....

BY JAMES FAIRLIE
28 April

The Arsenal beat Huddersfield Town by two goals to none in the final round of the competition for the Football Association Challenge Cup at Wembley Stadium on Saturday afternoon in the presence of the King and over 92,000 other spectators. The Cup has thus come back to London after nine years and for the third time only in 48 years. It was The Arsenal's first winning of the Cup, for they failed in the final round against Cardiff City just three years ago.

It was no easy victory for the winners. They were often hard put to it to keep the ball out of their goal, particularly in the second half. More than once a foot just got in the way to stop a shot. The ball often hovered uncannily in their goalmouth, but it did not seem to get the right bounce to the feet of the Huddersfield men. The Arsenal goalkeeper, Preedy, too, who at times cleared with rare brilliance and daring, was also at times rather uncertain and took risks which hardly deserved to succeed as they did. Three times he let the ball slip from his hands when he was trying to clear. Twice a partner got it away. The third time he pounced on it as it lay on the ground before the Huddersfield forwards who had him surrounded could get their feet to it. He was so beset that he could not clear, and fortunately for him one of his opponents in the eagerness of the moment tackled him in such manner as to merit a free-kick, and that gave Preedy a lucky escape from an awkward position. He had been hurt in the melee, which resembled a loose Rugby scrimmage, and it was a few moments before he could resume his place.

Still, The Arsenal did deserve to win, for in the first half they attacked with a zest and a dash that gave them the early lead of a goal which meant much. The play was then at its best and it was just as fine as anyone could wish to see. The Arsenal were then the better side, but after they had got that goal the attack seemed to pass over to the Huddersfield team and they did everything that players can do to win a match except score the goals. In the second half play was not nearly so good. Huddersfield pressed almost continuously till, just six minutes before the end of the game, The Arsenal scored their second goal in a lonely dash down the field by Lambert after a long, high tricky kick by James from halfway. That settled matters. It seemed to take all the sting out of

the Huddersfield attack and the game ended rather tamely.

There was one great player on each side. Others had bright moments and accomplished wonders from time to time, but these two kept it up from start to finish. They never varied. They were the men of the match. They were James of The Arsenal and Smith, the Huddersfield veteran of many Cup-ties. It was the skill and bold tactics of James that turned the scale in favour of his side. He himself scored the first goal, and it was he who made the second possible. To his remarkable control of the ball he added the craft that both sees and makes an opening. He was also an aid to the defenders, and once it was he who kicked the ball out of harm's way when danger threatened the goal. He had been fouled when the first goal came. He was on his feet in an instant, for he saw a chance, and without waiting for things to settle down he took the kick himself quickly. He passed the ball out to Bastin on the wing and Bastin, in place of going on himself, as the defence had expected, turned the ball back to James, who was still some way behind. James drove it low and hard into the net, with a swerve going away all the time out of Turner's reach. He had been too quick for his opponents, and he had shot without waiting to steady himself or place the ball conveniently. The Arsenal had long been under sore pressure when the second goal came. James saw a chance down the middle and getting the ball at halfway he kicked long and high straight down the field towards the goal. Lambert was off hot in pursuit. Somehow he slipped in between Goodall and Spence and got ahead of them in the race for the ball. Turner came out to meet him, but he had misjudged the time and Lambert was able to tap the ball past him through the goal.

Smith was the man of the Huddersfield team. He was a constant thorn in the side of the Arsenal defence and they could seldom keep him down. He was ever on the alert and when the ball came his way he made ground steadily. There was always danger when he was moving, but his centres to Jackson, who was waiting as usual near the goal, did not fall too well. Once early in the game, just before The Arsenal had scored, Jackson got his head to the ball, but it went just outside the post. Several times by running out Preedy was able to just touch the ball as it was crossing and divert it away from Jackson. It was not Jackson's lucky day. The play did not run much his way and he got little scope from John, who marked him well. Yet he threatened danger more than once, and several times in the first half he shot straight for goal, once finding Preedy waiting with outstretched arms to receive the ball when he had lofted it over the others

of the defence. Smith later began to shoot, too, from the left, and he tested Preedy frequently, one shot near the end being a fine low drive which was just cleared at the expense of a corner.

No others but James and Smith added to their reputations on the day's play. Yet on the whole, after a somewhat nervous start, it was a better display of football than is usually seen in the Cup final. Play became ragged in the second half and there was a lot of wild and loose kicking, but in the first it was at times unexpectedly brilliant. The Arsenal and Huddersfield attacked in turns, The Arsenal more daringly at the start. They then seemed the more likely to score, for several times they just missed the goal, one round of heading by Hulme, Lambert, and Bastin ending with the ball going just over. Parker had a chance with a free kick just outside the penalty area, but kicked over the bar. Parker had a hard game all through. The play ran to that side and he found Smith a big handful. He could not keep up the pace, but often by clever anticipation of the next movement he found himself in the right spot to clear. Hapgood did not have so much to do and he was a little uncertain at times, but John covered that wing well. Baker was not good in defence, but Seddon played like a centre full-back and was often hard by when things looked ugly for the side near the goal. Of the forwards, Hulme made some fine rushes but shot wildly. He missed one glorious chance from a centre by Bastin which Lambert left for him. Jack was far below his form and played as though he were far from fit. Lambert got the goal that was expected of him, and Bastin, well nursed by James, had an excellent first half but faded away afterwards.

Turner had a light afternoon compared with Preedy, and he was rarely put to the test. Both Goodall and Spence, without being brilliant, were sound, but Goodall was hardly up to his own standard in the Scottish match on the same ground at the beginning of the month. Campbell was the best of the half-backs, and his excellent plying of Smith with the ball assisted much in making that wing so dangerous. Wilson was the hardest worker, and Naylor had one fine shot at goal early in the game. Kelly was too slow, and hung far back, and gave little aid to Jackson. In the centre, Huddersfield were weak, and though Raw played hard, neither he nor Davies gave much trouble to the defence. If some of the strength of the side on the wings could have been transferred to the centre, things might have gone differently. The Arsenal won the match because they had an inside forward who could develop the attack and press it home to the utmost. Huddersfield tried to start things from the outsides, and the inside men could not carry them through.

MATCH FACTS

Arsenal 2   **Huddersfield Town 0**
James 16, Lambert 88

Arsenal: C. Preedy, T. Parker, E. Hapgood, A. Baker, W. Seddon, R. John, J. Hulme, D. Jack, J. Lambert, A. James, C. Bastin
Huddersfield Town: H. Turner, R. Goodall, B. Spence, J. Naylor, T. Wilson, A. Campbell, A. Jackson, R. Kelly, H. Davies, H. Raw, W.H. Smith
Referee: T. Crew (Leicester)
Attendance: 92,488

6

WALSALL v ARSENAL

FA CUP THIRD ROUND, 1933

In the eyes of many from the industrial North and Midlands, wealthy, aristocratic Arsenal symbolised the capital's apparent immunity from the effects of the Depression. There was, therefore, a burning desire to see them taken down a peg or two. Nevertheless, nobody thought they were in any danger when they met Walsall, mid-table in the third division north, in the third round of the FA Cup in 1932–33.

"Arsenal played like a dispirited and hopelessly beaten side, vastly different from Walsall, who did not carry a single weak man"

WALSALL 2
ARSENAL 0

FA CUP THIRD ROUND
14 JANUARY 1933
FELLOWS PARK

....

16 January

Walsall beat Arsenal by two goals to none at Walsall. Their players were mobbed and carried shoulder high to the cheers of some 12,000 excited spectators, who, with the final whistle, rushed on the pitch. No such result had been expected.

A victory for Arsenal had almost come to be taken for granted, even though they had to play on their opponents' ground, and accidents and illness had left their forces seriously depleted. All the honours of the game, however, went to Walsall. Their football was better, much more virile, and so roused to the occasion that from the start they had Arsenal in difficulties. Far from Arsenal being the better team, they were a side of many weaknesses, poor in defence and unconvincing in attack. Arsenal were quite unlike themselves. To attribute their defeat to the absence of such players as Hapgood, John, Hulme, and Coleman would be to deny justice to Walsall, who through their hard tackling, great speed, and boundless energy might have prevailed against the full strength of Arsenal. Arsenal lost because they were the inferior side: Black, a young Scot, who was playing in Hapgood's place at left back, had neither the speed nor the resource to hold in check the fast wing opposed to him; and at a moment when Arsenal seemed likely to get a goal to balance that which had been scored by Alsop, about 15 minutes after the change of ends, a penalty kick was given against him for a foul on the Walsall centre-forward, from which Sheppard beat Moss for the second time. That incident so demoralised Arsenal that they had even less of the play afterwards and invited a heavier defeat.

Sidey, who in the absence of John was at left half, was outclassed. Warnes, who was preferred to Hulme at outside right, was not a success, and Walsh, who was at centre-forward, was a poor leader, while Jack and James were for the most part held in check by the Walsall half-backs. Bastin alone of the Arsenal forwards, played up to his usual standard, and towards the close of the first half nearly scored with perhaps the best shot of the match.

From the kick-off Walsall, who were without Langford, probably the best of all their backs, whose place Bird took, had the Arsenal defence in trouble. Ball and Coward found it comparatively easy to get the better of Sidey and Black. Moss, well supported by Roberts and Male, prevented a goal, but generally Arsenal were kept on the defensive until the interval. Leslie, the Walsall centre half-back, did more than bring about the total eclipse of Walsh: by hard tackling he frequently kept

James and Jack in control. Salt completely mastered Warnes, and except for an occasional raid by Bastin, the play of Arsenal forwards would have had no redeeming feature. James and Jack schemed in vain, and only the untiring efforts of Roberts and the reliability of Male kept Walsall from setting up a winning lead before half-time. As it was the interval arrived with no score.

With the slope of the ground in their favour in the second half Arsenal for a time improved without, however, threatening to break down the defence of their opponents. Warnes was given a favourable opportunity to score, but he required too much room, and before he could shoot Salt bowled him over. Walsh also had chances, but Bastin alone seriously tested Cunningham, a vigilant, but by no means overworked goalkeeper. Having survived various attacks Walsall, through Alsop, scored with a shot unexpected but not hard. With half an hour still to go the chances were that Arsenal would at least force a draw. It was then that Black gave away the penalty kick. Sheppard made no mistake, and thereafter Arsenal played like a dispirited and hopelessly beaten side, vastly different from Walsall, who did not carry a single weak man. The winners were not clever or highly skilled footballers, but they thoroughly deserved to win.

MATCH FACTS

Walsall 2	**Arsenal 0**
Alsop 60, Sheppard 70 pen	

Walsall: J. Cunningham, J. Bennett, S. Bird, J. Reed, G. Leslie, H. Salt, C. Ball, W. Coward, G. Alsop, W. Sheppard, F. Lee
Arsenal: F. Moss, G. Male, T. Black, F. Hill, H. Roberts, N. Sidey, W. Warnes, D. Jack, C. Walsh, A. James, C. Bastin
Referee: A. Taylor (Wigan)
Attendance: 11,150

7

PORTSMOUTH v WOLVERHAMPTON WANDERERS

FA CUP FINAL, 1939

Dark clouds hung over Europe as Portsmouth and Wolverhampton Wanderers contested the FA Cup final. How many of those present at Wembley had an inkling that this would be the last of football's grand showpieces for seven years? With a brilliant young team riding high in the first division, Wolves were hot favourites – but the pressure of a cup final can sometimes prove overpowering.

"To be three goals down in a Cup final is enough to take the heart out of any side, and Wolverhampton deserve every credit for refusing to let it discourage them"

PORTSMOUTH 4 WOLVERHAMPTON WANDERERS 1

FA CUP FINAL
29 APRIL 1939
WEMBLEY STADIUM

....

BY DUDLEY CAREW, ASSOCIATION FOOTBALL CORRESPONDENT

1 May

Portsmouth beat Wolverhampton Wanderers in the final of the FA Cup at Wembley on Saturday by four goals to one in the presence of the King and Queen and about 100,000 spectators.

A score of four goals is unusual in the Cup final, but Portsmouth were well worth every one of them. Wolverhampton started off with the rush that was expected by those who had prophesied their victory and forced a corner in the first minute of the game. Portsmouth, however, refused to fight on the defensive, and before many minutes had passed the strength of their half-back line began to make itself felt, and that strength was decisive. The quick, hard, terrier-like tackling of Guthrie, Rowe, and Wharton threw the Wolverhampton attack completely off its balance, and only very occasionally did the Wolverhampton line bring off those smooth, rhythmic movements which have earned the team renown as well as goals this season. All through the game Portsmouth played the better balanced and more methodical game. Their marking was close and intelligent, and behind that splendidly sure and aggressive half-back line were a goalkeeper who never looked like making a shadow of a mistake and two backs who covered one another with perfect understanding. Barlow at inside-left was one of the most accomplished players on the field, and it was his astute passes which again and again set the Portsmouth line going, while Worrall's speed, footwork, and general football craft were a constant menace to the left wing of the Wolverhampton defence.

Of Wolverhampton it must simply be written that inspiration eluded them and that they were never really the masters of themselves or their nerves, to say nothing of Portsmouth. Cullis, although he strove valiantly in the second half to rally the side for a forlorn hope, was strangely uncertain of himself in the earlier stages of the game, and this uncertainty affected the whole scheme of the defence. The defenders individually did some good things every now and again, but the defence, as a whole, lacked the cohesion of that of Portsmouth. It was often drawn out of position

and the Portsmouth players were generally given too much room in which to manoeuvre. The Wolverhampton half-back line was too hard pressed to give its usual help to the forwards, and, when it did get the ball forward, it found a line at sixes and sevens with itself. Burton and Maguire were nothing like so effective as Worrall and Parker and the inside forwards showed a disquieting tendency to bunch. A team plays as well as the other side allows it to do, and the simple truth is that on Saturday Portsmouth hardly allowed Wolverhampton to play at all. Wolverhampton, it is true, contributed to their own undoing, but it must have been desperately hard to play against a team as confident as Portsmouth were.

It was a day straight out of winter with a cold, showery north-easterly wind, but Cup final crowds do not let details like the weather upset them, and the community singing went with all the familiar Wembley swing. The turf was, of course, spotlessly green, and for some time before the kick-off it was pleasantly decorated by the bands of the Royal Marines, the Irish Guards, and the Welsh Guards. The King received a great welcome when he went out to the two ranks of players, and punctually at 3 o'clock the game began.

Guthrie won the toss, but the wind was inclined to swirl and was of no great use to anyone. Wolverhampton, as has been stated, forced a corner in the first minute, and were generally aggressive, but Portsmouth were the first team really to settle down, and once the first few minutes were over there was little trace of nerves in the game they played. They produced sound, solid football, altogether too sound and solid for a young Wolverhampton side which plainly felt the greatness of the occasion. Once Cullis misjudged a pass back, Scott came out of goal but never got to the ball, and the general panic that momentarily affected the Wolverhampton defence was symptomatic of much of their football. Barlow once worked his way over to the left and got in a shot Scott did well to catch, but at the other end the Portsmouth defence blundered for once in its life and Dorsett found himself through. He tried a low cross-shot but did not really hit the ball and Walker was able to save although he had to concede a corner in doing so. Portsmouth opened the score after half an hour's play. The ball was kicked downfield to Anderson, and Anderson in his turn pushed it forward to Barlow. Cullis could not intercept the pass, and Barlow, who was unmarked, steadied himself and then drove the ball deliberately high into the net. There was a moment when Wolverhampton showed a flash of their greatness and a glorious movement ended with Burton driving in a low shot which Walker saved

cleanly, but there was no sort of doubt as to which was the better side, and, just before the interval, Anderson scored a second goal for Portsmouth. Anderson, after having one shot intercepted, managed to fasten on to the ball again, and, although Scott, who seemed to misjudge the whole position, got his fingers to the ball, he could not stop it from journeying to the back of the net. Portsmouth kicked off in the second half, and, almost from the kick-off they scored. Parker and Barlow took the ball cleverly down the field. Barlow shot hard, and Scott, who looked as though he should have saved, made a frantic grab at the ball while he was lying on the ground. It seemed that he might keep it on the right side of the line, but Parker rushed up and quickly settled any doubt there might have been.

To be three goals down in a Cup final is enough to take the heart out of any side, and Wolverhampton deserve every credit for refusing to let it discourage them. Their football continued to have obvious weaknesses, but, with Cullis coming up to encourage them, they fought back with spirit and after seven minutes they scored. A close passing movement ended with Dorsett in possession of the ball and he scored with a fine cross-shot which gave Walker no chance. Had Portsmouth faltered it is possible that Wolverhampton would have found their real fire and that the game would have had a remarkable ending, but all through the match Portsmouth had played the kind of game that does not falter at the hint of a crisis. The half-back line remained magnificent in its ruthlessness, and Wolverhampton were never allowed to feel that their goal would have the slightest influence on the destiny of the game. Indeed Portsmouth added to their lead with a goal which was, perhaps, the best of the match. Barlow sent the ball out to Worrall, Worrall ran strongly down the touchline and sent across a centre which Parker met with his head, and the ball went past Scott as though he had driven it with his foot. Cullis, moving more and more up the field, kept Wolverhampton hard at it, but the battle was lost and won, and, judging by Cup-tie standards, a remarkably good and enjoyable battle it was, even although there was seldom any doubt which captain would receive the Cup from the King.

MATCH FACTS

Portsmouth 4
*Barlow 29, Anderson 43,
Parker 46 71*

Wolverhampton Wanderers 1
Dorsett 54

Portsmouth: H. Walker, L. Morgan, W. Rochford, J. Guthrie, T. Rowe, G. Wharton, F. Worrall, J. McAlinden, J. Anderson, B. Barlow, C. Parker
Wolverhampton Wanderers: A. Scott, W. Morris, B. Taylor, T. Galley, S. Cullis, J. Gardiner, S. Burton, A. McIntosh, D. Westcott, R. Dorsett, E. Maguire
Referee: T. Thompson (Newcastle-upon-Tyne)
Attendance: 99,370

8

BLACKPOOL v BOLTON WANDERERS

FA CUP FINAL, 1953

Stanley Matthews, one of England's greatest and most popular footballers, was 38 and had already been on the losing side in two FA Cup finals when Blackpool reached the final again against Bolton Wanderers in 1953. It was Coronation year, which meant many more people had acquired televisions on which to watch the match – but could he make it third time lucky?

"It is by the power to call souls out of the abyss into life that greatness is judged"

**BLACKPOOL 4
BOLTON WANDERERS 3**

FA CUP FINAL
2 MAY 1953
WEMBLEY STADIUM

....

**BY GEOFFREY GREEN,
ASSOCIATION FOOTBALL
CORRESPONDENT**
4 May

The Cup Final of 1953 will live in memory. It will live with that 100,000 crowd compressed within the stately curve of a Wembley Stadium once more bathed in the spring sunshine of a Saturday; it will live with that other countless multitude that viewed it second-hand upon the magic screen of television. It will live not only because of its highly colourful and emotional climax, that saw Blackpool emerge from a losing position of 1–3 25 minutes from the end to pluck a glorious victory by four goals to three as the last seconds were being drained from the afternoon. It will live largely because here in the presence of the Queen and the Duke of Edinburgh the game of football, the game of the people, was crowned with all felicity in this year of Coronation and national rejoicing.

So Blackpool at the last came from the blue to gain their place in history for the first time. But where to begin the story of such an afternoon of contrast; of light and shade, of tragedy and error, of mediocrity and supreme quality? The thoughts go

GREAT INNINGS BY HARVEY

AUSTRALIANS THRASH BOWLING

A great innings by Harvey, who finished the day needing only four runs to gain his highest previous score of 205, enabled the Australians to recover twice against Leicestershire at Leicester on Saturday.

As at Worcester in their opening match, the first three Australian batsmen fell cheaply. Hate, McDonald, and Hassett all being back in the pavilion for 16. In each case weak shots were responsible, although one could sympathize with Hole in his unaccustomed position as opening batsman. He was first to go, bowled by a late inswinger from Lester's lowered lively left-hander.

Harvey and Miller put Australia back on the right road with a stand of 90 in the last of over a minute. Both attacked the bowling with excellent forcing strokes, and the Leicestershire attack seemed powerless to separate them when Miller was run out. There followed another partial collapse. Craig, after a few intrusive strokes, fell soon after Spencer took the new ball, and Archer, who had made a century at Worcester, never looked like staying long.

But Harvey remained dominant and, as so often happens, the Australians produced an unexpected man for the crisis. This time it was Davidson, a left-hander, who set about the bowling in fervidly that late in the second over faster than Harvey. In little over an hour these two demoralized Leicestershire by putting on 117, of which Davidson claimed 63, including a six and 11 4's. Harvey having passed 100 in three hours but stricken then took complete command and in another 100 minutes he doubled his score. By the close he had hit 27 4's.

M.C.C. v. YORKSHIRE
AT LORD'S

The heavy rain of Thursday and Friday made only three hours' cricket possible in the opening match of the season at Lord's but in that time Yorkshire dismissed M.C.C. for 87, and had time to begin their own innings. This fully justified Yardley's action in giving Yorkshire's opponents first innings when he won the toss. The M.C.C. batsmen could not find an answer to the left-arm spin of Wardle, who bowled eight overs before conceding a run and finished in unchanged spell with an analysis of 34-13—25—6.

TRIUMPH OF MATTHEWS AND BLACKPOOL

BOLTON BEATEN IN LAST MINUTE AT WEMBLEY

From Our Association Football Correspondent

The Cup Final of 1953 will live in memory. It will live with that 100,000 crowd compressed within the steely curve of a Wembley Stadium once more bathed in the spring sunshine of a Saturday; it will live with that other countless exultitude that viewed it second-hand upon the magic screen of television. It will live not only because of its highly colourful and emotional climax, that saw Blackpool emerge from a losing position of 1—3 25 minutes from the end to pluck a glorious victory by four goals to three as the last seconds were being drained from the afternoon. It will live largely because here in the presence of the Queen and the Duke of Edinburgh the game of football, the game of the people, was crowned with all felicity in this year of Coronation and national rejoicing.

Matthews putting across a centre challenged by Wheeler, the Bolton right half.

GOLF TITLE FOR MICKLEM

A THRILLING FINAL

FROM OUR GOLF CORRESPONDENT

G. H. Micklem became the new English golf champion on Saturday when he beat R. J. White on the 35th green at Royal Birkdale, and if, the next time he goes out, he casts an adoring glance at his jupiter it will not be surprising, for it contributed a great deal to his success.

SATURDAY'S RESULTS

F.A. CUP FINAL

FINAL TABLES
LEAGUE CHAMPIONSHIP

HARD COURT SINGLES WON BY MORTIMER

MISS HART ESTABLISHES A RECORD

FROM OUR LAWN TENNIS CORRESPONDENT

The National Hard Courts championship ended in a blaze of sunshine at Bournemouth on Saturday, an first time there was marked unanimity on the wisdom of the arrangements.

round in one's head as though they were coloured beads in a box.

First, perhaps, one should say, with a passing and kindly thought for Bolton, that seldom can there have been a more popular victory. Certainly there has never been one quite so dramatic. And never before has the lush stage of Wembley been so dominated by the performance of a single player. This popular sentiment and this performance embraced but a single subject – Stanley Matthews. This was his finest hour, and that it should come with such timing at such a moment at Wembley, when the eyes of the country were upon him in his third Cup Final, was a rightful consummation of a great career.

It is by the power to call souls out of the abyss into life that greatness is judged. So can Matthews be judged, for that exactly is what he achieved on this memorable Saturday. With 25 minutes left Bolton led by three goals to one and seemed assured of their fourth Wembley victory. Few then could cavil at their apparently unassailable position, for while two of their goals could be tabulated as gifts from a strangely hypnotised and unnerved Farm under the Blackpool crossbar – ever has Wembley been the graveyard of goalkeepers – against this there could be set the sad fact that from the opening quarter of an hour Bolton had been reduced to 10 effective men through a leg injury to Bell, their left-half.

Thus, with a disorganised team, they had taken what chances the gods had to offer, had played an open, fast game – with the long through pass to the dangerous Lofthouse as their sharpest dagger – and had worked themselves into a winning position, while their opponents time after time frittered away the openings Matthews created with deft artistry.

To understand the ending one must begin at the beginning. Within 90 seconds of the kick-off there came the first shaft of tragedy, Lofthouse lashed in a powerful low drive from 25 yards and Farm, perhaps taken by surprise and certainly beaten by a slight swerve off the pitch, allowed the swift-moving shot to glance off his arm into the net as he dived. Thus Blackpool, having scarcely touched the ball, at once gave Bolton a goal start. When Moir put Lofthouse clean through at the twentieth minute and the centre-forward, angling his shot past the advancing Farm, hit the far post a resounding thud the Blackpool fires were all but extinguished. But not quite, for in spite of everything, the fates were storing up their smiles for them until the climax, and this Lofthouse shot, as it proved, may well have been a turning point.

Certainly it looked like it when Blackpool, after some inept finishing by Taylor and Mudie, drew level for the first time 10 minutes before half-time. Again the imp of Wembley produced a freak goal, for now as

Mortensen, who had a fine match in every way, broke loose through the middle past Barrass and Ball and slammed a left-foot shot to the far post, the unfortunate Hassall, fast in retreat, ran straight across the line to divert the ball helplessly into his own net.

There is no defence against this sort of thing. But within four minutes Bolton were ahead again, and again Farm, still dazed by his error, was at fault. Langton curled a lob into the goalmouth where Moir, with quick perception, leapt across the face of Farm to divert the ball by perhaps the barest shade into the net. It was swift thought and action, no doubt, but a goalkeeper, especially of international standing, should never be caught in this way.

So Bolton led 2–1 at half-time in a match that thus far had produced too many moments of flat mediocrity. The goals were there, of course – and all the world loves a goal – but each was untidy. Bolton, with Bell limping at outside-left Langton inside him, and Hassall playing finely at left-half, clearly were the more workmanlike, for Blackpool as yet withheld in their finishing the promise of some cultured approach play, where the ball was stroked along the ground. Matthews, as opportunity offered, tempted each of his forwards to rise above himself at the crux, but with no response.

So it was that when Bell, soaring off like some gull with a stricken wing, gallantly headed Holden's cross past Farm to give Bolton a 3–1 lead 10 minutes

after the interval it looked all over. But it was now that the afternoon suddenly took on a new quality. The colours became brighter, the outlines sharper. It was Matthews the artist who effected the transformation. And so we came to the last breathless stage that will live on into history. The story book ending was at hand.

Matthews is a superb artist, a football genius beyond compare. He paints, as it were, in water-colours and not oils. His work always has had that beautiful bloom that oils cannot give. He has it within him to turn mice into horses, and nothing into everything. Now in those last 25 minutes he turned Blackpool into giants at a time when all his inspiration might well have drained away after earlier disappointment. Blackpool, in a word, began to hum like a machine in top gear – with the young Robinson at last recovered from his early anxiety – and suddenly the 10 gallant men of Bolton were no longer sufficient to stay the hand of events.

As Matthews suddenly took an acutely measured pass from the diminutive Taylor there were 22 minutes left. Once again he left the bewildered Ball stranded; not this time with a lazy inside swerve, or that famous shuffling outward flick, but by pure acceleration. In a flash he was gone and at top speed he chipped a perfect centre spinning unpleasantly under the far corner of the Bolton crossbar. Hanson no more than got his fingers to the ball and as it fell loose, about to pass outside the post, Mortensen, straining forward at full stretch, just managed to squeeze the ball home through the only space left to him. It was through the eye of a needle.

That was 2–3, and now there came a new hope as rising excitement flooded the arena like light, with Matthews reaching the heights of his creative instinct. Outside and inside, he kept bewildering opponent after opponent as a torrent of noise swelled up from the vast crowd. But still Bolton hung on bravely, with Wheeler, Barrass, and Hassall their heroes. Once Perry missed a "sitter" from Matthews, so did Mudie, and then Hanson saved brilliantly from Mortensen at point blank range.

Three minutes remained. Surely it was over now for all that Matthews, Johnston, Mortensen, and little Taylor had tried to do. But no. Suddenly there came an infringement against Mortensen on the edge of the penalty area, and before one could realise it there lay the ball in the back of the Bolton net, shot home like some red-hot thunderbolt by Mortensen himself from 20 yards; 3–3 and now extra time. But no again. With time measured in seconds Taylor again gave Matthews a lovely pass. Matthews, with supreme balance and control, now went inside Ball. As Barrass challenged he left the centre-half on the outside, streaked in to the byline, cut back a diagonal pass and Perry, putting away all past sins, shot home low past a defence cut to ribbons.

Blackpool had won unbelievably. Almost at once came the whistle to create an unforgettable last scene, for there, amidst all the roar and the clatter, and the long shadows of the Band of the Brigade of Guards in the centre of the sunlit field, was Matthews being carried shoulder high with his captain Johnston from the place of triumph, each with his hand upon the Cup.

Poor Bolton, they were left with the red hot cinders. But what a finish, and the most goals ever scored at Wembley!

MATCH FACTS

Blackpool 4	Bolton Wanderers 3
Mortensen 35 68 89, Perry 90	*Lofthouse 2, Moir 39, Bell 55*

Blackpool: G. Farm, E. Shimwell, T. Garrett, E. Fenton, H. Johnston, C. Robinson, S. Matthews, E. Taylor, S. Mortensen, J. Mudie, W. Perry
Bolton Wanderers: S. Hanson, J. Ball, R. Banks, J. Wheeler, M. Barrass, E. Bell, D. Holden, W. Moir, N. Lofthouse, H. Hassall, R. Langton
Referee: M. Griffiths (Abertillery)
Attendance: 100,000

HUNGARY'S VICTORY AT WEMBLEY

Hungary beat England in the match at Wembley yesterday by six goals to three. The picture on the left shows G. Grosics, the Hungarian goalkeeper, clearing a high centre as Robb, England's left wing, and Mortensen, the centre forward, go in to the attack. Right: Hungary's second goal. Merrick, England's goalkeeper, failing to stop a deflection off the foot of Eckersley, the left back.

NEW LINER.—An artist's impression of the new 22,000-ton Cunard liner Saxonia, which is expected to be launched early next year. She and her sister ship, the new Ivernia, will serve Quebec and Montreal from the United Kingdom.

PRINCESS MARGARET being welcomed on her arrival at the Stock Exchange yesterday.

FAT-STOCK SHOW.—Aberdeen Angus cattle in the judging ring at the Birmingham Agricultural Exhibition Society's fat cattle show which was opened in Bingley Hall yesterday. The show closes on Saturday.

WESTMINSTER VISIT:—The Moderator of the General Assembly of the Church of Scotland, Dr. J. Pitt-Watson (second from right), being greeted by Mr. Henderson Stewart, M.P., on his arrival at the House of Commons yesterday. On the left is Dr. E. F. V. Scott and next to him is Dr. J. Moffett.

THE TIMES CROSSWORD PUZZLE No. 7,387

ACROSS

1 They have reached their greatest heights (5, 3).
5 The label on a tin (5).
9 It's in the past but the play's may be now (4, 4).
10 So an extremist taken trouble to get loved (6).
12 A highly competitive event (3, 4).
13 "Hanging and wiving goes by destiny," she said (7).
14 Films notices (anag.) (12).
17 Designed to pull one over the Pons Asinorum, maybe (6, 6).
21 Quarles's poems (7).
23 17, lacking its power unit, backs to a weatherclock (7).
24 Spirit of opera (5).
25 An objection sounds intentional (8).
26 Macaulay or Aytoun, so to speak (5).
27 On this both 13 and 23 begin like 20 (8).

DOWN

1 Female method in Ireland (6).
2 See: it might be so easy (6).
3 This calendar's a bad record (7).
4 A gift that's strained ? (7, 5).
6 In which a road ran (7).
7 Here music-hall acts go down with the cheaper seats (5).
8 A chambermaid in college (8).
11 An evil of grain that is not to be pardoned (12).
15 The traditional "blunt instrument" (4, 4).
16 Cobblers' trade association ? (7).
18 Novel young lady who entered the world (7).
19 Did her two negatives make an affirmative ? (7).
20 Estimate (6).
22 Let sap rise in the shades (6).

SOLUTION OF PUZZLE No. 7,386

. In Crossword Puzzle No. 7,385 the solution of clue 23 down should have read SOUP.

9

ENGLAND v HUNGARY

INTERNATIONAL FRIENDLY, 1953

England felt so certain of their invincibility that they did not even bother to enter the first three World Cups. When they finally did take part – in 1950 – the resulting shambles was dismissed as a freak. After all, no foreign power had ever won on English soil. But when the brilliant Hungarians came to Wembley late in 1953 a day of reckoning was in store – and *The Times* correspondent Geoffrey Green was at his brilliant best.

"They shot with the accuracy and speed of archers.
It was Agincourt in reverse"

ENGLAND 3
HUNGARY 6

INTERNATIONAL FRIENDLY
25 NOVEMBER 1953
WEMBLEY STADIUM
....

BY GEOFFREY GREEN,
ASSOCIATION FOOTBALL
CORRESPONDENT
26 November

Yesterday by 4 o'clock on a grey winter's afternoon within the bowl of Wembley Stadium the inevitable had happened. To those who had seen the shadows of the recent years creeping closer and closer there was perhaps no real surprise. England at last were beaten by the foreign invader on solid English soil. And it was to a great side from Hungary, the Olympic champions, that the final honour fell. They have won a most precious prize by their rich, overflowing, and to English patriots, unbelievable victory of six goals to three over an England side that was cut to ribbons for most of an astonishing afternoon. Here, indeed, did we attend, all 100,000 of us, the twilight of the gods.

There is no sense in writing that England were a poor side. Everything in this world is comparative. Taken within the framework of British football they were acceptable. This same combination – with the addition of the absent Finney – could probably win against Scotland at

Hampden Park next April. But here, on Wembley's velvet turf, they found themselves strangers in a strange world, a world of flitting red spirits, for such did the Hungarians seem as they moved at devastating pace with superb skill and powerful finish in their cherry bright shirts.

One has talked about the new conception of football as developed by the continentals and South Americans. Always the main criticism against the style has been its lack of a final punch near goal. One has thought at times, too, that perhaps the perfection of football was to be found somewhere between the hard hitting, open British method and this other more subtle, probing infiltration.

Yesterday the Hungarians, with perfect teamwork, demonstrated this midway point to perfection. Theirs was a mixture of exquisite short passing and the long English game. The whole of it was knit by exact ball control and mounted by a speed of movement and surprise of thought that had an English team ground into Wembley's pitch a long way from the end. The Hungarians, in fact, moved the ball swiftly along the ground with delicate flicks or used the long pass in the air. And the point was that they used these variations as they wished, changing the point of attack at remarkable speed. To round it off – this was the real point – they shot with the accuracy and speed of archers. It was Agincourt in reverse.

One has always said that the day the continental learned to shoot would be the moment British football would have to wake up. That moment has come at last. In truth, it has been around the corner for some time, but there can no longer be any doubt. England's sad end on the national stage now proclaims it to the skies.

Outpaced and outmanoeuvred by this intelligent exposition of football, England never were truly in the match. There were odd moments certainly when a fitful hope spurted up, such as when Sewell put us level at one all at the quarter hour and later during a brave rally that took England to half-time 2–4 down. Yet these were merely the stirrings of a patriot who clung jealously to the past. The cold voice of reason always pressed home the truth.

Indeed from the very first minute the writing loomed large on Wembley's steep and tight-packed banks. Within 60 seconds Hungary took the lead when a quick central thrust by Bozsik, Zakarias, and Hidegkuti left the centre-forward to sell a perfect dummy and lash home, right foot, a swift rising shot to the top corner of Merrick's net. The ball was white and gleaming. It could have been a dove of peace. Rather it was a bird of ill-omen, for from that moment the Hungarians shot 10 times to every once of England.

Just before England drew level a sharp move of fascinating beauty, both in conception and execution, between Czibor and Puskas was finished off by Hidegkuti. But the Dutch referee gave the centre-forward offside, which perhaps was charitable as things ended. Yet the English reply when it did come also arrived excitingly, for Johnston, intercepting in his own penalty area, ran forward to send Mortensen through. A quick pass to the left next set Sewell free and that was one all as a low left-foot shot beat Grosics.

But hope was quickly stilled. Within 28 minutes Hungary led 4–1. However disturbing it might have been, it was breathtaking. At the twentieth minute, for instance, Puskas sent Czibor racing down the left and from Kocsis's flick Hidegkuti put Hungary ahead again at close range, the ball hitting Eckersley as he tried a desperate interception. Almost at once Kocsis sent the fast-moving Czibor, who entered the attack time after time down the right flank, past Eckersley. A diagonal ground pass was pulled back by Puskas, evading a tackle in an inside-right position – sheer jugglery, this – and finished off with a fizzing left-foot shot inside the near post.

Minutes later a free kick by the progressive Bozsik was diverted by Puskas's heel past the diving Merrick, and England, 4–1 down with the half-hour not yet struck, were an army in retreat and disorder. Certainly some flagging courage was whipped in that rally up to half-time by Matthews and Mortensen, both of whom played their hearts out, crowded as they were, but though it brought a goal it could no more turn back the tide of elusive red shirts than if a fly had settled on the centre circle.

After an acrobatic save by Grosics to a great header by Robb it was Mortensen, dashing away from a throw-in, losing then recovering the ball and calling up some of his dynamic past, who now set Wembley roaring as he sped through like a whippet to shoot England's second goal. But 2–4 down at half-time clearly demanded a miracle in the space left after some of the desperate escapes at Merrick's end that had gone hand in hand with the telling Hungarian thrusts and overall authority.

Within 10 minutes of the interval the past was dead and buried forever. A great rising shot by Bozsik as the ball was caressed back to him on the edge of the penalty area after Merrick had turned Czibor's header on to the post made it 5–2, and moments later Hidegkuti brought his personal contribution to three within a perfect performance as he volleyed home Hungary's sixth goal from a lob by Puskas. It was too much. Though Ramsey said the last word of all for England with a penalty kick when Mortensen was brought down half an hour from the end, the crucial lines had been written and declaimed long since by Hungary in the sunshine of the early afternoon. Ten minutes before the end Grosics, with an injured arm, surrendered his charge to Geller, his substitute, but by now a Hungarian goalkeeper was but a formal requirement.

So was history made. England were beaten at all points, on the ground, in the air, and tactically. Hidegkuti, a centre-forward who played deep in the rear supplying the midfield link to probing and brilliant inside-forwards and fast wingers, not only left Johnston a lonely, detached figure on the edge of England's penalty area but also scored three goals completely to beat the English defensive retreat. But Johnston was not to blame; the whole side was unhinged. The speed, cunning, and shooting power of the Hungarian forwards provided a spectacle not to be forgotten.

Long passes out of defence to five forwards who showed football dressed in new colours was something not seen before in this country. We have our Matthews and our Finney certainly, but they are alone. Taylor and Sewell, hard as they and the whole side now fought to the last drop, were by comparison mere workers with scarcely a shot between them at the side of progressive, dangerous artists who seemed able to adjust themselves at will to any demand. When extreme skill was needed it was there. When some fire and bite entered the battle after half-time it made no difference.

English football can be proud of its past. But it must awake to a new future.

MATCH FACTS

England 3	Hungary 6
Sewell 13, Mortensen 38, Ramsey 57 pen	*Hidegkuti 1 20 53, Puskas 24 27, Bozsik 50*

England: G. Merrick, A. Ramsey, W. Eckersley, W. Wright, H. Johnston, J. Dickinson, S. Matthews, E. Taylor, S. Mortensen, J. Sewell, G. Robb
Hungary: G. Grosics, J. Buzanszky, M. Lantos, J. Bozsik, G. Lorant, J. Zakarias, L. Budai, S. Kocsis, N. Hidegkuti, F. Puskas, Z. Czibor
Referee: L. Horn (Netherlands)
Attendance: 105,000

10

WOLVERHAMPTON WANDERERS v HONVED

CLUB FRIENDLY, 1954

Stan Cullis and Matt Busby, managers of Wolverhampton Wanderers and Manchester United – the two best teams in the country in the mid 1950s – were forward-thinkers who understood that the game had to look to new horizons. Cullis organised friendlies against top Continental teams, utilising the magical new medium of floodlights. One game, against Honved of Hungary, was to prove crucial in the founding of the European Cup.

"To snatch the final victory was a performance in skill, team spirit, and stamina that needed no batteries and pylons of glittering arc lamps to illuminate it"

WOLVERHAMPTON WANDERERS 3 HONVED 2

CLUB FRIENDLY
13 DECEMBER 1954
MOLINEUX
....

**BY GEOFFREY GREEN,
ASSOCIATION FOOTBALL
CORRESPONDENT**
14 December

So Wolverhampton Wanderers have done it again! First Moscow Spartak. Now Honved, from Budapest, the side containing seven internationals and six men of the fabulous Hungarian side who were at Wembley in November of last year. Yet at half-time, when Honved led by two goals to none under the floodlights of Molineux, one was prepared once more to write that night and day these Hungarians are the ones. But a superlative rally that gathered momentum all through a storming second half took Wolves just past the post by three goals to two, the last two decisive thrusts from Swinbourne coming within a minute of each other with just a fraction less than a quarter of an hour left for play.

Although it in no way minimises Wolverhampton's wonderful achievement, it must be said that mud was on their side. The Hungarians were certainly lost in the mire in the last half.

Wolverhampton did British football proud under the night sky. To recover two goals lost in the opening 14 minutes to such opposition, and then snatch the final victory was a performance in skill, team spirit, and stamina that needed no batteries and pylons of glittering arc lamps to illuminate it. Nor is it easy to identify any special hero in what so obviously was a team effort. But one cannot pass by Wright at the heart of the defence. He was a giant astride the blackened, scarred battlefield.

At the beginning Wright's tactics were to move far forward into midfield following the deep playing tactics of Machos, a centre-forward in the style of Hidegkuti. Behind Wright, Flowers kept watch for the central thrust of Kocsis, the real spearhead these days of Hungarian forward play. Later Wright changed his methods, leaving Flowers and Slater to kill the attack in its early midfield birth. Either way Wright was matchless, both from the ground and in the air and one could see that he has now appreciated how the Hungarians work into position for the final cutting through task.

Wolverhampton reached their heights in attack only after the interval, though there was a phase just before the change of ends when Farago was called upon for a series of brilliant saves from Swinbourne, Hancocks and Smith. It was the Hungarian goalkeeper then who kept the Honved 2–0 lead secure to half-time, though it was Swinbourne, the other real hero with Wright, who was finally to make the night his own.

But for all Wolverhampton's pressure and prodding in the first half it was Honved who showed the real class, the real touches of their deep artistry in unfriendly conditions. Their two goals could have been more, for the chances they made and lost were far more open and inviting than those created by Wilshaw or Swinbourne behind Lorant at the other end.

Yet what plain sailing it all seemed to be for Honved after the opening quarter of an hour and how little could we anticipate the violent twist in store. At the eleventh minute a lovely triangular move between Bozsik, Kocsis, and Budai down the right flank ended in a handling infringement by Flowers. Puskas, left-footed, took the free kick from the right of the penalty area and placed the ball perfectly for Kocsis – the greatest header in the world – to nod past Williams.

Four minutes later Bozsik and Kocsis again were at it, and there was Machos moving silently and swiftly through the middle to leave Williams helpless once again. Two up to Honved and all over, it seemed. It could have been, too, had not Williams twice turned aside shots from Czibor before the interval. Once a dazzling Honved attack saw Puskas set Kocsis free, but his shot stuck in the mud behind Williams.

These were the sudden breaks with sharp passes chipped through the air by a Honved forward line that looked only to attack and left the defence to look after itself. What they truly lacked now was the influence of a Hidegkuti to support Bozsik – a great ball player – in midfield. Otherwise it was the Wolves, using the open central spaces, who were seeing most of the ball.

But from the fifth minute of the second half the heroic tale began to unfold itself. Kovacs pushed Hancocks in the penalty area and the little winger gave the first wings to his side from the spot. From then on it was Wolverhampton, and only Wolverhampton, all the way. With seven corners in the next 25 minutes they rose to their heights; sweeping through the quagmire, Honved were on their heels in defence, Puskas was deep in the mud and a spent force; Kocsis tried the through pass to both wings, but now Wolverhampton knew the Honved trick of drawing forward the defence and splitting it from behind.

With 14 minutes left the explosive point was reached. Slater sent Wilshaw free with a perfect long pass down the left and Swinbourne was up to head in the cross past a scattered defence. Two all. But Wolverhampton were not content with that. They had scented victory a long way back and now they knew it was near. In the next minute it was there. Wilshaw broke free from a tackle on the half-way line, swept down in a long dribble, drew Lorant and sent Swinbourne through for a glorious winning goal. The roars must have echoed throughout the Midlands.

Yet as the clock reluctantly released the last dying seconds Honved in one last gasp all but arose to save their necks. Bozsik, always the cool artist in the mud, sent Czibor like lightning clean through the middle of the Wolves defence. But Williams met the moment of crisis with a clear judgment. His was the save of the night for by it he saved Wolverhampton their great victory.

MATCH FACTS

Wolverhampton Wanderers 3	Honved 2
Hancocks 49 pen, Swinbourne 76 77	*Kocsis 10, Machos 14*

Wolverhampton Wanderers: B. Williams, E. Stuart, W. Shorthouse, W. Slater, W. Wright, R. Flowers, J. Hancocks, P. Broadbent, R. Swinbourne, D. Wilshaw, L. Smith

Honved: L. Farago, L. Rakoczi, J. Kovaks, J. Bozsik, G. Lorant, N. Banyai, L. Budai, S. Kocsis, F. Machos (sub: L. Tichy), F. Puskas, Z. Czibor

Referee: R. Leafe (Notts)
Attendance: 55,000

11

ARSENAL v MANCHESTER UNITED

FOOTBALL LEAGUE FIRST DIVISION, 1958

In the winter of 1957–58, Manchester United were trailing Wolverhampton Wanderers in pursuit of a third successive League championship. But, having defied the Football League to take part, they were through to the last eight of the European Cup. After winning the home leg 2–1, they were due to travel to Belgrade to face Red Star in the second leg of the quarter-final. But first Busby's Babes faced a league game at Arsenal.

"The players came off arm in arm. They knew they had finally fashioned something of which to be proud"

ARSENAL 4
MANCHESTER UNITED 5

FOOTBALL LEAGUE,
FIRST DIVISION
1 FEBRUARY 1958
HIGHBURY

....

**BY GEOFFREY GREEN,
ASSOCIATION FOOTBALL
CORRESPONDENT**
3 February

There was a whiff of the old days at Highbury on Saturday. There must have been some premonition about it, too: the crowds fairly poured in, a 64,000 gathering filling to the rim of the stadium far up where it cut a grey sky. And they were fairly repaid with a feast as the giants of yesterday and today fought out a chivalrous wavering struggle.

There were two heroic phases. It will take a month of Sundays to forget them. The first came shortly after half-time when in the bat of an eyelid – precisely two minutes and 30 seconds on the stop watch – Herd and Bloomfield (twice) put the ball in Gregg's net three times to wipe out United's 3–0 lead at the interval. That set a spark to the gunpowder. It stirred some of the Arsenal atmosphere – if not the skill – of a quarter of a century ago when Hulme, Jack, Lambert, James, and Bastin were sweeping all before them.

It was admirable. But perhaps even more admirable was the Manchester reply. Lesser sides would have wilted in the face of such a cruel blast. The wall of noise that thundered over the stadium fed Arsenal's sudden ecstasy and added to the assault. But put to the touch United showed their mettle. As if they were nonchalantly dismissing a troublesome fly they suddenly spun two more intricate, precision moves to leap ahead again to 5–3. Here was their true pedigree, though Arsenal came once more to 4–5, leaving the end on a razor's edge.

Stumbling out of Highbury at the close one took away two clear impressions – that the old Arsenal spirit still remains for something fresh to be kindled under the new leadership of Bowen, who had an inspiring match at left half: and that Manchester United now appear to have committed themselves to all-out attack in their effort to overtake Wolves at the head of the Championship. It matches the Hungarian outlook of four years ago and seems to say in so many words "All right. If you score three, four or five, we will score, four, five or six."

Arsenal, too, caught much of this same buoyancy. Although three goals down at the interval they yet shared much of the pattern, as Bowen and the bustling Groves, wandering inwards from the right wing, drove them on. Where they failed over those early stages was a lack of penetration and ideas once the penalty area came in sight. There Herd, Bloomfield, Tapscott, and Nutt turned along the lines of latitude in a vain quest to search out the areas between Jones, Byrne, and the other Manchester defenders.

Gaps there were in the Manchester portcullis, but until that extraordinary upheaval later Arsenal failed to nose their way through.

How different was the Manchester attacking conception. With Taylor a mobile hub and Colman the link, Scanlon, Viollet, Charlton, and Morgans flew down the lines of longitude, switching the ball with a swift, flowing precision. Scanlon, for one, showed a clean pair of heels to everyone in sight, while young Charlton underlined his growing poise and stamina with a mature, powerful display as a foil to the nomadic Taylor and Viollet. His sharp shooting from any angle alone is worth a trick or two to this new young Manchester line that is rapidly finding the winged feet of a Mercury.

Their combined speed left Arsenal's timid finishing in a state of bankruptcy by the interval. First Edwards cruised up to the edge of the penalty area to shoot home a square pass from Morgans under Kelsey's late dive. That was after 10 minutes. By the half hour Arsenal had raised a counterattack and it was now that there came a typical Manchester riposte. At one end Gregg, with the speed of light, made a superb diving save to Groves's header. From his clearance Scanlon sprinted 70 yards down the left, chased all the way by Tapscott full tilt. Over flashed the centre and Charlton crashed the ball home. Bang. Instead of 1–all, it was 2–0 to United, and before half-time 3–0 when Taylor swept in Morgans's pass. By then, too, Charlton had had two certain goals diverted by the remarkable interceptions of Arsenal's full-backs covering a helpless goalkeeper.

So Manchester United settled down to coast home gently over the last half and the rest of us to some peaceful, academic browsing. Suddenly the peace was shattered. With half an hour left there came a huge explosion. Herd volleyed in a lob from the tireless Bowen; Bloomfield holed out Groves's clever header and almost at once proceeded to glance a deep centre from Nutt off his eyebrows past Gregg's dive – all these at close range. It was no hallucination. Here was reality. Arsenal were level at 3–all and Manchester had been taken by the ears. The crowd thundered like a turbulent sea.

Now the champions changed gear. Charlton fed the swift Scanlon, and little Viollet appeared like a jack-in-the-box to head them into the lead again. Next Colman sent Morgans away and Taylor, taking the last pass, cut in to beat Kelsey from an acute angle. That was 5–3 to the United, who had opened their eyes again. But Bowen and Groves, now a power at inside-right, still had something to say. They opened the way for Herd, and away went Tapscott to steer his shot inside the far post.

The thermometer was doing a war dance. But mercifully that was the finish. There was no breath left in anyone. The players came off arm in arm. They knew they had finally fashioned something of which to be proud.

MATCH FACTS

Arsenal 4
*Herd 58, Bloomfield 60 61,
Tapscott 76*

Manchester United 5
*Edwards 10, Charlton,
Taylor 44 71, Viollet 64*

Arsenal: J. Kelsey, S. Charlton, D. Evans, G. Ward, J. Fotheringham, D. Bowen,
V. Groves, D. Tapscott, D. Herd, J. Bloomfield, G. Nutt
Manchester United: H. Gregg, W. Foulkes, R. Byrne, E. Colman, M. Jones,
D. Edwards, K. Morgans, R. Charlton, T. Taylor, D. Viollet, A. Scanlon
Referee: G.W. Pullin (Bristol)
Attendance: 63,578

12

EINTRACHT FRANKFURT v REAL MADRID

EUROPEAN CUP FINAL, 1960

The fifth European Cup final was the first to be played in Britain and there was huge interest in seeing first-hand the exotic superstars of Real Madrid, who had won the first tournament in its first four years. Hampden Park was filled with what is still the largest attendance for a European Cup or Champions League final ... and they were not disappointed.

"Real opened rather like elder statesmen a little weary of great occasions but resolved to find their own tempo in their own good time"

EINTRACHT FRANKFURT 3
REAL MADRID 7

EUROPEAN CUP FINAL
18 MAY 1960
HAMPDEN PARK

....

19 May

In a European Cup final of high artistry, superb forward play, and astonishing goals, Real Madrid overwhelmed Eintracht of Frankfurt, maintained their dominance in this competition, and sustained their claim to being the finest football team in the world.

The match was a triumph for Puskas, formerly captain of Hungary, and one of the world's outstanding forwards who scored four goals. He,

Gento, and Di Stefano, who scored three times, were the irresistible striking forces for Madrid and in sustained passages in the second half the quality of their forward play and ball control was of such finely drawn skill, of such accuracy, imagination and, indeed impudence, as to bring thundering down around them vast waves of delighted appreciation from Hampden's mighty crowd.

Real opened rather like elder statesmen a little weary of great occasions but resolved to find their own tempo in their own good time. Eintracht, by contrast, were vigorous, open, and resolute in their play and quite unmindful, it seemed, of Real's fearful reputation. In the very first minute a Meier cross shot almost beat Dominguez, who only just touched it onto the bar and safety. The experienced Kress at outside right, with forceful dribbling and running, kept the Real defence at stretch and nervous. After 19 minutes Stein made a deep thrust on the right and Kress stole secretly through the central defence to volley the low cross home.

Real produced an immediate counter-attack. Dominguez cleared, Puskas headed on, and Gento was liberated behind the Eintracht defence, his shot clipping only just outside the far post. Canario on the right, for once bludgeoned and elbowed a path past Hoefer and Di Stefano swept home the low pass in the 27th minute. Three minutes later when Loy stopped, but failed to hold a Canario shot, Di Stefano was on hand to shoot the goal over the sprawling goalkeeper from two yards.

At the 44th minute Puskas scored a remarkable goal. Backing up a Del Sol attack he took possession a yard from the by-line eight yards from the near post. From this frightening position he hit the roof of the net with an awesome left-foot shot. Thus it was 3–1 Real at the interval.

When, at the fifty-fourth minute, Puskas scored from a penalty the contest dissolved into an exhibition. The fifth goal, six minutes later, was splendid. A clearance by Santamaria was taken 50 yards at great speed by Gento, who put over a short cross and Puskas headed home. Ten minutes later Puskas came with yet another. With his back to the goal he suddenly spun round and found with his left-foot shot the only possible fraction of target space at the angle of bar and post.

Stein scored for Eintracht and Di Stefano from the re-start promptly cut a path through to score with a hard shot. Stein scored another, but the night truly belonged to Puskas, one of the most dynamic personalities ever known in football, to Gento and Di Stefano and, of course, to Real Madrid who have now won all five European Cup finals played.

MATCH FACTS

Eintracht Frankfurt 3
Kress 18, Stein 72 75

Real Madrid 7
*Di Stefano 27 30 71,
Puskas 45+1 56 pen 60 71*

Eintracht Frankfurt: E. Loy, F. Lutz, H. Hofer, H. Weilbacher, H. Eigenbrodt, D. Stinka, R. Kress, D. Lindner, E. Stein, A. Pfaff, E. Meier
Real Madrid: R. Dominguez, Marquitos, J. Santamaria, Pachin, J.-M. Vidal, J.-M. Zarraga, Canario, L. Del Sol, A. Di Stefano, F. Puskas, F. Gento
Referee: J. Mowatt (Glasgow)
Attendance: 127,621

13

TOTTENHAM HOTSPUR v SHEFFIELD WEDNESDAY

FOOTBALL LEAGUE FIRST DIVISION, 1961

Once in a while a team emerges that sets new standards in how the game is played. Such a side was the Tottenham Hotspur combination assembled by Bill Nicholson at the start of the 1960s. Stylish, cool and led by the loquacious Danny Blanchflower, their ambition was to become the first to win the mythical League and FA Cup Double in the 20th century.

"So the first leg of the football spring double has been captured by a side who all through the season have shown a touch of the thoroughbred"

**TOTTENHAM HOTSPUR 2
SHEFFIELD WEDNESDAY 1**

FOOTBALL LEAGUE
FIRST DIVISION
17 APRIL 1961
WHITE HART LANE

....

**BY GEOFFREY GREEN,
ASSOCIATION FOOTBALL
CORRESPONDENT**
18 April

Tottenham Hotspur are champions and last night at White Hart Lane was in its way a night of nights for the men of north London, even though their victory over their nearest and fiercest rivals, Sheffield Wednesday, was not quite the match it ought to have been. Not that one expected very much else. There was too much at stake.

It was a nervy, and often far too passionate, battle played out in a hot, seething atmosphere of a 61,000 crowd which had about it something of the clamour of a Plaza de Toros. Still, Spurs have done it and the first to congratulate them at the end as the crowds tried to swarm on to the field past barriers of police were Sheffield Wednesday themselves, a hard, economical side with a great defence that had fought Spurs all the way.

At the finish when all the figures had disappeared from the battleground

WHITE HART LANE NIGHT OF NIGHTS

SPURS CHAMPIONS AFTER FIERCE FINAL STRUGGLE

From Our Association Football Correspondent

Tottenham Hotspur 2, Sheffield Wednesday 1

Tottenham Hotspur are champions and last night at White Hart Lane in its way a night of nights for the men of north London, even though their victory over their nearest and fiercest rivals, Sheffield Wednesday, was not quite the match it ought to have been. Not that one expected very much else. There was too much at stake.

It was a nervy, and often far too passionate, battle played out in a hot, seething atmosphere of a 61,000 crowd which had about it something of the clamour of a Plaza de Toros. Still, Spurs have done it and the first to congratulate them at the end as the crowds tried

LEADING POSITIONS

	P.	W.	D.	L.	F.	A.	Pts.
Tottenham Hotspur ...	39	30	4	5	111	49	64
Sheffield Wednesday...	39	22	12	5	74	41	56
Wolverhampton W'ders	40	24	7	9	96	70	55
Everton ...	40	23	6	14	81	67	46
Burnley ...	38	19	6	13	93	72	44
Manchester United ...	40	17	8	15	81	71	42

to swarm on to the field past barriers of police were Sheffield Wednesday themselves, a hard, economical side with a great defence that had fought Spurs all the way.

At the finish when all the figures had disappeared from the battleground the great crowds were crying: " We want Danny, we want Danny ", but this was a not a night on which the Tottenham captain Blanchflower was at the scintillating peak of his form. Nor need one be surprised, for it was not the sort of struggle in which his refined artistry could live for too long, with the pace and the fierceness of the tackling such as they were. So the first leg of the football spring double has been captured by a side who all through the season have shown a touch of the thoroughbred. It is only when they have fallen from their own high pinnacle that one has tended to be critical, but taken over eight months of a hard testing season in all kinds of conditions and tension theirs has been a masterly effort.

Now they stand within 90 minutes of the twentieth century has so far proved to be a mirage. Whether Spurs can pull it off now remains to be seen. Leicester City still have much to say about that and we must wait now until May 6. Yet it is a season on which Tottenham can look proudly; the season when they won their second championship just 10 years after 1951 when their present manager was a playing member of that earlier triumphant team.

VASTLY EXCITED

Tottenham have broken all kinds of records so far. Looking back one can remember their 16 unbeaten matches from the opening day of the season, which in itself was a new mark in history; they have 30 wins to their name already, which is more than any side has ever had in the First Division; they have set up a club record of 111 goals; and they have been watched by over two million people. A greater figure than has ever before watched a club in a League season. Now remains the double to be snatched and only three more points from their three remaining matches to beat Arsenal's total of 66 points set up in 1931.

A quarter of an hour after the end last night, when the players came out of the directors' box to take their bows from a cheering, vastly excited populace, one could look back rather more disinterestedly on a tense and passionate game in which there were several stirring duels. Smith against Swan, colleagues of the England side, down the middle; Mackay against Craig, two Scotsmen; and the withering speed of Jones, who, cleverly fed by White, was the real mainspring of Tottenham's great fight here.

And, my goodness, how they had to fight. At the half-hour, with Tottenham on top, breaking up the Spurs' delicate

rhythm with their sharp tackling, the men of Yorkshire took the lead when Megson flashed home a rebound from the edge of the penalty area following a free kick by Fay.

Tottenham at that point looked in real trouble with Blanchflower only occasionally able to exert his steadying influence. Then came the dramatic turn. It was all contained within the last three minutes of the dying half. First Ellis, who nine times out of 10 had the measure of Norman in the air—put only in the air—headed Wilkinson's cross beyond everyone, but it hit the Tottenham post and was scrambled away. A minute later Baker's long upfield clearance was flicked backwards by little Dyson as he beat the massive Swan in the air and there was Smith hooking the ball over Megson with his right foot and smashing it into the roof of Springett's net with his left.

One—all, and White Hart Lane was a sea of waving figures, yet nothing compared with the scene just on the stroke of half-time. It was then that Blanchflower, taking a free kick, signalled Norman up into the Wednesday penalty area. Blanchflower placed the ball perfectly. Norman headed sideways and there was Allen with a superb volley, taken shoulder high, crashing the ball again past Springett. One could hardly hear oneself speak during the interval.

At last Tottenham were ahead and once they had got the scent they were always just that much smoother at the change of ends to hold on to their prize. But not before Smith had once crashed into another colleague of his in the England side, Springett, who was off the field for five minutes being rapidly repaired while Johnson took over the green sweater under the Wednesday crossbar. If there were any heroes at this last turn of the card they were Jones, for Tottenham, and Swan, for Sheffield Wednesday, who played as fine a game as I have ever seen from him at centre-half. Now for May 6.

TOTTENHAM HOTSPUR.—Brown; Baker, Henry; Blanchflower, Norman, Mackay; Jones, White, Smith, Allen, Dyson.
SHEFFIELD WEDNESDAY.—Springett; Johnson, Megson; Swan, Kay; Finney, Craig, Ellis, Fantham, Wilkinson.
REFEREE.—T. W. Dawes (Norfolk).

RANGERS DRAW AT HALIFAX

Queen's Park Rangers, who easily beat Halifax Town 5—1 at Loftus Road on Saturday, were fortunate to share points in a rearranged Third Division fixture against the same opponents last night. In spite of being handicapped by an injury to their left back, Hudson, Halifax were the superior team and only splendid goalkeeping by Drinkwater saved Rangers from defeat. Holmes scored from a penalty in the first half for Halifax and Andrews equalized after the interval. The dropped point leaves Walsall favourites to accompany Bury into the Second Division. They have one more point than Rangers.

	Home			Away							
	P.	W.	D.	L.	W.	D.	L.	F.	A.	Pts.
Bury	43	14	5	2	11	5	6	101	53	60
Walsall	43	13	5	2	9	2	12	92	60	51
Queen's Park R.	43	11	6	4	6	9	7	88	55	49
Watford	43	11	4	6	6	4	12	77	64	42

In a scrappy match at Stockport, a goal by the Northampton Town centre forward, Edwards, earned them a 1—1 draw and enhanced their chances of promotion to the Third Division.

	Home			Away							
	P.	W.	D.	L.	W.	D.	L.	F.	A.	Pts.
Peterborough Utd	43	17	4	1	9	6	6	123	61	62
Crystal Palace	43	13	5	3	6	6	10	98	68	49
Northampton T.	43	14	4	4	4	9	8	84	48	49
Bradford	43	14	4	3	3	7	12	76	62	45
York City	43	16	3	3	1	6	14	80	77	43

DRYSDALE CUP SQUASH

The results in the Drysdale Cup junior squash rackets Competition at the R.A.C. yesterday were:—

FOURTH ROUND.—C. J. Clabbon (Brighton) beat A. C. Flint (Greshaw's) 9—2, 9—1, 9—1; G. Sanders (Cumberland) beat V.M.G. Wand (Loretto) 6—9, 9—6, 9—4; G. C. Aylward (Tonbridge) beat D. L. Pennington (Ardingly) 10—8, 9—1, 9—1; J. D. Fairburn (Halbury) and J.R.C. beat G. N. Stiff (Southampton) 9—7, 9—5, 9—4; R. Kaye (Oldham) beat A. A. Shaw (Millfield) 9—1, 9—1, 9—1; E. R. Phazey (Eton) and L. Crisford (Uppingham) beat R. Tubolz (St. Edward's) 9—0, 9—4, 9—2; E. R. Phazey (Eton) beat Long Brieish (late Eton) 9—4, 9—2; R. J. Wheeler (E.C.S.) beat R. L. Ellis (Watford) 9—2, 9—2; H. C. Pascoe (Copenhagen) beat C. M. Graham (Eton) 9—3, 9—4, 9—2.

Jubilant Sheffield Wednesday and disconsolate Tottenham Hotspur after Megson had scored Sheffield's goal at White Hart Lane last night. The pensive figure in the foreground is Mackay.

LACROSSE LOGIC CONFOUNDED

SOUTH SUCCEED AFTER 59 YEARS

FROM OUR LACROSSE CORRESPONDENT

The South's lacrosse team confounded all forecasts at Elmers End on Saturday by winning 3—0 against what was reported to be the finest North team for many years. The South thereby gained their first victory in the series since 1902, a precedent is unlikely anyone present remembered.

That both teams were strong was undisputed. That the recent improvement in the South's team standards would lead to a close match was obvious. That the suspect South attack—not so weakened as might have been expected by the replacement of the injured Gillette by Pritchard —would score few goals against the North's tough defence was inevitable. That everything made abnormal North victory likely, since their attack could hardly fail to achieve at least six goals, was therefore logical.

What was not foreseen was that the South's defence could play so furdily and unerringly, that the Oxford and Cambridge tourists could have learnt so much in America, and that the South would be so much fitter than their opponents. Honours went to Shaw, Wilkinson, Arnold, Leord and Bibby, five resilient, big-hearted backs who subdued the North's forwards.

QUICK GOALS

They all marked their men closely, handled, cleared and covered expertly, checked and foraged vigorously, and never spared themselves. Behind them, Allsop in goal coped calmly with the few good shots, cleared constructively, and played with inspiring confidence. Ahead, Richardson contained McDiarmid, the North's centre.

When the first quarter ended fairly at 0—0, the South were content. With still no score by half-time, they were curious as to the possibilities. But it needed three goals in seven exciting minutes during the third quarter—a long shot by Richardson, who shortly afterwards gave a perfect pass to Warrington for a goal from the crease, and finally another long shot, from Lyons —to give the South the scent of victory.

The fourth quarter was played in relative silence as the tension mounted and anxiety grew. Finally the South, almost embarrassed by their success, were able to walk off proud and worthy winners past their surprised opponents.

SOUTH.—R. T. Allsop (Cambridge University); D. T. Wilkinson (Oxford University), J. Lord (London University), G. D. Arnold (Purley); C. A. Shaw (Cambridge University), H. Bibby (London University), A. J. Richardson (Norwood); J. K. Roberton (Hampstead); A. R. Lyons (Cambridge University), I. J. Lyons (Purley) (captain), G. H. Metcalfe (Purley), M. Warrington (London University).
NORTH.—G. E. Allison (Old Hulmeians); F. M. McClymon (Old Hulmeians), R. M. Threlfall (Old Hulmeians), R. R. Clayton (South Manchester and Wythenshawe) (captain), W. K. Cowperthwaite (Mellor), J. Jordan (Manchester University); C. G. Bowker (South Manchester and Wythenshawe), D. McDiarmid (Mellor), R. T. Pennington (Old Hulmeians), H. L. Bennett (Old Glovians), A. E. Morland (Old Hulmeians).

CRICKET

ST. KITTS.—Leeward Islands.—Sir Kitts, 155 (Barber 5 for 27, Wells 3 for 40; Walker 2 for 8, Wheatley 2 for 28) and Barber 3 for 19; Swarbrick v M.C.C., 235 for 5 dec.

TODAY'S FIXTURE.—Cambridge University Freshmen's Trial.

RUGBY UNION.—PUBLIC SCHOOLS SINGLES FINAL (at Whitgift School).—P. Mellor (Bedford) beat R. F. Bulgin (Marlborough Taylors') 11—6, 8—11, 11—3).

TOP SEEDS OUT OF RACKETS

TEETH DRAWN FROM SINGLES

FROM OUR RACKETS CORRESPONDENT

The amateur rackets singles championship, which made a tentative start at Queen's Club during the weekend while the chief interest was centred on the doubles, will be continued there each day this week, a light schedule of eliminating matches working up to the semi-final round on Saturday and the final on Sunday.

What had promised to be an especially appetizing competition, with a record entry of 32, has had its main teeth drawn at the last moment by the unavoidable removal of the premier players. G. W. T. Atkins, the champion and indisputably the favourite, has had to withdraw because of a business trip abroad, and J. R. Thompson, seeded at the opposite pole, has scratched with a strained elbow which was seen to be causing him discomfort in the doubles.

These two between them have won the event for each of the past nine years.

Moreover, C. J. Swallow, who was never a certain runner this year but was originally entered in the draw as third seed, has left the field under pressure of examinations, and other notable absentees include C. T. M. Pugh and J. M. G. Tildesley.

The competition as a whole is therefore lamentably pollarded, leaving Gracey, Bridgeman, and Milford as the leading contestants in the top half and Milne, and Leonard with the best chance down below. It would indeed be rare tournament if Milford, who was champion as long ago as 1930, and Milne, fresh from winning the public schools singles, are left to dispute the title on Sunday, but stranger things could happen in rackets.

ABOVE USUAL LEVEL

Milne has already cleared one steep hurdle in beating Connell in the closest match so far. It was sad to see the loser leave the event in the opening round, for he is always good to watch and was unlucky in the sense that he was well capable of beating many of those who have gone farther, but Milne just got home in five games. Both players missed a great many chances, hitting down at critical moments or failing to take advantage of gaping openings for a kill, but there were many splendid strokes, each maintaining a punishing pace and not sparing himself in covering the court.

Gracey went on his way competently enough at the expense of Warburg, who kept his end up well in the second game, but Leonard was fully extended by Hogben. This, another unfortunate meeting at this stage, was well above the usual level for a first round match, as was to be expected from these two. Leonard had the heavier service and was also the more aggressive in his return, though there was little between them in the rallies.

RESULTS.—R. M. K. Gracey beat D. J. Warburg (9—4, 15—5, 15—6); R. D. Leonard beat J. F. R. Hogben (15—4, 15—8, 15—9, 15—8); G. W. A. Milne beat G. C. Connell (7—15, 15—12, 15—5, 16—13, 15—9).

NEW £5,700 GOLF TOURNAMENT

MATTHEWS LEARNS LESSON

LAWN TENNIS VETERAN FINALLY FALTERS

F. Wallis, who was playing lawn many years before the British hard court champion, S. Matthews, was born, gave Matthews a hard time on the Connaught hard court at Chingford, Essex, yesterday. Wallis won nine games in a row to lead 3—1 in the second round match by 6—1, 6—3 in the final set before Matthews won second round match by 6—1, 6—3.

Matthews looked to have the match well in hand. He took the first set 6—1, Wallis, top-spinning the ball to a lilzing length and slowing the game to his own pace, forced his opponent make many errors. Before Matthews knew what was happening, he had lost the set to love and was 0—3 down in the second set.

Matthews then pulled himself together. Instead of trying for outright winning, he kept the ball in play, realizing that the longer the rally lasted the less chance he had of winning. So it was Wallis, his reserves of stamina gone, not put the same bite into his play and he lost the next six games.

Matthews is 15. Two others of the age gave impressive performances. Stilwell (Essex) recovered from deficit in the third set to beat G. Lancashire), the Army champion, 1—6, 8—6, and Miss F. Truman, Essex, the younger sister of Britain's bee ace, Miss C. C. Truman, beat Hewitt (Essex) by 6—4, 6—1.

G. Sanders, who reached the Cumberland Club tournament week, had an easy win in the men's. He took seven successive games from to beat E. Jones (Hertfordshire) by 6—1. Another convincing winner women's singles was British junior pion Miss R. A. Blakelock. Miss dropped only the fourth game of to beat Miss R. Hunt (Surrey 6—0.

Speedy progress in the men's was made by M. A. Otway, the National player, who, with a bye in round, played through two singles loss of only four games to reach quarter-final round.

CONNAUGHT RESULTS

MEN'S SINGLES

R. F. Hancock (Essex) beat C. W. Larient shire) (6—7, 6—1).
R. J. Jarrett (Derbyshire) beat A. C. Camps (6—6, 6—1).
C. K. Applewhaite (Lancs) beat B. Citron (9 (6—2, 6—2).
A. O. Lucas (Suffolk) beat W. S. Ghai (Essex (6—2, 6—4).
Lord Mexborough (Yorks) beat T. K. Clap (6—2, 6—2).
A. G. Irwin (Essex) beat J. W. Richardson (4 (6—2, 6—1).
W. J. Hodgkinson (Devon) beat R. A. F. (Essex) (6—2, 7—5, 6—4).
R. J. Aguirre (Essex) beat A. Garrell (Essex) (6—1, 6—1).
R. Gorevito (Australia) beat M. A. Inward (5, 6—4).
G. W. Stilwell (Essex) beat G. W. Stubbs (6—2, 8—6, 8—6).
R. F. Walton (Warwickshire) beat J. E. (Essex) (9—7, 3—6, 6—2).
R. Rick (Middlesex) beat D. Pay (Middlesex) (6—2, 6—4).
A. P. Billingham (Northants) beat J. MIllne (6—0, 6—4).
C. Bee (Surrey) beat P. Wing (Essex) (6—3, 6—4).
R. K. Collins (Essex) beat E. C. Harradine (6—2, 6—4).
R. Condy (Ireland) beat A. A. Peirce (Essex) (6—2, 6—2).

SECOND ROUND

S. Matthews (Lancs) beat F. J. Wallis (Essex) (6—1, 6—3).

the great crowds were crying: "We want Danny, we want Danny", but this was a not a night on which the Tottenham captain Blanchflower was at the scintillating best we know of him. Nor need one be surprised, for it was not the sort of struggle in which his refined artistry could live for too long, with the pace and the fierceness of the tackling such as they were. So the first leg of the football spring double has been captured by a side who all through the season have shown a touch of the thoroughbred. It is only when they have fallen from their own high pinnacle that one has tended to be critical, but taken over eight months of a hard testing season in all kinds of conditions and tension theirs has been a masterly effort.

Now they stand within 90 minutes of the League and Cup double, which throughout the twentieth century has so far proved to be a mirage. Whether Spurs can pull it off now remains to be seen. Leicester City still have much to say about that and we must wait now until May 6. Yet it is a season on which Tottenham can look back proudly; the season when they won their second championship just 10 years after 1951 when their present manager was a playing member of that earlier triumphant team.

Tottenham have broken all kinds of records so far. Looking back one can remember their 16 unbeaten matches from the opening day of the season, which in itself was a new mark in history; they have 30 wins to their name already, which is more than any side has ever had in the First Division; they have set up a club record of 111 goals; and they have been watched by over two million people, a greater figure than has ever before watched a club in a League season. Now remains the double to be snatched and only three more points from their three remaining matches to beat Arsenal's total of 66 points set up in 1931.

A quarter of an hour after the end last night, when the players came out of the directors' box to take their bows from a cheering, vastly excited populace, one could look back rather more disinterestedly on a tense and passionate game in which there were several stirring duels. Smith against Swan, colleagues of the England side, down the middle; Mackay against Craig, two Scotsmen; and the withering speed of Jones, who, cleverly fed by White, was the real mainspring of Tottenham's great fight back.

And, my goodness, how they had to fight. At the half-hour, with Wednesday on top, breaking up the Spurs' delicate rhythm with their sharp tackling, the men of Yorkshire took the lead when Megson flashed home a rebound from the edge of the penalty area following a free kick by Kay.

Tottenham at that point looked in real trouble with Blanchflower only occasionally able to exert his steadying influence. Then came the dramatic turn. It was all contained within the last three minutes of the dying half. First Ellis, who nine times out of 10 had the measure of Norman in the air – but only in the air – headed Wilkinson's cross beyond everyone, but it hit the Tottenham post and was scrambled away. A minute later Baker's long upfield clearance was flicked backwards by little Dyson as he beat the massive Swan in the air and there was Smith hooking the ball over Megson with his right foot and smashing it into the roof of Springett's net with his left.

One-all, and White Hart Lane was a sea of waving figures, yet nothing compared with the scene just on the stroke of half-time. It was then that Blanchflower, taking a free kick, signalled Norman up into the Wednesday penalty area. Blanchflower placed the ball perfectly, Norman headed sideways and there was Allen with a superb volley, taken shoulder high, crashing the ball again past Springett. One could hardly hear oneself speak during the interval.

At last Tottenham were ahead and once they had got the scent they were always just that much smoother at the change of ends to hold on to their prize. But not before Smith had once crashed into another colleague of his in the England side, Springett, who was off the field for five minutes being rapidly repaired while Johnson took over the green sweater under the Wednesday crossbar. If there were any heroes at this last turn of the card they were Jones, for Tottenham, and Swan, for Sheffield Wednesday, who played as fine a game as I have ever seen from him at centre-half. Now for May 6.

MATCH FACTS

Tottenham Hotspur 2	**Sheffield Wednesday 1**
Smith 42, Allen 43	*Megson 28*

Tottenham Hotspur: W. Brown, P. Baker, R. Henry, D. Blanchflower, M. Norman, D. Mackay, C. Jones, J. White, R. Smith, L. Allen, T. Dyson
Sheffield Wednesday: P. Springett, P. Johnson, D. Megson, B. Hill, P. Swan, A. Kay, A. Finney, R. Craig, K. Ellis, J. Fantham, D. Wilkinson
Referee: T.W. Dawes (Norfolk)
Attendance: 61,200

14

TSV 1860 MUNICH v WEST HAM UNITED

EUROPEAN CUP WINNERS' CUP FINAL, 1965

Playing stylish, progressive football with a twist of Continental sophistication, West Ham United, under the management of Ron Greenwood, were one of the most attractive teams in England in the 1960s. After winning the FA Cup in 1964, they qualified for the European Cup Winners' Cup and reached the final which, fortuitously, was staged at Wembley.

"I wonder if one day next July Moore, West Ham's captain, who gave a storming, immaculate display last night, will also lead his England team up to the royal box to collect the World Cup"

WEST HAM UNITED 2
TSV 1860 MUNICH 0

EUROPEAN CUP
WINNERS' CUP FINAL
19 MAY 1965
WEMBLEY STADIUM

**BY GEOFFREY GREEN,
ASSOCIATION FOOTBALL
CORRESPONDENT**
20 May

The European Cup Winners' Cup is back in England. It has been taken away, for the moment at least, from the Latin nations. After Tottenham Hotspur, who beat Atletico Madrid in Rotterdam in 1963, it was the turn of West Ham United to set the light glowing in London last night.

Before a wildly excited crowd of 100,000 who paid £76,000 for their pleasure, they beat a fine Munich side under the floodlights of Wembley. Never was money better spent. This was a night when the true supporter of the game, who lives on the terraces through the winter, was at last given his rightful place in the national theatre of the game. Seldom before can Wembley have heard such a rich, vibrant noise from beginning to end.

The match we saw last night was more than a triumph for West Ham. It was a triumph for the game of football itself. Apart from some body checking by Kohlars, the German

SPORTING NEWS

WEMBLEY FINAL A TRIUMPH FOR FOOTBALL

WEST HAM RISE TO VICTORY WITH BOLD IMAGINATION

From Our Association Football Correspondent

West Ham United 2, T. S. V. Munich 0

The European Cup Winners' Cup is back in England. It has been taken away, for the moment at least, from the Latin nations. After Tottenham Hotspur, who beat Atlético Madrid, in Rotterdam in 1963, it was the turn of West Ham United to set the light glowing in London last night.

Before a wildly excited crowd of 100,000 who paid £76,000 for their pleasure, they beat a fine Munich side under the floodlights of Wembley. Never was money better spent. This was a night when the true supporter of the game, who lives on the terraces through the winter, was at last given his rightful place in the national theatre of the game. Seldom before can Wembley have heard such a rich, vibrant noise from beginning to end.

The match we saw last night was more than a triumph for West Ham. It was a triumph for the game of football itself. Apart from some body checking by Kohlars, the German left back, who frequently ran Sealey off the tracks, the Hungarian referee scarcely had anything to do as he kept close control over two sides intent upon the ball rather than the men. Here was a vast British crowd seeing a final victory on their own soil. They were gracious in their applause for both victor and vanquished.

I wonder if one day next July Moore, West Ham's captain, who gave a storming, immaculate display last night, will also lead his England team up to the royal box to collect the World Cup. That is far ahead, and perhaps too much to think about. But here at least, laid before us, was a match that decorated the Wembley stage. It was a magnificent game, and if West Ham took too long to make the final thrust, that was the only flaw I could find in their football.

CROWD HELD

Their football was bold and imaginative; the outlines of their break from defence into attack were always sharper than Munich's. West Ham's was a polished performance, indeed, but the match as a whole got the crowd by the throat from the beginning.

The thickset Germans, in pure white, played the triangular wall-pass exquisitely. Rebele, a danger on the left wing, and Brunnenmeier interchanged passes at top speed across the field with the inside forwards, Kuppers and Grosser, forcing West Ham into several dangerous positions. Yet by half time Brown, Moore, Peters and the rest had read these lines of approach and were pouncing on them, nipping the moves in the bud just when they looked like coming to full flower.

West Ham could have been two up before the interval when, first, at the quarter-hour, Sissons glided across from Dear just past the post with only the prehensile Radenkovic in front of him. That was a sitter, and poor Sissons held his head in his hands.

FRESH VITALITY

All too soon Sealey and Dear made a hash of an open goal from a cross by Sissons. We began to wonder whether they would pay for these omissions in the end. It was all high-speed action from the start, and the Germans themselves were far from idle. Twice Standen had to make point-blank parries from terrific shots by Brunnenmeier and Grosser.

But it was always West Ham who brought a new dimension to the game and a fresh vitality; it was this new dimension, playing with numbers, playing with angles, switching positions to mesmerize the opposition, that finally began to take its toll. The paradox so far was that there had been no goals when there might have been a hatful. In the first 10 minutes of the second half poor Sissons, taking a through pass from Hurst, hit the far post with a crack. Then Radenkovic made the second of two magnificent diving saves from Hurst.

All the time the Germans, with Brunnenmeier and Rebele reacting to the promptings of their progressive wing halves, still had things to say for themselves. Twice Standen had to make last ditch saves. The first, from Grosser, from close in after a 50-yard dribble; then, even more dramatically, from Kuppers after the inside right had slipped past the goalkeeper's dive only to be robbed at the last second in front of an open goal by Standen's foot.

The final threads were now being drawn tighter and closer by West Ham, however. Driven on by Moore, who played a giant's part, backed up tirelessly by Peters and Kirkup—a splendid performance this—the goal that West Ham so deserved finally came. With 20 minutes left Boyce intercepted a German pass out of defence, broke into an open space, drew Kohlars, and sent Sealey in. Radenkovic could only have heard the winger's angled shot as it hit the roof of his net.

DOUBLE SUMMERSAULT

Sealey did a double somersault in joy, the stadium exploded with noise, and within 90 seconds West Ham had scored again. They seemed to hover for a moment, then rise like a phoenix as Peters flicked on a free-kick by Moore for Sealey once more to stab the ball in. It was all over. But still poor Sissons's luck would not change as a withering right-foot shot from the edge of the penalty area almost bent the angle of Radenkovic's goalpost. And it was Radenkovic again who saved a shot by Dear, close in, after a flowing move between Sissons, Peters, Sissons, and Moore.

The West Ham clans were singing "Eee Aye Adio we've won the Cup" as, at the end, Moore received his cup from the president of U.E.F.A. He held it aloft after a victory lap and the lights shone on it. This was the end of their present road. All along the route they have played intelligent, intellectual football, and we may hope that the reflections of it will go wider throughout the British game.

To round off what will be one of the memorable nights was the way Wembley cheered the losers from the field; the way the Munich banners saluted West Ham in their hour; and how Olympic Way itself was lined by cheering thousands waving farewell to the German supporters in their coaches going home.

WEST HAM UNITED.—Standen; Kirkup, Burkett; Peters, Brown, Moore; Sealey, Boyce, Hurst, Dear, Sissons.

T.S.V. MUNICH.—Radenkovic; Wagner, Kohlars; Benn, Reich, Luttrop; Heiss, Kuppers, Brunnenmeier, Grosser, Rebele.

REFEREE.—I. Zsolt (Hungary).

UNITED WIN ON AGGREGATE

Manchester United 0, Strasbourg 0

The strength of the Strasbourg defence and failings near goal prevented Manchester United scoring in the first half of the Inter Cities Fairs Cup quarter-final at Old Trafford last night. Three times threatening through passes by Herd were cut out, although twice it needed a foul on Best to halt progress.

Manchester United increased their pressure as the half went on, and Schuth made excellent saves from Stiles and Herd.

Strasbourg showed plenty of neat mid-field play but lacked pace near goal, as was shown when Biernet, the centre forward went through only to have the ball taken from his toes by Foulkes.

Another narrow escape for Strasbourg came in the fifty-seventh minute, when Schuth pushed out a shot by Charlton for Herd to hit the upright, and another Charlton shot beat the goalkeeper but rebounded from the inside of the post.

Strasbourg were rarely seen in attack, and near the end Stiles and Charlton both shot over the Strasbourg goal from easy positions.

The five goals gained from the first leg qualify Manchester United for the semi-final against the Hungarian club, Ferencvaros.

MANCHESTER UNITED.—P. Dunne; Brennan, A. Dunne; Crerand, Foulkes, Stiles; Connelly, Charlton, Herd, Law, Best.

STRASBOURG.—Schuth; Gonzales, Sbaiz; Steiber, Devaux, Kaebel; Gress, Merschel, Biernet, Szczepaniak, Hausser.

REFEREE.—Mr. F. Geluck (Belgium).

YESTERDAY'S RESULTS

EUROPEAN CUP WINNERS' CUP.—FINAL.—West Ham United 2, T.S.V. Munich 0.

INTER CITIES' FAIRS' CUP.—Manchester United 0, Strasbourg 0 (Manchester United won 5—0 on aggregate); Atletico Madrid 3, Juventus 1 (first leg).

SCOTTISH SUMMER CUP.—Dundee United 3, Aberdeen 0; St. Johnston 2, Dundee 3; St. Mirren 1, Partick 1; Third Lanark 5, Airdrie 2; Motherwell 3, Kilmarnock 0; Hearts 2, Dunfermline 2; Falkirk 1, Hibernian 3.

Sealey (No. 7), the West Ham right winger, turns with his arms raised in triumph after scoring the second of two goals against T.S.V. Munich at Wembley last night. On his left is Peters, who gave him the opportu

RUSSELL BACKBONE OF MIDDLESEX

BUSINESSLIKE OPENING WITH BREARLEY

LORD'S.—Northamptonshire, with nine first innings wickets in hand, are 261 runs behind Middlesex.

A solid, sometimes stolid, century by Russell formed the backbone of the effort which kept Middlesex at the crease for the best part of the day. It may seem churlish to attribute dull batting to a player who has made 156 out of 246 in four hours and 40 minutes, massively buttressing his innings with 24 fours.

Nevertheless, there were times when play seemed like a ship becalmed in the doldrums, and even so naturally aggressive a player as Clark took 40 minutes to put together his first eight runs. In the last hour of the innings, however, his attacking spirit revived and, with Murray, he put on 45 runs in 40 minutes. Titmus's declaration gave Northamptonshire less than half an hour's batting and Prideaux opened with Reynolds, instead of Milburn, who was suffering from a pulled leg muscle.

PLEASANT ACTION

A businesslike, if unexciting first wicket partnership between Russell and Brearley gave Middlesex a reasonable start. Bailey, who shared the opening attack with Crump, made his first appearance last season and took five wickets in an innings three times in his first four games. He has a pleasantly rhythmic action and bowled his overs accurately, without receiving any help from a placid pitch.

When P. J. Watts replaced Crump, Brearley twice on-drove him for four and when Scott and Steele came on, Russell played a succession of bright strokes, bringing up the 50 with a firm cover drive in just over the hour and going on to reach his own half century out of 86 with another four, his seventh. At 89, Brearley drove Steele straight to the pavilion rails, but off the next ball he gave a non-violent return catch.

SLOW START

Luncheon was reached with a respectable score of 100 for one, but in the third over afterwards White swung round at a ball from P. D. Watts and, somewhat incredibly, hit it to the wicketkeeper. Parfitt was unaccountably slow in making a start and in the first hour of the afternoon the treatment of the bowling was not so much flattering as positive obsequious. For long periods the batting was as grey as the skies above.

At 148 Parfitt gently turned a ball into the hands of backward short leg, but then Russell suddenly quickened his pace and completed a meritorious hundred. His 15 fours included many fine strokes but, in three hours and a half, even these seemed widely spaced. His third 50 was compiled in much more entertaining fashion than his earlier two and, when he was out to a well-judged running catch at cover, he had added another nine to his total of boundaries.

With Russell out, Clark and Murray

WORCESTERSHIRE CRAMPI BY THEIR OWN FEARS

From a Staff Reporter

THE OVAL.—Surrey, with all first innings wickets in hand, are 203 runs behind Worcestershire.

So far this season Worcestershire have shown little of the form which won them the championship last summer and Surrey have done little to justify their rating as strong challengers for that title.

Yesterday Worcestershire's batsmen continued to struggle, but the Surrey attack fully justified Stewart's decision to field. The opening bowlers, swinging the ball well in a helpful atmosphere, captured two early wickets and then the spinners took over to reduce the scoring rate to a crawl. Harman and Pocock, the young Surrey hopes, both bowled particularly well.

In the two hours of the morning Worcestershire scored 46 runs for the loss of three wickets. For most of the time the rate of overs kept pace with the runs, and for a brief while was in the lead. Of the 41 overs 24 were maidens. Ten of these were bowled consecutively by the spinners while the score stood at 30. Harman conceded one four for one wicket in eight overs.

In the second period the scoring rate was a little more than doubled, 101 runs being added. The 100 itself came up at last off the sixty-sixth over at 23 minutes past three. D'Oliveira was caught early on. Headley went to his 50 with a cracking off drive for four after three hours and 40 minutes. He added 10 more before giving a catch after tea to end a stay of four hours and 20 minutes, which included nine fours. Richardson reached his 50 just before the interval in the comparatively scintillating time of 90 minutes. He added no more.

CHIEF CULPRITS

These, then, are the main details of as depressing a batting display as can have come from reigning county champions. If there has been worse, one can but be grateful for not having seen it. The wicket was described by the players as "puddingy". The ball was slow to come on to the bat. Once the slow bowlers came on the wicket was found to be conducive to spin, but the ball turned only a little, and then slowly. But none of these facts is sufficient to justify such an abysmal scoring rate.

The simple truth is that well though the Surrey bowlers bowled the Worcestershire batsmen made things difficult for themselves. Harman made the odd ball pop, and from that moment the pitch was treated with a respect it did not deserve. The batsmen played in fear of what might happen, and their forebodings their style to such an extent became stagnant.

From this criticism Kenyon anc must be exempted, because they b in the opening half-hour, though unlikely to be proud of the stro brought his downfall. He dangle on the line of the off stump and penalty. Arnold, though, bowl better balls without success, and his two wickets.

Perhaps the saddest feature of was that the chief culprits of W shire's submission to spin were the most attractive stroke-maker game today, Graveney, the elegant who has the temperament of Indian cricketers, and D'Oliveira.

Graveney began with a ring to like a well-tuned bell. Here was of beauty, but a joy for but a sh He briefly showed his effortless then retreated into his shell to in five minutes short of an hour. got a beauty from Harman which late.

OUT OF CHARACT

Headley took some quarter of a get off the mark. D'Oliveira too Both were utterly restrained and c out of character. Latterly we saw off drives from Headley but D after one square cut off Pocock, patience with that bowler and gav to Harman at mid off.

Headley, when he finally left th admitted in the pavilion that even long an innings, his timing still there. Richardson began like a pl is out of form, found it, particula hitting 12 in an over off Pocock, got out like a novice with a lof into the covers.

Gibson ran through the tail to fi five for 35.

WORCESTERSHIRE.—FIRST INN

*D. Kenyon, c. Edrich, b. Arnold ..
M. J. Horton, c. Long, b. Arnold ..
R. G. A. Headley, c. Long, b. Gibson
T. W. Graveney, c. Long, b. Harman
B. D'Oliveira, c. Harman, b. Pocock
D. W. Richardson, c. Stewart, b. Gibson
†R. Booth, c. Smith, b. Gibson ..
D. N. F. Slade, c. Tindall, b. Gibson
N. Gifford, c. Storey, b. Gibson ..
L. J. Coldwell, b. Storey .. ..
J. A. Flavel, not out .. ..
Extras (b. 7, l.-b. 5, w. 2, n.-b. 3)

Total .. ..

FALL OF WICKETS.—1—10, 2—11, 3— 5—151, 6—168, 7—192, 8—205, 9—207, 10—

BOWLING.—Arnold, 23—6—55—2; Gibso 35—5; Storey, 20.1—6—39—1; Harman, 13- Pocock, 20—13—26—1; Tindall, 6—0—18—

SURREY.—FIRST INNINGS

W. A. Smith, not out .. ..
J. H. Edrich, not out .. ..

Total (no wkt.) .. ..

*M. J. Stewart, S. J. Storey, K. F. Barringto Tindall, D. Gibson, †A. Long, G. Arnold, and P. I. Pocock to go in.

UMPIRES.—W. H. Copson and R. S.

DOCILE PITCH SPOILS COWDRE DECISION TO FIELD

GRAVESEND.—Kent, with all first innings wickets in hand, are 346 runs behind Leicestershire.

Hallam played a captain's part ing his side together on the few o that the bowlers looked at all c and he must have been well pleas left back, who frequently ran Sealey off the tracks, the Hungarian referee scarcely had anything to do as he kept close control over two sides intent upon the ball rather than the men. Here was a vast British crowd seeing a final victory on their own soil. They were gracious in their applause for both victor and vanquished.

I wonder if one day next July Moore, West Ham's captain, who gave a storming, immaculate display last night, will also lead his England team up to the royal box to collect the World Cup. That is far ahead, and perhaps too much to think about. But here at least, laid before us, was a match that decorated the Wembley stage. It was a magnificent game, and if West Ham took too long to make the final thrust, that was the only flaw I could find in their football.

Their football was bold and imaginative; the outlines of their break from defence into attack were always sharper than Munich's. West Ham's was a polished performance, indeed, but the match as a whole got the crowd by the throat from the beginning.

The thickset Germans, in pure white, played the triangular wall-pass exquisitely. Rebele, a danger on the left wing, and Brunnenmeier interchanged passes at top speed across the field with the inside forwards, Kuppers and Grosser, forcing West Ham into several dangerous positions. Yet by half-time Brown, Moore, Peters and the rest had read these lines of approach and were pouncing on them, nipping the moves in the bud just when they looked like coming to full flower.

West Ham could have been two up before the interval when, first, at the quarter-hour, Sissons glided a cross from Dear just past the post with only the prehensile Radenkovic in front of him. That was a sitter, and poor Sissons held his head in his hands.

All too soon Sealey and Dear made a hash of an open goal from a cross by Sissons. We began to wonder whether they would pay for these omissions in the end. It was all high-speed action from the start, and the Germans themselves were far from idle. Twice Standen had to make point-blank parries from terrific shots by Brunnenmeier and Grosser.

But it was always West Ham who brought a new dimension to the game and a fresh vitality; it was this new dimension, playing with numbers, playing with angles, switching positions to mesmerise the opposition, that finally began to take its toll. The paradox so far was that there had been no goals when there might have been a hatful. In the first 10 minutes of the second half poor Sissons, taking a through pass from Hurst, hit the far post with a crack. Then Radenkovic made the second of two magnificent diving saves from Hurst.

All the time the Germans, with Brunnenmeier and Rebele reacting to the promptings of their progressive wing halves, still had things to say for themselves. Twice Standen had to make last-ditch saves.

The first, from Grosser, from close in after a 50-yard dribble; then, even more dramatically, from Kuppers after the inside right had slipped past the goalkeeper's dive only to be robbed at the last second in front of an open goal by Standen's foot.

The final threads were now being drawn tighter and closer by West Ham, however. Driven on by Moore, who played a giant's part, backed up tirelessly by Peters and Kirkup – a splendid performance this – the goal that West Ham so deserved finally came. With 20 minutes left Boyce intercepted a German pass out of defence, broke into an open space, drew Kohlars, and sent Sealey in. Radenkovic could only have heard the winger's angled shot as it hit the roof of his net.

Sealey did a double somersault in joy, the stadium exploded with noise, and within 90 seconds West Ham had scored again. They seemed to hover for a moment; then rise like a phoenix as Peters flicked on a free-kick by Moore for Sealey once more to stab the ball in. It was all over. But still poor Sissons's luck would not change as a withering right-foot shot from the edge of the penalty area almost bent the angle of Radenkovic's goalpost And it was Radenkovic again who saved a shot by Dear, close in, after a flowing move between Sissons, Peters, Sissons, and Moore.

The West Ham clans were singing "Eee Aye Adio we've won the Cup" as, at the end, Moore received his cup from the president of UEFA. He held it aloft after a victory lap and the lights shone on it. This was the end of their present road. All along the route they have played intelligent, intellectual football, and we may hope that the reflections of it will go wider throughout the British game.

To round off what will be one of the memorable nights was the way Wembley cheered the losers from the field; the way the Munich banners saluted West Ham in their hour; and how Olympic Way itself was lined by cheering thousands waving farewell to the German supporters in their coaches going home.

MATCH FACTS

West Ham United 2	TSV 1860 Munich 0
Sealey 70 72	

West Ham United: J. Standen, J. Kirkup, J. Burkett, M. Peters, K. Brown, R. Moore, A. Sealey, R. Boyce, G. Hurst, B. Dear, J. Sissons
TSV 1860 Munich: P. Radenkovic, M. Wagner, W. Kohlars, S. Bena, H. Reich, O. Luttrop, A. Heiss, H. Kuppers, R. Brunnenmeier, P. Grosser, H. Rebele
Referee: I. Zsolt (Hungary)
Attendance: 97,974

15

ENGLAND v WEST GERMANY

WORLD CUP FINAL, 1966

The appointment of Alf Ramsey as England supremo in 1962 marked a radical departure for the national game: for the first time the manager was allowed to choose the players. Boldly, Ramsey predicted that his team would win the World Cup on home soil in 1966. The campaign began slowly but gained momentum until, on July 30, the nation stopped to see if England could defeat West Germany and be crowned champions of the world.

"That was it, we thought. Wembley shuddered like some great monster turning in its sleep"

ENGLAND 4
WEST GERMANY 2

AFTER EXTRA TIME

WORLD CUP FINAL
30 JULY 1966
WEMBLEY STADIUM

....

BY GEOFFREY GREEN, FOOTBALL CORRESPONDENT

1 August

England, the pioneers of organised football and the home of the game, are the new World Champions for the first time. They are still pinching themselves.

So, too, are others of us, the sceptics, who from the start thought the feat beyond our reach. But it is no dream. If England, perhaps, did not possess the greatest flair, they were the best prepared in the field, with the best temperament based on a functional plan. Further to that, they built up to a peak. The timing of it was good.

West Germany, twice semi-finalists in other years and the surprise holders of 1954, when they upset the magnificent Hungarians, were beaten fair and square in a match of high drama. A squally afternoon of showers and sunshine was rich with excitement and some passing controversy that tested the stamina and will-power of both sides, to say nothing of the 93,000 crowd ranged around Wembley's steep banks and

RAMSEY PROVED RIGHT IN WORLD CUP

England surmount final test of morale

FROM OUR FOOTBALL CORRESPONDENT

England 4, West Germany 2

England, the pioneers of organized football and the home of the game, are the new World Champions for the first time. They are still pinching themselves.

So, too, are others of us, the sceptics, who from the start thought the feat beyond our reach. But it is no dream. If England, perhaps, did not possess the greatest flair, they were the best prepared in the field, with the best temperament based on a functional plan. Further to that, they built up to a peak. The timing of it was good.

West Germany, twice semi-finalists in other years and the surprise holders of 1954, when they upset the magnificent Hungarians, were beaten fair and square in a match of high drama. A squally afternoon of showers and sunshine was rich with excitement and some passing controversy that tested the stamina and will-power of both sides, to say nothing of the 93,000 crowd ranged around Wembley's steep banks and the 400 million others watching on television around the world.

The climax came in a punishing period of an extra half-hour after the Germans had first led and then saved their necks with an equalizing goal at 2—2 a mere 15 seconds from the end of normal time.

WORLD CHAMPIONS

BANKS

COHEN J. CHARLTON WILSON

STILES MOORE

R. CHARLTON PETERS

BALL HURST HUNT

To have the Cup thus apparently dashed from their lips at the very moment of victory was a deep test of England's morale. Psychologically Germany should have had the edge in that extra time. But Moore and his men rose magnificently to the challenge. Only the two sets of actors down on that green stage could have truly felt the bitter disappointment or the elation of that moment.

But as England were yet girding themselves for the extended test Mr. Ramsey, their manager, walked calmly among his men to say: "All right. You let it slip. Now start again!" They did. They reacted vigorously. How some of them found the resilience and the stamina finally to outstay a German side equally powerful physically, equally determined, equally battle-hardened, was beyond praise.

All were heroes: none more so than Moore as he drove his side on; than the little flame-haired Ball, a real ball of fire this great day, as he covered every blade of grass on Wembley's wide spaces; than the intelligent Peters; than Hurst—preferred to Greaves at the eleventh hour as a striker—who crashed in two goals during extra time to become the first man to hit the net three times in a World Cup final.

STORYBOOK ENDING

For Hurst, for Moore, the captain, and for Ramsey, the inscrutable manager, this indeed was a storybook ending. If there are no substitutes for gods, equally there are no substitutes for courage and temperament. England had those in full measure.

Thus the 1966 championships were crowned worthily in the presence of the Queen and the Duke of Edinburgh. Earlier irritations were forgotten and the best now lingers on. And never has Wembley itself provided a more emotional setting. From early afternoon the atmosphere was electric. It fairly crackled. The terracing was a sea of waving flags, the standards of two nations; the noise was a wall of sound that drowned the flutterings of one's heart. High in the stands there came the beating of a drum, a deep, pulsating thud, almost tribal.

It set the mood of a throbbing match, climaxed in the sunshine of the end when the Germans, honourable losers, made their own farewell lap of the stadium to a warm reception and followed amid thunderous roars as the stadium rose to Moore holding the golden, winged trophy in triumphal circuit. Honour and justice were done in that proud moment beyond many dreams.

So for the sixth time in eight World Cup finals the side that scored first were finally vanquished. It was the Germans who thus followed history when they broke the ice at the thirteenth minute. The pitch, made treacherous by two earlier showers, was ripe for error. At that moment Wilson, misjudging his leap to Seeler's deep cross from the left, headed down to the feet of Haller and there was the No. 8—one of Germany's telling factors at the side of Overath, Beckenbauer, Held, and Seeler—to steer home a quick diagonal shot beyond Banks's groping fingers.

That tiny error opened the way. Wilson quickly pushed the incident to the back of his mind and though Germany, by the interval, could claim a slight advantage in possession and use of the ball it was England that had quickly drawn level—within six minutes, in fact. An infringement by Overath on Moore brought a free kick to the left; England's captain, quickly spotting a gap in the square formation of the German defence, instantly floated a 35-yard kick through the middle and there was Hurst, again making yards from the right as he had done a week earlier against Argentina, to guide in his header.

There, at 1—1, it stood at half-time with several other narrow squeaks survived at each end. Once, Banks somehow made two point-blank, reflex saves in as many seconds from Overath and Emmerich; at the other end Tilkowski parried a left foot rocket from Hunt as Peters freed his man.

TRIBAL THROB

More slanting rain greeted the start of the second half, glinting through the sunshine to say that somewhere there was a fox's wedding. For a spell the struggle marked time as the opposing forces regrouped for the break-through. The crowd, still vibrant, sang "Oh my, what a referee!" as the Swiss made some pernickety decisions. Bobby Charlton, following a deep cross from Peters on the left, once missed the far post by a whisker. Only 18 minutes remained then. But that tribal drum began to throb again and almost at once England answered its call.

With 13 minutes to go Ball, the effervescent, the irrepressible, often tackling back to help the defence like Bobby Charlton, now forced a corner on the right. He took the kick himself: the ball, helped on, reached Hurst, whose first-time shot was blocked by Hottges. Suddenly, there was Peters all alone with the rebound in front of Tilkowski and the next second his shot billowed the net. It was West Ham United again.

That was it, we thought. Wembley shuddered like some great monster turning in its sleep. But the Germans were not done yet. Stiles, Moore and the rest covered England's rear as even the fair-haired Schnellinger came up to reinforce the last efforts of the tireless Haller, Overath, Held and Beckenbauer.

SAD THING

With the last minute already unwinding itself the Cup was almost in Moore's grasp. Then it happened. One moment England's balloon of hope was floating gaily, or with the appearance of gaiety. The next, pop, there it was, a wrinkled, sad thing upon the floor.

An infringement, wrongly, I think, given against Jack Charlton's header as Seeler made a back for him, led to Emmerich blasting his free kick into the wall of English defenders. Held blazed at the rebound, the ball spun across Banks's goalmouth—not without a suspicion of German hands on the way—and suddenly Weber was on hand to win a mêlée at close range as he joyfully shot Germany level.

Those bitter 15 seconds might have destroyed England, as they just had time to kick-off before the start of extra time. But they did not. Rolling up their sleeves and turning down their stockings as the threat of cramp drew near on the porous pitch they stuck to their planned approach—Moore and Stiles, blandly shrewd, mopping up the German central thrusts; Bobby Charlton and Peters providing from midfield; Ball, unbelievably, everywhere like a wasp; Hurst and Hunt the hammer men at the front.

To add to the swaying excitement of a match of tiny errors punished there came one final point for debate. Extra time approached its mid-way as Stiles, now a five-barred gate, set Ball free with a long pass down the right. Over came the instant centre, Hurst trapped, swivelled and thundered his shot to the underside of Tilkowski's crossbar. The ball hurtled down to be headed clear by Weber.

Was it over the line or not? It was all a matter of speed of eye. It looked good. The referee consulted his Russian linesman. The wait was agonizing. The answer was "goal!" The Germans protested as England, 3—2 ahead, rejoiced and the stadium erupted.

WEST HAM MOVE

How both sides saw out the last stages of a punishing two hours was beyond praise. But the final stroke of all was perhaps the best as the book was snapped shut. Again with only seconds to go it was England's turn to write finis to it all

Again it was Hurst who did so imperiously. In another West Ham move he took a deep pass from Moore through the extended German defensive lines—now committed to last despairing attack—drove himself onwards to end with a rasping left foot shot that rattled Tilkowski's net.

The matter was decided, dismissed. England's players had proved Ramsey right. The Cup belonged to them and later they belonged to the jubilant, chanting crowds of the capital on what was another V.E. night.

ENGLAND.—Banks; Cohen, J. Charlton, Wilson, Stiles, Moore (captain), Peters, R. Charlton, Ball, Hurst, Hunt.

WEST GERMANY.—Tilkowski; Hottges, Schultz, Weber, Schnellinger, Beckenbauer, Haller, Seeler, Held, Overath, Emmerich.

REFEREE.—G. Dienst (Switzerland).

WORLD CUP RESULTS

GROUP 1

	Englan	Uruguay	Me ico	Franc:	Points
England ..	–	0-0	2-0	2-0	[illegible]
Uruguay ..	[illegible]	–	0-0	2-1	4
Mexico ..	0-2	[illegible]	–	1-1	2
France ..	-2	-2	1-1	–	

GROUP 2

	W Germany	Argentina	Spain	Switzerland	Points
W. Germany ..	—	0-0	2-1	5-0	5
Argentina ..	0-0	—	2-1	2-0	5
Spain	1-2	1-2	—	2-1	2
Switzerland ..	0-5	0-2	1-2	—	0

GROUP 3

	Portugal	Hungary	Brazil	Bulgaria	Points
Portugal ..	—	3-1	3-1	3-0	6
Hungary ..	1-3	—	3-1	3-1	4
Brazil	1-3	1-3	—	2-0	2
Bulgaria ..	0-3	1-3	0-2	—	0

GROUP 4

	Russia	N Korea	Italy	Chile	Points
Russia	—	3-0	1-0	2-1	6
N. Korea ..	0-3	—	1-0	1-1	3
Italy	0-1	0-1	—	2-0	2
Chile	1-2	1-1	0-2	—	1

QUARTER-FINALS

England .. .. 1 Argentina .. 0
Russia .. .. 2 Hungary .. 1
Portugal .. 5 North Korea .. 3
West Germany .. 4 Uruguay .. 0

SEMI-FINALS

West Germany .. 2 Russia 1
England .. .. 2 Portugal .. 1

THIRD PLACE

Portugal .. 2 Russia 1

Mr. Ramsey, his dream achieved, with the Jules Rimet trophy held by Moore, the England captain. At right is Stiles.

THE ARCHITECT OF VICTORY

He won his players and they brought him his reward

FROM OUR FOOTBALL CORRESPONDENT

Three years ago when Alf Ramsey was appointed England team manager in succession to Walter Winterbottom he made what seemed a dangerous statement. "England will win the World Cup", he said.

Every year since, and sometimes month by month, he has stuck to guns that threatened to be spiked. Certainly there were some of us who felt he was living under a sword of Damocles of his own making.

But he has triumphed and I, for one, salute him, having doubted him. The sword has been swept away and replaced by a laurel wreath. Having reached the pinnacle now, sharing the past achievements of men like Vittorio Pozzo, of Italy, Vicente Feola, the Brazilian, and Sepp Heberger, of west Germany, it is anyone's guess what his next move may be. Being the intractable, withdrawn man he is we shall doubtless all be left guessing.

When asked this very point after Saturday's final he replied: "Everyone seems concerned about what I'm going to do. But there is another World Cup in Mexico in four years. It's good to have won at home; it would be good to win there. . . ."

One could put two and two together and get the wrong answer, just as it could be wrong to heed the whispers that link his name with Arsenal.

Dagenham-born, meticulous in appearance, precise and thoughtful in all he does, matching his play in other days as a studious full back for Southampton, Tottenham Hotspur and England, I have known him for all but 20 years. Although always friendly, if vaguely detached, I know him no better now than then. He has said: "After one year as England's manager I was told to grow another skin. I have done that." I believe him.

Yet talking with him into the early hours once last December the night England beat Spain 2—0 in the bitter temperature of a freezing Madrid, I believed momentarily to have penetrated behind his mask of bland reserve. It was the night the new Ramsey style, carefully planned, of perpetual motion on the field, at last emerged. His 4—3—3 plan really worked; every player clicked together in a way that is often hard to explain in football; everything went right. He talked of "this precious gem", shaping his hands in front of him as if around an imaginary football. For once there was a momentary gleam of sensitive satisfaction behind his wary eyes.

If he has mistrusted the press generally, and with reason since few supported his ideas until recently, at least he won over his players earlier. Three summers ago, during the "Little World Cup" in Brazil, there was in fact a splinter, breakaway faction within his party. That was followed by a temporary withholding of the re-appointment of Moore as captain at the start of the next season.

Yet Ramsey duly earned the respect of his crew. Entirely professional in all his planning, he has proved himself a players' man. At times they may have thought him unduly harsh, but it was always for the good of the whole and they came to recognize that.

LOYALTY AND EFFORT

Given to doctrinaire, puritanical, even apparently humourless, he has nonetheless dedicated himself to one end—victory. A lone wolf, he yet managed to build up a team spirit among his men unknown before in any international squad. The stars and the reserves were treated alike; he protected each with the same vigour and asked in return 100 per cent loyalty and effort. The answer to it all was seen at Wembley. That was England's secret.

Perseverance, planning, the trying out of 51 different players in his search for the right World Cup team blend, he has won, too, the loyalty of his assistants. When Harold Shepherdson, his chief trainer, leapt to his feet as Germany equalized on Saturday seconds before full time, all the seemingly unemotional Ramsey said was: "Sit down!" It was an order obeyed.

Analysing the 6—3 defeat of England by Hungary at Wembley in 1953, a match in which he played and suffered, he once said to me: "Four of those Hungarian goals came from outside our penalty area. We should never have lost."

Few perhaps, would agree with him there. But then many thought he had burnt his boats over the past three seasons by his prediction over the World Cup of 1966. Yet, in the end, our Alfred did not burn anything—his boats or his cakes.

THE WORLD SAYS 'WELL DONE'

England were hailed yesterday as true champions after their victory in the World Cup final. General world opinion was summed up by the Stockholm newspaper *Aftonbladet* which said: "The cup is at home and deservedly so. . . . England deserved victory not only yesterday but in the entire tournament for they were the best team. . . ."

Millions of people watched the match live on television in Europe and millions more saw it in Mexico, Canada and the United States via the Early Bird communications satellite. Many cities in western Europe reported deserted streets as people clustered round television and radio sets for the match. And from around the world came tributes to England and to their manager Alf Ramsey. *Reuter* Correspondents reported these comments:—

Soviet Sports (Moscow).—"England were worthy winners, gaining their victory both convincingly and attractively."

L'Humanite Dimanche (Paris).—"England well deserved the world cup. It was a triumph of strength and determination . . ."

La Suisse (Geneva).—"The English not only built up a superior volume of play, but showed greater staying power. About the middle of the second half the Germans seemed worn out." It singled out Alan Ball as the man of the match "always in the right place at the right time".

Tribune de Lausanne (from Maurice Simon, a confirmed doubter of Ramsey's methods).—"The only thing I can do is to go barefoot wearing a hair shirt, together with some of my colleagues who like me will have to rub their foreheads in the dust before the new god the English have found for themselves—Ramsey."

L'Avvenire d'Italia (Bologna)." We hoped the best man would win and the best man did win."

Diario de Noticias (Lisbon).—"The victory of the English, though their third goal may have aroused many doubts, was fair, though not playing a match at the level of champions, England were the best team . . ."

Marca (Madrid).—The key to England's World Cup victory was fighting spirit and physical fitness. But it attacked Swiss referee Gottfried Dienst for allowing England's third goal—"a phantom goal" it called it.

El Pais (Uruguay).—"England's most glorious day—champions of the world for the first time. Uruguay was the only team the champions could not defeat. The masters of football are now undisputed."

In Brazil England's victory came as no surprise, although in contrast to the huge excited crowds who thronged the streets for the public relays of Brazil's games few stood by the loud speakers in Sao Paulo and Rio de Janeiro to listen to commentary on the final. In Chile motorists tooted their horns to celebrate the victory and in Mexico *El Sol de Mexico* said: "It was a grand match."

But from Argentina came a sour note. Still smarting at their defeat by England in the "Battle of Wembley", newspapers in Buenos Aires spoke of Saturday's final as "a farce". One paper headlined its report, "Lucky Pirates".

YACHTING

Leading 5.5 metres helmsmen miss signal

FROM OUR YACHTING CORRESPONDENT—COPENHAGEN, JULY 31

Misunderstanding and recriminations once again marred the Royal Danish Yacht Club's centenary regatta here today. Arguments about a controversial signal, which the leading 5.5 metres helmsmen failed to notice, overshadowed the fine victory of Bob Mosbacher of the United States in the fourth race of the European Dragon championship.

The signal was hoisted to indicate that the position of the finishing line had been changed, after a sharp windshift, in order to provide a proper beat on the final leg. Provisions for such a step had been made in the sailing instructions, and the race committee were evidently quite within their rights.

Unfortunately, however, the committee vessel was moored too far away from the leeward mark and, even if the flag signal was visible, the new course direction could only be read with binoculars. Unaware of the alteration, the leading group sailed on to where they thought the finishing line should be, only to find a handful of spectators as bewildered as themselves.

DAILY TROUBLE

The resulting frustration has, sad to say, increased the general atmosphere of disenchantment. Not a day has passed yet without some trouble, and several people are suggesting that the yacht club has bitten off more than it can chew. Reluctant though one is to criticize such charming hosts, it is difficult to avoid the impression that the organization of communications are not all that they might be.

Crown Prince Harald of Norway, the leader of the first round, was among the 5.5 metres helmsmen who were led astray But the most disappointed man was Bobby Symonette, of the Bahamas, who seemed to have a good race well won on the final leg. He, among others, is determined to persuade the committee to stick to an Olympic course for the world championships later this week, and not to make any alterations during a race.

Windshifts are, of course, all too common and there is nothing duller than a race which develops into a succession of reaches. But to ask helmsmen and crews to notice a change of course while concentrating on a tricky manoeuvre at the leeward mark is almost certainly unwise. The hazards are clearly shown in the confusion that surrounded Friday's Dragon racing and the decision, late that evening, to declare the second race in the European championships void.

Another request is likely to be for the committee vessel to be moored at the starboard end of the line. To date it has been moored at the port end which makes the starting signal difficult to hear and increases the risk of jostling and barging.

There was certainly some scrambling at the start of today's Dragon championship race, amid angry shouts a Swedish boat Joy III (Jan Georgii) struck the counter of a Dutch rival, tore a spreader off the mast of the British Jerboa (P. Dyas), and finally ploughed into a French boat, ripping a large hole in her side.

In contrast, another Swedish contestant, Debutant (J. Sunderlin) which is one of the chief contenders for the title, was quickly away from the melee along with Williwaw of the United States a few yards to leeward, and both were in the first half-dozen at the windward mark.

EUROPEAN DRAGONS CHAMPIONSHIP.—SATURDAY (third race).—Chok (A. Birch, Denmark), 1; Williwaw (G. S. Friedrichs, U.S.), 2; Annie VI (R. Senet, France), 3; Debutant (J. Sunderlin, Sweden), 4; Friendship (O. Wetterberg, Sweden), 5; Maj-Britt (A. Holm, Denmark), 6. BRITISH PLACINGS.—Jerboa (P. Dyas), 8; Tara (Sir G. Smith), 10; Sandpiper (N. Streeter), 25. SUNDAY (fourth race).—Aphrodite (R. Mosbacher, U.S.), 1; Maj-Britt, 2; Chok, 3; Debutant, 4; Josephine (H. Jensen, Denmark), 5; Tara (Sir Gordon Smith, G.B.), 6. BRITISH PLACINGS.—Sandpiper, 13; Jerboa, retired.

DRAGONS SOUND WEEK SATURDAY (Second Race).—Esquire (F. Schack, Denmark), 1; Kalorius III (A. Pehrsson, Denmark), 2; N. 233 (E. Wilk-Hansen, Norway), 3. BRITISH PLACINGS.—Salamander II (R. D. Judah), 7; Karen II (K. L. Gumley), 8; Nortle (W. D. Citron), 10; Sirius (P. D. Lloyd), 11. SUNDAY (Third Race).—Mugico (H. Schult, W. Germany), 1; Kismet II (R. Lehtinen, Finland), 2; Bajade VIII (P. Nielsen, Denmark), 3. BRITISH PLACINGS.—Medusa (J. O. T. Hughes), 9; Salamander II, 16.

5.5 METRES (ROYAL SWEDISH YACHT CLUB CUP) SATURDAY (Second Race).—Figaro (F. Olsen, Norway), 1; Nirvana IV (A. Courdevey, Switzerland), 2; Chaje III (J. Nemes, Finland), 3; Yeoman XII (R. Aisher, G.B.), 5. SUNDAY (Final Race).—Web IV (W. Bernstein, Denmark), 1; Web III (P. Elvstrom, Denmark), 2; Vamp XII (R. E. Turner, U.S.), 3. Yeoman XII, 13.

FINNS.—SATURDAY.—Flodebollen (C. B. McCurrach, S. Africa), 1; Farmer (H. Wind, Denmark), 2; Musketeer (B. L. Saffery-Cooper, G.B.), 3; Trade Wind (R. H. A. Hart, G.B.), 10. SUNDAY.—Fluer (H. Wind, Denmark), 1; Flodebollen (C. B. McCurrach, S. Africa), 2; US 707 (H. Sprague, U.S.), 3.

505s.—SATURDAY.—Razzle-Dazzle (D. Bowles, G.B.), 1; D. 1901 (J. Eppers, Denmark), 2; D. 2305 (H. Fogher, Denmark), 3. SUNDAY.—Nanok II (M. Bierre Petersen, Denmark), 1; D. 2305 (H. Fogh, Denmark), 2; D. 1901 (J. Eppers, Denmark), 3. Razzle-Dazzle (D. Bowles, G.B.) 5. BRITISH PLACINGS.—Trade Winds (R. H. A. Hart, G.B.), 10; Musketeer (B. L. Saffery-Cooper, G.B.), 12.

ROUNDABOUT'S FINE DISPLAY

There was a good day's racing at Cowes yesterday. The main events were won by Zillah (D. R. Maddox) in the 22.5ft. to under 29ft. cruiser class; Roundabout (Sir Max Aitken) in the 19ft. to under 22.5ft.; Medina II (Marquess of Milford Haven) in the Darings; Marenda in the International One Designs; and Penguin Too in the Dragons.

The weather was mainly bright but squally, based on a force four south-westerly—a typical Cowes cocktail: In the cruiser starts, run off in four classes, there was considerable loose scrummaging at the Squadron end of the line. In spite of flagrant infringements of port and starboard rules, everybody seemed to take an easy attitude to their rights of protest.

After the cruisers, the new International Tempest class took off, fielding six starters and making a better fist of this operation than they did in yesterday's race. The Tempest appearance at Cowes is a gallant effort, but on its present showing the new Olympic two-man boat looks unlikely to supplant the Star.

The I.O.D. Mitzi (G. Blaxter) had passed Marenda and looked all set for a first gun. As so often happens at Cowes, however, the last beat was decisive, and Marenda regained the lead to finish first. These and Penguin Too's Dragon victory were the highlights of the inshore brigade.

The cruiser could be watched slogging out their 25-mile course covering Solent Banks. But more interest was aroused as the following divisions passed through the line. The outstanding performance of the day in this sector was by Sir Max Aitken's Roundabout, which sailed into Cowes from Copenhagen on Saturday afternoon. She made a restrained start, but passed boat after boat to finish first by over six minutes on corrected time and take the Festival of Britain Cup back in her locker.

TENNIS

BRUSSELS.—GALEA CUP.—Great Britain beat Poland, 3—2. Results:—D. Lloyd lost to B. Lewandowski (6—4, 1—6, 3—6); G. Battrick lost to T. Nowicki (2—6, 6—4, 7—9); Battrick and Lloyd beat Lewandowski and Nowicki (7—5, 8—6, 6—1); Lloyd beat Nowicki (8—6, 1—6, 6—4); Battrick beat Lewandowski (3—6, 6—4, 6—2).

BASEBALL. — NATIONAL LEAGUE. — Philadelphia Phillies 4, Pittsburgh Pirates 1; Cincinnati Reds 5, Houston Astros 1; New York Mets 6, Chicago Cubs 3; St. Louis Cardinals 3, Los Angeles Dodgers 1; Atlanta Braves 6; San Francisco Giants 5 (and 15—2). AMERICAN LEAGUE.—California Angels 2, Cleveland Indians 1; Minnesota Twins 7, Baltimore Orioles 6; Chicago White Sox 6, New York Yankees 0; Boston Red Sox 8, Washington Senators 2; Kansas City Athletics 2, Detroit Tigers 1.

the 400 million others watching on television around the world.

The climax came in a punishing period of an extra half-hour after the Germans had first led and then saved their necks with an equalising goal at 2–2 a mere 15 seconds from the end of normal time.

To have the Cup thus apparently dashed from their lips at the very moment of victory was a deep test of England's morale. Psychologically Germany should have had the edge in that extra time. But Moore and his men rose magnificently to the challenge. Only the two sets of actors down on that green stage could have truly felt the bitter disappointment or the elation of that moment.

But as England were yet girding themselves for the extended test Mr Ramsey, their manager, walked calmly among his men to say: "All right. You let it slip. Now start again!" They did. They reacted vigorously. How some of them found the resilience and the stamina finally to outstay a German side equally powerful physically, equally determined, equally battle-hardened, was beyond praise.

All were heroes: none more so than Moore as he drove his side on; than the little flame-haired Ball, a real ball of fire this great day, as he covered every blade of grass on Wembley's wide spaces; than the intelligent Peters, than Hurst – preferred to Greaves at the eleventh hour as a striker – who crashed in two goals during extra time to become the first man to hit the net three times in a World Cup final.

For Hurst, for Moore, the captain, and for Ramsey, the inscrutable manager, this indeed was a storybook ending. If there are no substitutes for gods, equally there are no substitutes for courage and temperament. England had those in full measure.

Thus the 1966 championships were crowned worthily in the presence of the Queen and the Duke of Edinburgh. Earlier irritations were forgotten and the best now lingers on. And never has Wembley itself provided a more emotional setting. From early afternoon the atmosphere was electric. It fairly crackled. The terracing was a sea of waving flags, the standards of two nations; the noise was a wall of sound that drowned the flutterings of one's heart. High in the stands there came the beating of a drum, a deep, pulsating thud, almost tribal.

It set the mood of a throbbing match, climaxed in the sunshine of the end when the Germans, honourable losers, made their own farewell lap of the stadium to a warm reception and followed amid thunderous roars as the stadium rose to Moore holding the golden, winged trophy in triumphal circuit. Honour and justice were done in that proud moment beyond many dreams.

So for the sixth time in eight World Cup finals the side that scored first were finally vanquished. It was the Germans who thus followed history when they broke the ice at the thirteenth minute. The pitch, made treacherous by two earlier showers, was ripe for error. At that moment Wilson misjudging his leap to Seeler's deep cross from the left, headed down to the feet of Haller and there was the No. 8 – one of Germany's telling factors at the side of Overath, Beckenbauer, Held, and Seeler – to steer home a quick diagonal shot beyond Banks's groping fingers.

That tiny error opened the way. Wilson quickly pushed the incident to the back of his mind and though Germany, by the interval, could claim a slight advantage in possession and use of the ball it was England that had quickly drawn level – within six minutes, in fact. An infringement by Overath on Moore brought a free kick to the left; England's captain, quickly spotting a gap in the square formation of the German defence, instantly floated a 35-yard kick through the middle and there was Hurst, again making yards from the right as he had done a week earlier against Argentina, to guide in his header.

There, at 1–1, it stood at half-time with several other narrow squeaks survived at each end. Once, Banks somehow made two point-blank, reflex saves in as many seconds from Overath and Emmerich; at the other end Tilkowski parried a left foot rocket from Hunt as Peters freed his man.

More slanting rain greeted the start of the second half, glinting through the sunshine to say that somewhere there was a fox's wedding. For a spell the struggle marked time as the opposing forces regrouped for the breakthrough. The crowd, still vibrant, sang "Oh my, what a referee!" as the Swiss made some pernickety decisions. Bobby Charlton, following a deep cross from Peters on the left, once missed the far post by a whisker. Only 18 minutes remained then. But that tribal drum began to throb again and almost at once England answered its call.

With 13 minutes to go Ball, the effervescent, the irrepressible, often tackling back to help the defence like Bobby Charlton, now forced a corner on the right. He took the kick himself: the ball, helped on, reached Hurst, whose first-time shot was blocked by Hottges. Suddenly, there was Peters all alone with the rebound in front of Tilkowski and the next second his shot billowed the net. It was West Ham United again.

That was it, we thought. Wembley shuddered like some great monster turning in its sleep. But the Germans were not done yet. Stiles, Moore and the rest covered England's rear as even the fair-haired Schnellinger came up to reinforce the last efforts of the tireless Haller, Overath, Held and Beckenbauer.

With the last minute already unwinding itself the Cup was almost in Moore's grasp. Then it happened. One moment England's balloon of hope was floating gaily, or with the appearance of gaiety. The next, pop, there it was, a wrinkled sad thing upon the floor.

An infringement, wrongly, I think, given against Jack Charlton's header as Seeler made a back for him, led to Emmerich blasting his free kick into the wall of English defenders. Held blazed at the rebound, the ball spun across Banks's goalmouth – not without a suspicion of German hands on the way – and suddenly Weber was on hand to win a melee at close range as he joyfully shot Germany level.

Those bitter 15 seconds might have destroyed England, as they just had time to kick-off before the start of extra time. But they did not. Rolling up their sleeves and turning down their stockings as the threat of cramp drew near on the porous pitch they stuck to their planned approach – Moore and Stiles, blandly shrewd, mopping up the German central thrusts; Bobby Charlton and Peters providing from midfield; Ball, unbelievably, everywhere like a wasp; Hurst and Hunt the hammer men at the front.

To add to the swaying excitement of a match of tiny errors punished there came one final point for debate. Extra time approached its mid-way as Stiles, now a five-barred gate, set Ball free with a long pass down the right. Over came the instant centre, Hurst trapped, swivelled and thundered his shot to the underside of Tilkowski's crossbar. The ball hurtled down to be headed clear by Weber.

Was it over the line or not? It was all a matter of speed of eye. It looked good.

The referee consulted his Russian linesman. The wait was agonising. The answer was "goal!" The Germans protested as England, 3–2 ahead, rejoiced and the stadium erupted.

How both sides saw out the last stages of a punishing two hours was beyond praise. But the final stroke of all was perhaps the best as the book was snapped shut. Again with only seconds to go it was England's turn to write finis to it all.

Again it was Hurst who did so imperiously. In another West Ham move he took a deep pass from Moore through the extended German defensive lines – now committed to a last despairing attack – drove himself onwards to end with a rasping left foot shot that rattled Tilkowski's net.

The matter was decided, dismissed. England's players had proved Ramsey right. The Cup belonged to them and later they belonged to the jubilant, chanting crowds of the capital on what was another V.E. night.

MATCH FACTS

England 4
Hurst 18 101 120, Peters 78

After extra time

West Germany 2
Haller 12, Weber 89

England: G. Banks, G. Cohen, J. Charlton, R. Wilson, N. Stiles, R. Moore,
M. Peters, R. Charlton, A. Ball, G. Hurst, R. Hunt
West Germany: H. Tilkowski, H.-D. Hottges, W. Schultz, W. Weber, K.-H. Schnellinger,
F. Beckenbauer, H. Haller, U. Seeler, S. Held, W. Overath, L. Emmerich
Referee: G. Dienst (Switzerland)
Attendance: 96,924

16

CELTIC v INTER MILAN

EUROPEAN CUP FINAL, 1967

The European Cup final of 1967, the first to feature a British club, threw up a fascinating culture clash. Inter Milan, winners in 1964 and 1965, were wealthy, sophisticated and – under the management of Helenio Herrera – wedded to a grimly attritional defensive style. At Celtic, meanwhile, Jock Stein had assembled a team of players drawn entirely from the Glasgow area who employed a joyful, freewheeling brand of attacking football.

"So Lisbon, Estoril, and the little fishing village down this coast, tonight belong to Glasgow"

**CELTIC 2
INTER MILAN 1**

EUROPEAN CUP FINAL
25 MAY 1967
NATIONAL STADIUM, LISBON

**BY GEOFFREY GREEN,
FOOTBALL CORRESPONDENT**
26 May

There is always a first time. Celtic, having swept Scotland clean of every prize, have now also swept the Continent. By their great victory here today in the National Stadium over Internazionale, Milan they have become the first British side to be champions of Europe.

When McNeil, the Celtic captain, at last held the trophy aloft in the glinting sunlight of a lovely evening, the 70,000 crowd stood to him as one man for there was no doubt where Portuguese hearts now lay. They remembered how Inter only two years ago had, by subtle negotiation, made Benfica, the local heroes, play the European final in Milan.

But that is past and now, at last, the Latin domination of this European competition has been broken. After years of rule by Real Madrid, then Benfica and the two clubs of Milan, the emphasis of power has switched. And the Scots have now won a place of honour that can never be taken from them.

The scenes at the end were almost tribal. Thousands of Celtic supporters invaded the pitch waving their banners and uttering wild whoops of joy. Hundreds knelt to kiss the ground and having cut slices from the turf of Wembley last month, these Scotsmen now did the same to the Cumberland soil of the stately National Stadium here.

So Lisbon, Estoril, and the little fishing village down this coast, tonight belong to Glasgow. And amidst all the bedlam the words of Jock Stein, Celtic's proud manager, to me earlier this winter come echoing back: "I would like to play Inter just once," he said, "on a neutral ground. They can shut up the game for 20 minutes and then turn on the tap to suit themselves. But we will make them work all the way for every minute and I would like to see their answer."

We got it today. The size of Celtic's performance can be measured by one fact, Milan have been champions of Europe three times in the last four years and this was only their second defeat in continental competitions in all that time.

True, today they were without Suarez, their commander-in-chief in midfield. He was absent injured. Jair, too, their Brazilian right wing, was missing. Without Suarez they had nothing to contribute in ideas for attack or control. They seemed a side suddenly without heart or skill, a side filled with apprehension.

By half-time they looked to be in extremis, and as the second half unfolded under a continuous Celtic bombardment, the Italian trainer was busy dousing his players with water in the hot sunshine that should have been their ally. Long before Celtic equalised half an hour from the end, and finally took the victory with only five minutes left, Inter looked ravaged and unlovely. Not even talented men like Mazzola, Corso, or Facchetti could bring a breath of wind to their sails.

Here was a wonderful team feat by Celtic. To recover from the psychological disadvantage of conceding a penalty kick after only seven minutes when Craig upended Cappellini and Mazzola stroked home his shot from the spot, was a performance indeed. But the longer the struggle unwound, the surer it was that Celtic would win.

If any one man deserved a crown of his own, it was Gemmell. Working on a long-standing plan deeply laid and worked out in the hope that Inter would have no counter, he swept time and again into attack down the left flank, overlapping the men in front and supplementing the 4–2–4 formation. Craig also followed suit on the right, helping the darting footwork of Johnstone. This bemused Milan and helped undermine their packed defence in depth.

For four-fifths of the evening it was Celtic, as surge after surge of attacks beat down a defence like waves crashing against a rock. That rock was

Sarti under the Milan crossbar. But for a series of dramatic saves and the help of his woodwork – struck twice on either side of the interval, first by Auld and later by Gemmell – it might have been almost a rout.

But to return to Gemmell. Every time he thrust forward, a big blond cat was set among the Italian pigeons, and when at last Craig, also up in attack, pulled the ball back diagonally from the right, there was Gemmell roaring through the middle to send home a thunderbolt for 1–1.

As the stadium exploded, with thousands of Scots dancing Highland jigs on the terracings, Celtic swept on. With Gemmell and Craig were Murdoch, Auld, and Johnstone as other master figures. Little Johnstone, perhaps, was the first to set the mood. In the opening minute he beat Burgnich in a close dribble, four times inside and out, to bring an ominous frown to Italian brows.

Celtic took the cue and built on it. They finally got their reward five minutes from the end when Gemmell again came up the left and pulled the ball back to Murdoch, whose flashing, low shot was diverted home to the corner by Chalmers. Moments later it was over. The field was full of dancing kilts.

MATCH FACTS

Celtic 2	Inter Milan 1
Gemmell 63, Chalmers 84	*Mazzola 7 pen*

Inter Milan: G. Sarti, A. Picchi, T. Burgnich, A. Guarneri, G. Facchetti, G. Bedin, M. Corso, M. Bicicli, S. Mazzola, R. Cappellini, A. Domenghini
Celtic: R. Simpson, J. Craig, T. Gemmell, R. Murdoch, W. McNeill, J. Clark, J. Johnstone, W. Wallace, S. Chalmers, B. Auld, B. Lennox
Referee: K. Tschenscher (West Germany)
Attendance: 45,000

17

BENFICA v MANCHESTER UNITED

EUROPEAN CUP FINAL, 1968

After the devastation of the Munich air crash, it took Matt Busby years to build another great Manchester United side. But by the mid 1960s a new generation of players were emerging – including the fabulous George Best – and United were once again winning domestic titles and challenging Europe's elite. In 1968, ten years after Munich, he finally led his team to a European Cup final.

"There have been many occasions of Wembley to remember, but few, apart perhaps from the final of the World Cup itself and the Stanley Matthews epic of 1953, to equal last night"

BENFICA 1
MANCHESTER UNITED 4

AFTER EXTRA TIME

EUROPEAN CUP FINAL
29 MAY 1968
WEMBLEY STADIUM

....

BY GEOFFREY GREEN,
FOOTBALL CORRESPONDENT
30 May

At last Manchester United have climbed their Everest and after 11 years of trial and effort their dreams have come true. Last night they became the first English club to win the European Cup when they beat Benfica, of Lisbon, the holders of 61 and 62 and so followed the breakthrough achieved last year by Celtic against Inter Milan.

So the crown sits on the heads of the first English club to enter this competition, seeing its wide horizons and the possibility of it on a world scale. And having now won, with a dramatic burst of seven minutes in the first half of extra time, they have helped to beat back the Latin domination that for so long had taken Continental football by the throat.

Next Manchester United will challenge Estudiantes, of Argentina, for the world club championship next season, a season that will see both United and City of Manchester treading the paths of Europe. What rivalry that will engender in the year to come.

There have been many occasions of Wembley to remember, but few, apart perhaps from the final of the World Cup itself and the Stanley Matthews epic of 1953, to equal last night. Out of nothing eventually there grew a dramatic climax. The first half was episodic and a busy dullness as a spate of ruthless tackling by the Portuguese defence and a symphony of whistling by the Italian referee broke the match into a thousand pieces.

A waiter might well have dropped a tray of glasses, such was the clatter, the crash and the bang of it all, with football secondary and both teams clearly out of humour with each other and with officialdom. Yet this merely proved to be the crucible. Out of the fire and the cruelty there finally lived something to remember.

It came to a boil in extra time as Manchester United, once heading for victory but robbed of their prize 10 minutes from the end of normal time, suddenly found a fresh wind that took them home in full sail. In a magical spell of seven minutes Best, Kidd and then Charlton struck like cobras to add to the goal which Charlton had first glanced in with his head to give them the lead soon after the change of ends of the first half.

In those moments the world shifted on its axis and Wembley all at once became a place for men with steady limbs and firm hearts. Life frequently ends things with a whimper rather than a bang. When for so long it had been a whimper now we actually did end with an explosion.

For so long there were butterflies at the pit of the myriad stomachs and suddenly it was all over. The barber shop critic, that powerful thinker, who said that United would win in extra time, was indeed proved to the hilt and I shall willingly submit to a shave from his razor.

When the untidy, often ugly, baggage of that opening half had been brushed out of the way the match at last began to find its stature as the blue shirts of Manchester United finally found rhythm, pattern and purpose.

Earlier Sadler, put clean through by Kidd, had shot past the Benfica post to miss a dolly. At this level it was equivalent to dropping Sobers in the slips. One cannot afford to do that and it seemed that United could yet pay the price, for Eusebio was constantly prowling like a caged, hungry animal threatening danger, which he showed after only 10 minutes from the kick off when he almost splintered Stepney's crossbar with a thunderbolt from 20 yards.

Yet when Dunne and Sadler worked a movement down the left and over came Sadler's cross for Charlton, rising on spring heels, to glide the ball home off his thinning head, it seemed that United were heading for their long-awaited glory.

It should have been theirs, too, without the need of extra time had not Sadler again given Henrique the chance to save an open goal with his feet after Best had mesmerised and opened the defence with a dazzling dribble and a shot which the goalkeeper could only partially parry.

Then there was Best himself, dancing clear of everyone and trying to dribble past the goalkeeper with a delicate touch only to be robbed at the last inch. So when all this had come and gone and United had failed to drive in their nails, there came the crux of the battle. With 10 minutes left the giant Torres rose like some Eiffel Tower to a diagonal cross to the right and head the ball square for Graca to crack in the equaliser.

How United survived those last 10 minutes of normal time only Stepney, under their crossbar, may be able to tell. But I doubt if even he knew much about two saves – both of instant reflex action – which somehow or other kept out scorching shots from Eusebio in the last three minutes before the whistle as Eusebio went through the United defence like a knife through butter. In my book United owe Stepney a debt this night for those two remarkable parries when all seemed lost.

So out of a gathering darkness, as Benfica seemed to gather new strength and a new poise, United rose. Once more as in Spain in their return leg with Real Madrid they fell back on their morale and unconquerable spirit.

Again it made giants of men who seemed to have given their last ounce of strength as they searched for the final yard to the summit. The scene before the beginning of extra time resembled some battlefield as the players of both sides fell back upon the velvet surface of Wembley seemingly exhausted, their limbs taut with cramp and their last fibres of strength apparently gone.

But suddenly there came the miracle. Within seven minutes of the beginning of extra time United found their Camelot. First Kidd nodded backwards a long clearance from Stepney from one end: at the other suddenly the dark-haired Best had wriggled his way like some will-o'-the-wisp past two tackles, drawn the goalkeeper in close to him as does the matador draw in the bull.

With a delicate, elusive swerve Best was past Henrique and he drove in the knife coldly and clinically. Almost at once Charlton's corner from the left was headed by Kidd to bring a brilliant save from Henrique, but the young Manchester man was alert to his duty. On his nineteenth birthday he rose like a salmon once more at the second attempt to nod in the rebound.

That was 3–1 and hardly had the cheering died than Kidd and Charlton worked another smooth movement down the right. Over came Kidd's cross and Charlton, somehow, with a wonderful, glancing flick, turned the ball into the far top corner for 4–1.

That was it and as the teams changed over once more for the second bit of that extra time Wembley once more resembled a battlefield as the players were given their last ministrations. It was over, apart from one more remarkable save by Stepney, left-handed, low down and at point- blank range from Eusebio. No wonder at the end Matt Busby said: "I am the proudest man in England tonight."

So an emotional night reached its climax. The struggle itself was crystallised with a duel at one end between the giant Torres and the black panther Eusebio against Foulkes and Stiles. The fact that neither, in the end, scored left the United men as the victors, though somehow I would have dearly wished a goal from Eusebio before the end as a tribute to his marvellous power and poetic movement.

At the other end it was the elusive Best, being chopped, harried and bruised from start to finish as he tried to bring his artistry to full flower. But soon, trying to dominate his ruthless opponents, he began to play with a kind of fury which overstretched itself as he attempted to beat the hordes of Benfica off his own bat.

Perhaps the greatest eye-opener of the struggle was Aston at outside left. Without any flowery touches, time after time he cut the right flank of the Portuguese defence open by sheer, uncomplicated speed. It was simple enough. He merely pushed the ball past Adolfo and showed his heels to the Portuguese. Long before the end the packed stadium was chanting his name. Certainly this will be a night for him to remember among the many others.

At the back Dunne was also masterly, as he covered every stray opening that presented itself at the rear of the faithful Foulkes and the abrasive Stiles, who had a face-to-face duel with Eusebio.

Crerand, too, was calmly masterful as he ranged the central areas at the side of Charlton. But I suppose in the end this could be said to have been Charlton's night. With two goals off his own bat it was he who went at last to collect the giant European trophy as the stadium rocked with joyful noise.

Behind him weary, but happy, straggled his side, and when the moment for the lap of honour arrived, Charlton himself was too tired to carry the giant cup around the stadium. He handed it over to his lieutenants and slowly trotted at the rear, no doubt thinking of all the years that had gone to make up this moment of glory.

So ended a dramatic night, when the banners waved and turned this great stadium at Wembley into a scene of carnival.

MATCH FACTS

Benfica 1   After extra time   **Manchester United 4**
Graca 79   *Charlton 53 99, Best 92, Kidd 94*

Manchester United: A. Stepney, S. Brennan, P. Dunne, P. Crerand, W. Foulkes,
N. Stiles, G. Best, B. Kidd, R. Charlton, D. Sadler, J. Aston
Benfica: J. Henrique, A. Calisto, H. Fernandes, J. Santos, F. Cruz, J. Graca,
M. Coluna, J. Augusto, J. Torres, Eusebio, A. Simoes
Referee: C. Lo Bello (Italy)
Attendance: 92,225

18

CELTIC v LEEDS UNITED

EUROPEAN CUP
SEMI-FINAL, 1970

For much of 1969–70, Don Revie's Leeds United looked on course for an unprecedented treble of the League championship, FA Cup and European Cup. But then their legs began to buckle under the strain. They were overtaken by Everton in the first division, drew with Chelsea in the FA Cup final and then lost the first leg of their "Battle of Britain" European Cup semi-final against Celtic. Work on Celtic Park meant the second leg was moved to Hampden Park where Leeds attempted to salvage their season.

"Bremner illustrated the point with his magnificent goal which should deserve a page of its own within the long history of Hampden Park"

CELTIC 2
LEEDS UNITED 1

CELTIC WIN 3–1 ON AGGREGATE

EUROPEAN CUP SEMI-FINAL
15 APRIL 1970
HAMPDEN PARK

....

**BY GEOFFREY GREEN,
FOOTBALL CORRESPONDENT**
16 April

By their victory at Hampden Park last night and the single goal triumph at Elland Road a fortnight ago, Celtic have now moved into the final of the European Cup. So on May 6 they will appear at the climax of this competition for the second time since 1967 and now the scene will be the San Siro Stadium, Milan.

It was these Scots who first broke the Latin grip on this competition four seasons ago and now, unless something untoward happens, it looks as though they will bring the trophy home north of the border once more when they meet the Dutchmen, Feyenoord.

So Leeds, who have been living on a razor's edge for the last month, playing last night their sixtieth game of the season and their seventh vital cup tie in 32 days, have now failed to surmount two of the three peaks at which they have aimed so bravely this season. One remains for them. The replay of the FA Cup final against Chelsea at Old Trafford in a fortnight's time.

But at this moment, poor chaps, they must be feeling rather like Sisyphus. But they have character and nothing will daunt their future. But will they win a single prize yet? We shall see. Yet at half-time last night when they led 1–0 through a dramatic, even sensational, goal by Bremner at the quarter hour it looked remarkably, against the odds, as if they had taken the high road to Scotland.

They survived a most fearsome onslaught by Celtic for nearly the whole of those opening 45 minutes; they were back on their heels as Murdoch, Connelly and Auld dominated midfield denying any mastery by Bremner and Giles and came through some desperate moments especially when first Madeley and then Cooper kicked scoring shots off the line.

When Bremner emerged from Celtic's onslaught, when the Scots sought a quick breakthrough, it seemed that some work of noble note may yet be done as the Leeds captain shot home a magnificent goal from fully 30 yards.

As Hunter intercepted a throw-in by Gemmell and punished some loose play between Hughes and Auld, the England wing half slipped the ball to his captain. Bremner, selling two dummies and breaking free of any harrying tackles, bore in for some 10 yards and let fly an arrow to the far top corner of the Celtic goal. The shot crashed home from the inside of the angle and crossbar as Williams and the rest of the Celtic men stood open-mouthed.

It was a Bobby Charlton thunderbolt of his heydays. And there, by that slender thread, Leeds held on to the interval with the whole tie itself delicately balanced on an aggregate score of 1–1. But truth to tell the Yorkshiremen were indeed lucky to be so placed. Minute after minute the Celtic storm beat around their ears.

In a thunderous opening there were desperate escapes from McNeill and then Gemmell as Sprake lost the ball in the goalmouth and was rescued by Charlton and then Bremner as his defenders kept out shots from the Celtic left back. In that start Celtic forced six corners within the opening eight minutes and it looked as if Leeds were to be pulverised. But they are never more dangerous than when their backs are to the wall and Bremner illustrated the point with his magnificent goal which should deserve a page of its own within the long history of Hampden Park.

But before half-time came there was that save by Madeley, who recovered magnificently to scrape the ball off the Leeds line following a masterly move between Connelly, Hughes and

Lennox; and then that recovery by Cooper again off the line as Gemmell flashed in a free kick by Auld.

However, if the Scots were harbouring any secret fears they were swept away within the opening eight minutes at the change of ends. Almost straight from the restart Hay pushed a short corner on the right to Auld and as his left foot cross swung inwards there was the tall, powerful Hughes to head Celtic level and put them 2–1 ahead on aggregate. Almost at once came a second blow as Hughes, going like an express train, felled Sprake and the goalkeeper was taken from the field of battle on a stretcher, with Harvey taking his place under the crossbar.

Hardly had Harvey arrived there was little Johnstone – as always as elusive and as annoying to Leeds as some wasp at a picnic – to worm his way brilliantly down the right, push a diagonal pass inwards for Murdoch coming up full steam to crash in goal number two. That was 3–1 ahead for Celtic and for all Leeds' brave efforts to pull something back before the finish it was beyond their power.

In the last 20 minutes Bates substituted for Lorimer and took over in midfield with Bremner going into attack in a last forlorn hope. But it was over and everyone knew it. So a fine match ended on a night of electric atmosphere, where the Hampden roar of a 134,000 crowd became a solid wall of noise that burnt the night away. Here were the Ladies from Hell letting rip in conditions that were perfect for football – early rain turning Hampden's green pitch into a billiard table where the ball moved fast and true, unlike the pudding that had been Wembley.

At the end with the crowd roaring "Easy! Easy!" the Celtic men knew that it had been nothing of the sort. Although they had dominated they had had to fight every inch of the way to win their domination against a fine side of method.

The heart of Celtic's brilliant performance lay in the right-wing quartet – Johnstone's brilliant close and elusive dribbling that from beginning to end had slowly sapped Leeds' strength; the overlapping and penetration of Hay from full back, and the central prompting of Murdoch and the tall, stately and beautifully balanced Connelly.

All this was a monument to human endeavour and skill under great pressures in a match of disciplined behaviour symbolised by the friendly and admiring swapping of shirts, man for man, as both teams embraced and congratulated each other at the end. But when Celtic did their lap of honour and the Glasgow skies shook we knew there had been a just and rightful winner.

MATCH FACTS

Celtic 2
Hughes 47, Murdoch 51

Leeds United 1
Bremner 14

Celtic: E. Williams, D. Hay, T. Gemmell, R. Murdoch, W. McNeill, J. Brogan,
J. Johnstone, G. Connelly, J. Hughes, B. Auld, B. Lennox
Leeds United: G. Sprake (sub: D. Harvey, 48), P. Madeley, T. Cooper, W. Bremner,
J. Charlton, N. Hunter, P. Lorimer (sub: M. Bates, 70), A. Clarke, M. Jones,
J. Giles, E. Gray
Referee: M. Kitabjian (France)
Attendance: 133,961

19

BRAZIL v ENGLAND

WORLD CUP GROUP MATCH, 1970

England travelled to the 1970 World Cup in Mexico with what many believed was a stronger squad than the one that had won the trophy four years earlier. They were drawn in the same group as favourites Brazil and when the two met under a blazing midday sun in Guadalajara they produced an epic struggle.

"In the feet of men like Pele, Jairzinho and Rivelino, shooting from long range, there is packed dynamite"

**BRAZIL 1
ENGLAND 0**

WORLD CUP GROUP MATCH
7 JUNE 1970
JALISCO STADIUM,
GUADALAJARA

....

**BY GEOFFREY GREEN,
FOOTBALL CORRESPONDENT**
8 June

By their narrow victory with a goal from the ever dangerous Jairzinho, before the 75,000 full house at Jalisco Stadium here today, Brazil have now moved more firmly to the top of Group 3 in the World Cup.

Brazil now have both feet in the quarter-final round, where I duly expect England to join them with a concluding victory over their last opponents next Thursday, Czechoslovakia. That, however, lingers in the future.

Meanwhile, we never seem able to beat these Brazilians. In eight meetings so far, we have won only once, and that at Wembley in the 1950s. As it is, Brazil picked their fifth win against England as though in a matter of sheer chances it was something like picking a man's pocket. England, this day, in the mere matter of chances, might well have won and certainly drawn. But that is to cry over spilt milk. If you cannot take what there is to offer in this game then you must pay the price.

Over the last stages, when Moore and his men bent their every fibre

England refuse to abdicate in defeat

From GEOFFREY GREEN, Football Correspondent

Guadalajara, June 7

Brazil 1, England 0

By their narrow victory with a goal from the ever dangerous Jairzinho, before the 75,000 full house at Jalisco Stadium here today, Brazil have now moved more firmly to the top of Group 3 in the World Cup.

Brazil now have both feet in the quarter final round, where I duly expect England to join them with a concluding victory over their last opponents next Thursday, Czechoslovakia. That, however, lingers in the future.

Meanwhile, we never seem able to beat these Brazilians. In eight meetings so far, we have won only once, and that at Wembley in the 1950s. As it is, Brazil picked their fifth win against England as though in a matter of sheer chances it was something like picking a man's pocket. England, this day, in the mere matter of chances, might well have won and certainly drawn. But that is to cry over spilt milk. If you cannot take what there is to offer in this game then you must pay the price.

Over the last stages, when Moore and his men bent their every fibre to rescue their cause, Ball and Astle—what a blinding error of his as he must have closed his eyes close in before an open goal—both missed fine chances. And then, again, as time ran out, there was Ball again with bad luck, that time to hit the Brazilian crossbar.

Still, it was no abdication in a match of endless activity. The Brazilians got the bit between their teeth for a magical spell just after the interval. But England's foolproof, sound defensive game never allowed the foe to run away with it. Already I have tried to embellish the saga with the chances that came England's way. However, they proved their power to endure and to resist.

In simple terms, here was a match between a better team, England, and better creative artists, Brazil. These Brazilians are a currency that no foreign exchange can control. When all seems at peace, and the opposition is lulled into a sense of safety, in a flash they can spread the game before their opponents like the evidence of case. So it was on this occasion when Pelé, Jairzinho, Tostao and Rivelino suddenly produced the rabbit out of the hat.

To be fair to Brazil, they missed their midfield mind reader Gerson. Without him they retreated rather more than usual. However, they were challenged all the way by the sustained qualities of courage, stamina and clear headedness of this whole England side, where Moore skilfully marshalled his forces at the rear and where Mullery covered every inch of the field as he shadowed the explosive Pelé wherever he moved.

This was a battle with honours even if not score.

In the feet of men like Pelé, Jairzinho and Rivelino, shooting from long range, there is packed dynamite. The inner cells of their genius and their great seams of expression are not yet exhausted. But though England today were again a team and a team of heroes who missed the boat, they may yet get their own back on Brazil.

I remember the World Cup of 1954, when Hungary swamped west Germany in their early group and then west Germany won the final itself against those Magyars. Who is to know, something like that may yet happen again. History can sometimes, indeed often repeat itself.

All through the night excitement and the nervous tensions had built up. The noise of klaxons and motor car horns, the shouting and razamataz, had gone into the early hours, forcing some of the England players to change their bedrooms.

Missing from the Brazilian ranks was Gerson, their midfield commander-in-chief—a great loss to them, making them, perhaps, more defensive minded, with Paulo Cezar lacking those long-range, penetrating passes that seem to move on a radar beam. For England, Wright was Cooper's partner at full-back, in place of the injured Newton.

For ten minutes England dictated, with Peters, Ball and Lee keeping Felix on his toes. Then, suddenly, out of all this came one of those explosive moments which on their day can set the Brazilians apart. The tall, long striding, powerful Jairzinho bore excitingly past Cooper and Moore to the right byeline. His centre was pitched towards the far post some seven yards out. Up went Pele with a swift, searching downward header. It looked all the world a goal, but somehow Banks, with a remarkable leap and sleight of hand, tipped the ball round the post to make one of the world-class saves of his life.

By half-time, with not a goal scored, England had done their fair share of the attacking. Firm at the back, and reading all the quick wall passing of Rivelino, Tostao and Pele, they answered in wider terms as Bobby Charlton, Ball and Peters kept the attack on the move.

Taking nothing out of themselves, England read all the lines of the Brazilian approach play, with Charlton looking younger than ever as he twice swept into the Brazilian goalmouth. He forced Felix to dive at his feet and later, on a 40-yard run, he hurdled two cruel tackles before shooting over.

The Brazilian danger to England lay in the constant threat of either Jairzinho or Paulo Cezar getting past Cooper and Wright on the byeline. More than once they did this, but each time the English covering in the middle was quick. Twice, indeed, it was England who cut out the better chances over the last 20 minutes to the interval.

Once Lee flicked on a cross by Wright for Peters to head over, the sort of offering he can often take at home; and once again from Wright, Hurst flicked on, and there was Lee, close in, to send his diving header straight at Felix. As the England man tried to reach the rebound, he kicked the goalkeeper on the head, receiving a warning from the Israeli referee while Felix received lengthy repairs.

Expectancy hung in the air at the change of ends. Almost at once the action began to mount, with England beginning to look as if they might tire while the Brazilians began to turn the screw with teasing, taunting little triangles of progressive football. There was no lack of range in their movements which more and more became moulded and luminous.

A sudden long-range flash by Paulo Cezar was tipped low round the post by Banks; a long through pass by Pelé, quick as a hawk to see an opening, found Jairzinho raking through on his own to the edge of the penalty area, but Banks was too quick for him as the goalkeeper challenged to kick the ball clear in the nick of time.

With half an hour left, Pele turned the screw one thread tighter as he took on four Englishmen in the space of ten yards to burst through. Only Mullery's constant shadowing and limitless capacity to recover rescued his side with a last retrieving tackle. Within seconds Banks was forced to punch out a left foot rocket from Rivelino, and now we seemed to sense that England's wall was about to collapse.

At the height of the bombardment, Brazil at last broke through with just under half an hour left. Tostao began the move with some clever footwork and body swerving on the left. His cross was finely placed. Pele sideslipped one way like a falling leaf, flicked the ball the other, and there was Jairzinho with three giant strides to move in for the kill with his rising cross-shot. From less than ten yards, Banks had no chance.

ENGLAND.—G. Banks; T. Wright, T. Cooper, A. Mullery, B. Labone, R. Moore, F. Lee (sub., C. Bell), A. Ball, R. Charlton (sub., J. Astle), G. Hurst, M. Peters.

BRAZIL.—V. Felix; R. Brito, W. Piazza, Carlos Alberto, T. Clodoaldo, R. Jairzinho, P. Cezar, A. Tostao (sub., M. Roberto), Pele, R. Rivelino, S. Everaldo.

Referee.—Abraham Klein (Israel).

Jairzinho (No. 7), the scorer of Brazil's goal, runs off in triumph, leaving Banks, England's goalkeeper, sitting ruefully on the ground and Mullery (left) looking despairingly at the ball. No. 11 is Martin Peters.

Mexican fiesta

From FRANK KEATING

Mexico City, June 7

El Salvador 0, Mexico 4

Mexico comprehensively defeated El Salvador in a carnival atmosphere here this afternoon.

Mexico went ahead on the stroke of half-time, after which El Salvador refused to kick off again. They spent four minutes appealing to the referee: some lay on the field in anguish and most of them were in tears. The referee solved his dilemma by whistling for half-time.

All Mexico had been saving up for today. If the football world had been awaiting happenings at Guadalajara since the numbers were drawn out last winter, that certainly didn't include the host nation. This was always going to be their day. Whatever else happened, even if—saints preserve us—their team failed to qualify for the quarter finals, there was to be a fiesta today. If no one else, at least they would hammer El Salvador.

The Mexican manager, Cardenas, had had a week of it. After the sterile opening game against Russia—now interpreted as a fine result after the happenings here yesterday afternoon — public opinion had daily picked a new side for him. All the new combinations included Enrique Borja, whose popularity—and wage packet—reaches George Best proportions.

Cardenas bowed to the clamour and picked not only Borja, but two other front runners who hadn't played last week, Padilla and Gonzalez. Clearly he planned to celebrate the fiesta with a hatful of goals.

Within seconds of half-time Valdivier scored, finding an open goal after a cross from the left. The stadium erupted. So did the Salvador team. The ball was left in the net as Magana raced to the middle to appeal to the referee. The whole side followed him to the centre and refused to start. This went on for four minutes until Mr. Kandil blew for half-time.

Within a minute of the restart Valdivier did it again. He rounded a slack defence about 20 yards out and made for goal before angling the ball wide of Magana.

Borja did not come out for the second half. He was replaced by Lopez, who wasn't long in making his presence felt at the party for, after 15 minutes, he rose beautifully to touch the ball on to Fragoso's right foot. Three nil

Cardenas brought off Lopez and substituted Basagruen. Within minutes he scored the fourth goal with an acute shot from 15 yards

Bulgaria swept aside

From ROGER MACDONALD

Leon, June 7

West Germany 5, Bulgaria 2

West Germany remain a team to be reckoned with in the World Cup. Sweeping aside the shadows of their match against Morocco, they put Bulgaria out of the competition with a performance of power and purpose. Not even the acrobatics of Simenov could withstand the lightning thrusts of Libuda, with the endless promptings of Beckenbauer from behind.

Libuda's darting runs soon stretched the Bulgarian defence, forcing Simenov into a flying interception. Then a free kick by Lohr almost pierced the wall, and Beckenbauer, elegant as ever, tried a one-two with Muller which Muller bungled hopelessly. Germany's pressure was relentless in the early stages and the horns of their supporters kept up a shrill monotone.

Then Bulgaria, totally against the run of play, took the lead after 12 minutes. Germany lined up in dilatory fashion to a free kick well outside the penalty area, and Asparoukhov side-footed the ball to Nikodimov, who shot well wide of the unsighted Meier.

But Germany were soon level. Libuda, showing astonishing speed for the conditions, outran and out-elbowed the full back to hit a low cross of such power that Simenov dropped the ball over his own line before a defender booted clear. Referee de Mendibil had to consult a linesman, but there was no doubt it was a goal

Germany lost their early nerves and put the pressure on Bulgaria's defence with some delightful passing at high speed. Libuda looked a match-winner on the right wing, no matter the odds. He took the ball past Gaganelov, lost his footing, but somehow wriggled back to his feet and rounded the full back, leaving Muller to beat Simenov at point blank range.

Then Libuda set off on another sinuous dribble and was brought down just inside the area. Muller made no mistake from the penalty spot

Bulgaria tried manfully to reduce the deficit, but Germany were equal to everything in defence and commanding in the field. Seeler leaped over a foul tackle to start a move which led to Muller crossing low from the left, and Seeler ran half the length of the field to sweep the ball home.

Sweden fail to hold lead

Israel 1, Sweden 1

Toluca, June 7.—In this cruc[ial] Group 2 match, Sweden, w[ho] were favourites to improve the[ir] position in the table and the[ir] hopes of going into the quarte[r] final round, failed to consolida[te] their goal lead in the secon[d] half. In the event, both sid[es] virtually ended their chances going into the next round.

The Israelis looked the bett[er] team at the start and Spiegler a[nd] his forwards had a number of go[od] chances as the Swedish defen[ce] struggled to find their form. In [a] gruelling first half the shorter m[en] from Israel, all a head smaller th[an] the Swedes, launched a series [of] attacks in the first 15 minutes.

The strong Swedish backs ha[d] their work cut out. Fiegenbaum, [in] the sixth minute, headed right in[to] the hands of the Swedish goa[l]keeper Gunner Larsson.

Israel's golden opportunity cam[e] in the forty-second minute whe[n] Fiegenbaum found himself faci[ng] the goalkeeper after a bad Swedi[sh] defensive error. But Larsso[n] blocked the shot with his foo[t]. The Swedes were unable to pier[ce] the tough Israeli defence, wh[o] threw themselves in despera[te] tackles at the feet of the Swedi[sh] forwards.

Israel's goalkeeper, Vissok[er], had his worst moment in t[he] twenty-fifth minute, when he tipp[ed] a shot from Turesson over th[e] bar. In the fortieth minute B. Larsson hit the side netting fro[m] a sharp angle, and three minute[s] earlier Kindvall's drive also we[nt] wide.

Turesson opened the scoring [in] the 54th minute, but three minute[s] later Spiegel levelled for Israel. [In] the 67th minute, chaos raged o[n] the field with players clashing eve[n] when the ball was not in play. Th[e] referee had to call in the linesme[n] to find out what was happenin[g]. The referee then had a discussio[n] with the team captains and aske[d] them to cool down.

SWEDEN.—S. G. Larsson; H. Selander, [.] Axelsson, R. Grip, T. Svensson, B. Larsso[n,] O. Kindvall, O. Persson (sub., S. Palsson), [.] Nordahl, T. Turesson, J. Olsson.

ISRAEL.—I. Vissoker, F. Bar, D. Prim[o,] S. Rosen, S. Rozenthal, I. Shum, G. Spieg[ler,] J. Fiegenbaum, M. Spiegler, J. Schwager, [.] Vollach.

Referee.—S. Tarekgn (Ethiopia).—Reut[er] and U.P.I.

Remaining fixtures

WEDNESDAY

Group 1.—Russia v. El Salvador.
Group 2.—Uruguay v. Sweden.
Group 3.—Brazil v. Rumania.
Group 4.—Peru v. west German[y].

THURSDAY

Group 1.—Mexico v. Belgium.
Group 2.—Israel v. Italy.
Group 3.—England v. Czechoslovakia.
Group 4.—Morocco v. Bulgaria.

to rescue their cause, Ball and Astle – what a blinding error of his as he must have closed his eyes close in before an open goal – both missed fine chances. And then, again, as time ran out, there was Ball again with bad luck, that time to hit the Brazilian crossbar.

Still, it was no abdication in a match of endless activity. The Brazilians got the bit between their teeth for a magical spell just after the interval. But England's foolproof, sound defensive game never allowed the foe to run away with it. Already I have tried to embellish the saga with the chances that came England's way. However, they proved their power to endure and to resist.

In simple terms, here was a match between a better team, England, and better creative artists, Brazil. These Brazilians are a currency that no foreign exchange can control. When all seems at peace, and the opposition is lulled into a sense of safety, in a flash they can spread the game before their opponents like the evidence of case. So it was on this occasion when Pele, Jairzinho, Tostao and Rivelino suddenly produced the rabbit out of the hat.

To be fair to Brazil, they missed their midfield mind reader Gerson. Without him they retreated rather more than usual. However, they were challenged all the way by the sustained qualities of courage, stamina and clear headedness of this whole England side, where Moore skillfully marshalled his forces at the rear and where Mullery covered every inch of the field as he shadowed the explosive Pele wherever he moved.

This was a battle with honours even if not score.

In the feet of men like Pele, Jairzinho and Rivelino, shooting from long range, there is packed dynamite. The inner cells of their genius and their great seams of expression are not yet exhausted. But though England today were again a team and a team of heroes who missed the boat, they may yet get their own back on Brazil.

I remember the World Cup of 1954, when Hungary swamped West Germany in their early group and then West Germany won the final itself against those Magyars. Who is to know, something like that may yet happen again. History can sometimes, indeed often repeat itself.

All through the night excitement and the nervous tensions had built up. The noise of klaxons and motor car horns, the shouting and razzmatazz, had gone into the early hours, forcing some of the England players to change their bedrooms.

Missing from the Brazilian ranks was Gerson, their midfield commander-in-chief – a great loss to them, making them, perhaps, more defensive minded, with Paulo Cezar lacking those long-range, penetrating passes that seem to move on a radar beam. For England, Wright was Cooper's partner at full-back, in place of the injured Newton.

For ten minutes England dictated, with Peters, Ball and Lee keeping Felix on his toes. Then, suddenly, out of all this came one of those explosive moments which on their day can set the Brazilians apart. The tall, long striding, powerful Jairzinho bore excitingly past Cooper and Moore to the right bye-line. His centre was pitched towards the far post some seven yards out. Up went Pele with a swift, searching downward header. It looked all the world a goal, but somehow Banks, with a remarkable leap and sleight of hand, tipped the ball round the post to make one of the world-class saves of his life.

By half-time, with not a goal scored, England had done their fair share of the attacking. Firm at the back, and reading all the quick wall passing of Rivelino, Tostao and Pele, they answered in wider terms as Bobby Charlton, Ball and Peters kept the attack on the move.

Taking nothing out of themselves, England read all the lines of the Brazilian approach play, with Charlton looking younger than ever as he twice swept into the Brazilian goalmouth. He forced Felix to dive at his feet and later, on a 40-yard run, he hurdled two cruel tackles before shooting over.

The Brazilian danger to England lay in the constant threat of either Jairzinho or Paulo Cezar getting past Cooper and Wright on the bye-line. More than once they did this, but each time the English covering in the middle was quick. Twice, indeed, it was England who cut out the better chances over the last 20 minutes to the interval.

Once Lee flicked on a cross by Wright for Peters to head over, the sort of offering he can often take at home; and once again from Wright, Hurst flicked on, and there was Lee, close in, to send his diving header straight at Felix. As the England man tried to reach the rebound, he kicked the goalkeeper on the head, receiving a warning from the Israeli referee while Felix received lengthy repairs.

Expectancy hung in the air at the change of ends. Almost at once the action began to mount, with England beginning to look as if they might tire while the Brazilians began to turn the screw with teasing, taunting little triangles of progressive football. There was no lack of range in their movements which more and more became moulded and luminous.

A sudden long-range flash by Paulo Cezar was tipped low round the post by Banks; a long through pass by Pele, quick as a hawk to see an opening, found Jairzinho raking through on his own to the edge of the penalty area, but Banks was too quick for him as the goalkeeper challenged to kick the ball clear in the nick of time.

With half an hour left, Pele turned the screw one thread tighter as he took on four Englishmen in the space of ten yards to burst through. Only Mullery's constant shadowing and limitless capacity to recover rescued his side with a last retrieving tackle. Within seconds Banks was forced to punch out a left foot rocket from Rivelino, and now we seemed to sense that England's wall was about to collapse.

At the height of the bombardment, Brazil at last broke through with just under half an hour left. Tostao began the move with some clever footwork and body swerving on the left. His cross was finely placed. Pele side slipped one way like a falling leaf, flicked the ball the other, and there was Jairzinho with three giant strides to move in for the kill with his rising cross-shot. From less than ten yards, Banks had no chance.

MATCH FACTS

Brazil 1
Jairzinho 59

England 0

Brazil: Felix, C. Alberto, W. Piazza, Brito, Everaldo, Clodoaldo, Jairzinho, P. Cezar, Tostao (sub: M. Roberto, 68), Pele, R. Rivelino
England: G. Banks, T. Wright, R. Cooper, A. Mullery, B. Labone, R. Moore, F. Lee (sub: J. Astle, 64), A. Ball, R. Charlton (sub: C. Bell, 64), G. Hurst, M. Peters
Referee: A. Klein (Israel)
Attendance: 70,950

MONDAY JUNE 15 1970
NO. 57,892 NINEPENCE

THE TIMES

IN BUSINESS NEW
SHARE PRICES
YEAR'S L

Conservative anger with Powell over rift on immigrants

Hush-up on fraud, MP says

From Our Correspondent

Skipton, June 14

Mr. George Burnaby Drayson, who has been Conservative M.P. for Skipton, Yorkshire, for the past 25 years, said today that in view of the attack, made on Mr. Enoch Powell he felt compelled to disclose a matter he had known of for a long time.

"After Mr. Powell's first and timely speech on the whole issue of immigration," Mr. Drayson said, "and its likely effect on the future of some of our towns and cities and our country, I was told that instructions had been issued to civil servants in the Ministry of National Insurance and the National Assistance Board that no more prosecutions should be instituted against immigrants for frauds on the department without reference to the department without reference to a superior, lest, no doubt, the evidence which these prosecutions would disclose might further exacerbate race relations."

He added that the phrase used was: "They are getting away with murder—and we are not allowed to prosecute" Mr. Drayson said he was challenging Mr. Wilson or Mr. Crossman to deny that any such instructions had ever been issued by any of their officials anywhere in the country.

The Race Relations Bill could discriminate against the British citizen if there was any interference with the normal procedure for instituting prosecutions for fraud and abuses in connexion with false claims for benefit under National Insurance or supplementary benefit schemes by adopting a different standard of procedure for coloured immigrants compared with ordinary British citizens.

"I will have no hesitation in disclosing the source of my evidence, in confidence, to Mr. Wilson or Mr. Crossman, should they ask for it, on the understanding, of course, that no disciplinary action would be taken against any official who might be involved", he said.

THE REST OF THE NEWS

Ceylon: Mrs. Bandaranaike to declare a republic ... 6

Germany: Local elections rebuff for Brandt ... 1

Chemical Engineering: Four-page special report in Business News

Weather forecast: Dry 2

Arts .... 10 | Forces
Bridge .... | Appointments 10
Honours 11, 12 | Letters 9
Business | Obituary 10
News ..... 17-24 | Overseas News 6
Court, Social 10 | Sport ... 13, 14
Crossword .. 16 | TV and Radio 15
Election News ... | The Times
.... 7, 8 | Diary ... 8
Engagements 10 | 25 Years Ago 10
Entertainments 10 | Weather ... 2
European News 6 | Wills 10
Home News 2, 4 |

FOR THE RECORD

The Times today and tomorrow will record the main events from the four days last week when the paper was not published

Today:

Business news contains the principal financial, industrial and economic news together with Friday's stock market prices in London.

Main items of foreign news, page 6. Enoch Powell's speeches from Thursday and Saturday, page 8. Other election speeches, page 7. Solution to last Tuesday's crossword, page 16.

Tomorrow:

Patrick Brogan's Rural Drive resumes from Glasgow. Home specialities bring news in their fields up to date.

Operation Seashore, held out today because of pressure on space will appear on June 22.

There was hostile reaction throughout the Tory Party yesterday to Mr. Enoch Powell's action on Saturday in widening the division between himself and the Shadow Cabinet on immigration policy.

A Gallup Poll survey in 50 key marginal seats, published in The Daily Telegraph today, shows a Labour lead of 7 per cent, an increase of 4 per cent in a week.

Breach seen as open fight for leadership

BY DAVID WOOD

Mr. Heath and Mr. Powell are at daggers drawn for all to see in the general election campaign moves into its closing days. Many observers outside the Conservative Party believe an open struggle has begun for mastery of a parliamentary party that may go back to Westminster broken from the polls on Thursday. But Mr. Heath and the Shadow Cabinet are profoundly convinced that Mr. Powell has for all time put himself beyond the pale as a challenger for the party leadership.

Bitterly critical messages flowing into Central Office yesterday for Mr. Barber, the party chairman, and Mr. William Whitelaw, the chief whip, from former Conservative M.P.s and candidates, as well as local leaders of the rank and file, are regarded as conclusive proof that the Conservative Party will not easily forgive Mr. Powell's timing of the deepening of his festering differences with the Shadow Cabinet.

I am told that the party, which always likes to keep family quarrels private, is showing extreme anger with Mr. Powell. This hostile reaction was so easily predictable during a make-or-break election that some very good judges cannot believe that Mr. Powell could mistake the nature of the Conservative Party in such a grievous way if he really is challenging for the leadership against Mr. Heath.

It is held that Mr. Powell cannot have saved 20 years in the Conservative Parliamentary Party without seeing what is plain to every other member of it: that the best recommendation for choice as leader, whether by "evolution" or direct election, is public loyalty to men and party, above all in bad or difficult times.

This analysis of the general election moves appeared to be general within the Shadow Cabinet and the party management over the weekend. Certainly it is to be noted that when Mr. Heath put out a measured statement in reply to Mr. Powell yesterday he took care to consult all members of the Shadow Cabinet.

ally, by telephone, or indirectly. It was a reply to Mr. Powell's speech on "the enemy within the gates", delivered in Birmingham on Saturday.

While he worked in London yesterday on his final election broadcast on television tonight, Mr. Heath knew that he would be hurried again at his campaign briefing in London this morning to explain why he has not renounced support as Conservative leader for Mr. Powell's candidature.

He will answer, as he did several times last week when Powellism dominated all other issues, that Conservative candidates are chosen by autonomous local associations, and that historically the Conservative Party does not impose an absolute party line on those who support it.

But this morning Mr. Heath intends to go beyond that. He will restate succinctly his position on immigration, and will then insist that he is not going to allow obsessive questions about Mr. Powell to overshadow all the fundamental issues on which the electorate ought to be making up its mind.

Mr. Wilson and Labour Ministers will feel under no such constraint. Last week they made daily capital out of Mr. Powell's speech wondering whether Britain's enemies might have infiltrated into the Home Office to mislead the public about the numbers of Commonwealth immigrants in Britain.

Mr. Wilson now has a much better opportunity to damage Mr. Heath and the Conservative collective leadership. He can present the dispute between Mr. Heath and Mr. Powell, as Mr. Denis Healey did at the weekend, as the unmistaken sign of a fight to the death by Powellites and right-wingers for the control of the Conservative Party.

This gift to Mr. Wilson arrives at a time when, in contrast, Conservative Party managers tacitly admit that their one last hope of avoiding humiliating defeat is organizational supremacy. The best use is being made by Mr. Barber of a series of local newspaper polls, which suggest that the Conservatives are in the lead, no matter what the general trend may be.

Meanwhile, two of the national opinion surveys, have reported hopelessly irreconcilable findings. N.O.P. for the Daily Mail on Friday put the Labour lead at 12.4 per cent, which would give a Commons majority of 150 seats or more. Gallup in the Sunday Telegraph yesterday showed a reverse trend, with the Labour lead cut back to 2.5 per cent

Unionists driven to Paisley: Minority view by David Triesman ... 7

News Team on Powell, his speeches and reactions ... 8

Leading article; letters ... 9

Müller sends the ball past Bonetti to score West Germany's winning goal in extra time against England in the World Cup quarter-final at Leon yesterday.

Dental union will curb treatment

A thousand British dentists will be told by the General Dental Practitioners' Association today to carry out only urgent dental treatment. Work on dentures and crowns is likely to be affected. Only patients in pain and members of priority groups will be exempt from the ban.

A statement said: "The association decided that until the recent pay award of the review body on doctors' and dentists' remuneration is implemented in full they will recommend members not to carry out uneconomic items of treatment."

The association is to press for a Royal Commission to "review the tripartite contract between the dental profession, the public and the central body."

The Junior Hospital Doctors' Association said yesterday the B.M.A.'s referendum on resignations was "premature."

B.M.A. view hardens, page 2.

Libya blacklists Leyland

Tripoli, Monday morning.—The Libyan Government has blacklisted 50 foreign companies, including the British Leyland motor company, and banned all dealings with these firms because of their links with Israel.—A.P.

Eight arrested in Ulster clash

Catholic youths stoned troops and police in Dungiven, co. Londonderry, yesterday as about 1,000 Orangemen paraded through the predominantly Catholic town.

One policeman was injured and eight arrests were made.

The Times

From today the price of The Times will be 9d. This is the price which the National Board for Prices and Incomes itself has justified in their report on the costs and revenue of national newspapers issued four months ago in February.

England out of World Cup

BY A STAFF REPORTER

England and west Germany fashioned another breathtaking World Cup football match yesterday. As at Wembley four years ago, the struggle was taken to extra time; but this time Germany had their revenge by winning 3—2.

The parallel with Wembley was even closer. For England again led 2—1 with only a few minutes left. But first Uwe Seeler, the German captain, put his side level, and in extra time Gerhard Müller, Seeler's successor in the centre of the German attack, booted home the winning goal from close range.

It was a bitter setback for England, who had for much of the match put their critics at recent origin only, to flight with a wealth of splendid football. Their captain, Bobby Moore, with Bogota now a distant memory, played a superb part in frustrating the German attack, who had scored more goals than any other country in the competition so far.

Alan Mullery, the Tottenham Hotspur captain, had put England surprisingly ahead—surprisingly, in that Mullery is not renowned for his goal scoring. Martin Peters, another Tottenham man, added to England's score in the second half.

England then went on to defence, and perhaps thereby contributed to their own downfall. They were unlucky to have to play the match without Gordon Banks, who had been struck by a stomach complaint the previous night.

Peter Bonetti is a fine replacement for Banks; but the suspicion lingered that Banks, with his genius as a goalkeeper, might have prevented one or two goals.

But there need be no excuses or scapegoats. Germany were worthy winners and England played fully to their capacity.

Two hours in the heat and at an altitude of 6,000ft. are punishing conditions for European footballers, and both team managers, Sir Alf Ramsey and Herr Helmut Schön, were highly critical.

The Germans have only two days in which to recover before their semi-final against Italy at Guadalajara. The same applies to Italy, of course; but they won comfortably 4—1 against Mexico at Toluca yesterday, without having to exert themselves, and over a span, of course, of only an hour and a half. It will be interesting to see if Germany will be able to stand the pace again on Wednesday.

In the other quarter-final ties played yesterday, Brazil, the favourites, beat Peru 4—2 at Guadalajara, and now go to Mexico City on Wednesday to face Uruguay, who yesterday beat Russia in Mexico City by a single goal in extra time.

Match report, page 13.

Bobby Moore case search

Buenos Aires, June 14

The police are now looking for a Colombian woman in connexion with the theft of a bracelet that led to an accusation being made in Bogota last month against Bobby Moore, the England football captain.

The police said that the woman had tried to sell a bracelet of emeralds and diamonds similar to the £600 one missing from a Bogota shop. Mr. Moore was released by a Colombian investigating magistrate on May 28.

More prices to be raised

By Our Business News Staff

Three nationalized industries are likely to ask for Government permission to raise prices shortly after the election. Coal, steel and postal charges are likely to be increased if the requests are granted.

The moves come as upward price movements are being announced in the private and public sectors. Freight routes by rail and sea are to go up, and many foods, including sausages, coffee, soups, confectionery and frozen foods, as well as detergents are to cost more.

Business News, page 17.

Husain faces new crisis after split in Army loyalty

From PAUL MARTIN

Amman, June 14

As peace returned to Jordan today King Husain faced a new crisis inside his kingdom. This followed an abortive rebellion by unnamed units loyal to his uncle, Major-General Sharif Nasser bin Jamil, the dismissed Commander-in-Chief, and last night's unsuccessful attempt on the life of Major-General Mashour al-Haditha, the moderate Chief of Staff. There is a strong suspicion that the two incidents are connected.

In a statement broadcast over Amman radio today, the King called on the Army and security forces to exercise the utmost self-control and demanded complete obedience to his orders. Referring to the latest threats to the delicate cease-fire between the Palestinian guerrillas and the Jordan Army, after a week of fighting had left more than 300 dead and 700 wounded in the capital, King Husain said: "The mutiny was aimed at making us responsible for what we refused to be accused of. We have foiled the attempts of the plotter and the executioner together."

During the fighting, Major Robert Perry, the assistant military attaché at the American Embassy, was shot dead when guerrillas broke into his home.

The dismissed Commander-in-Chief and Major-General Zayed bin Shaker, the commander of the Royal Armoured Brigade, whose units shelled refugee camps during the fighting, were held responsible for the most serious crisis Jordan has yet faced.

As this challenge to authority from inside the ranks of his armed forces has shown, the King now finds himself caught between the military of the

guerrilla extremists and fiercely anti-guerrilla elen in the Army.

Although the circumstance the attempt on Genera Haditha's life are far from it is understood that his car fired on by a lone gunma he was on his way to breal rebellious armoured unit their way to Amman.

In his first public appea Amman today, the King, by Arafat, the leader of Al F claimed at a press conferer Amman that the Pales guerrillas had been respot for restoring order in Am He said the future depended whether there is good will m will". He alleged that armed confrontation in streets of the capital was result of "an American spiracy" aimed at liquid the guerrilla movement.

Referring to the Musli report that the 82nd Air Division had been alerted a height of the Jordan crisis in American citizens at Jordan attempts of the plotter and the executioner together.

The guerrillas announce they had executed two men found guilty of raping American women during chaos that accompanied the days of battle in Amman

Amman, June 14.—Hundr heavy machineguns fire heard tonight in Amman th in a day of calm. Tracer b lit up the sky after the fi and a spokesman for Palestine Armed Struggle mand said the firing was at area of Jebel Nazha, in northern part of the c (Reuter)

British hostages tel of frightening orde

A dozen Britons, who had been held hostage in an Amman hotel for nearly 48 hours by Palestinian guerrillas, flew into Heathrow airport, London, last night.

They talked of bullet-spattered windows, massive robberies by the Jordanian Army, street fighting and of armed guards sitting beside them at breakfast. They blamed the Jordan Government forces for the latest flare-up in the capital and said it was a direct result of the heavy shelling of Palestinian refugee camps.

Among the group was 42-year-old Dr. John Smile, of Wimpole Street, London, a consultant at the Middlesex Hospital. He telephoned the British Embassy

to pass on the guer demands after they had cap the Philadelphia Hote Amman.

He said: "The demand specific: that the Govern forces cease their shelling o refugee camps immediately the hotel would be blown And they brought in a lot dynamite and placed it in lobby to back up their m ment."

The guerrillas, men and "armed to the teeth" with machineguns and grenades, burst into the ho the morning just as he was ing for an official visit the home of a Jordan friend.

Nasser speech, page 6; le article, page 9. Picture, p

Wilson 'panic' taunt

From HUGH NOYES

Bristol, June 14

Mr. Wilson's his sabbatical sally before polling day ended in Bristol today with the radio blacked out with stickers bearing the cryptic letters "E.H. for P.N." and a large "Vote Tory" was scrawled in lipstick on the rear window.

For the benefit of whistle watchers, the egg cannot is now 13, with yet another missing the Prime Minister a range of 5ft. and bouncing off a police inspector. On other fronts, two Tory cars trying to harass the cavalcade ran into each other and the ceiling of a Labour committee room fell in just before the Prime Minister arrived "Should indicate a landslide" Mr. Wilson said.

The Prime Minister gave his roadside and committee room speeches today to rub salt into the wounds festering in the Tory Party over the speeches of Mr. Enoch Powell. At every step he taunted the large numbers of Tory hecklers over their "divided loyalties"

"We have had nothing from them so far today except monosyllabic inuntations". Mr. Wil-

son shouted, against a steady chant of "Wilson Out", "There is nothing more frightening", he added, as the baying continued, "than seeing the gentlemanly party when it is getting panicky and hysterical"

"Mr. Powell has been complaining about an attack on democracy. He thinks he has seen this in various ways—Northern Ireland, strangely-What he is complaining about are the people who just don't listen to reason

Soviet 'meddling' upsets Sir Alec

BY OUR POLITICAL STAFF

Russia's invitation to Mr. Wilson to make an official visit to Moscow next month caused much resentment among Conservative leaders yesterday.

Sir Alec Douglas-Home, former Prime Minister and the Conservative spokesman on foreign affairs, issued a statement saying that he regretted "that Russia should attempt to prejudge the decision of the British people in the election".

Members of the Shadow Cabinet say that usually foreign governments take great care to see that none of their actions can be interpreted as an intervention in an election in another country. The Russians have usually been scrupulously correct, and their present action is regarded as important.

Mr. Smirnovsky, the Russian Ambassador, went at his own request to Downing Street to see Mr. Wilson on Saturday—the very day that Mr. Heath was

warning the electorate of a lessening of Britain's influence in the world under Labour.

The ambassador asked Mr. Wilson to make the visit under a long-standing invitation already given some time ago in principle but in view of political uncertainties no dates could be fixed.

The Soviet move suggests that the Russians assume that Mr. Wilson will win Thursday's election. If Mr. Wilson were to lose they would presumably withdraw this invitation.

The invitation had then ex-

tended by Mr. Kosygin last summer and was made through Mr. Wedgwood Benn, Minister of Technology, when he was in Moscow. It was accepted in principle but in view of political uncertainties no dates could be fixed.

Apparently Mr. Wilson went out of his way on Saturday to emphasize to the ambassador that the taking up of the invitation—which is up Mr. Wilson as Prime Minister—must depend on the outcome of the election.

20

ENGLAND v WEST GERMANY

WORLD CUP QUARTER-FINAL, 1970

A week after their defeat by Brazil, England travelled to Leon for a quarter-final reunion with their 1966 final opponents West Germany. It was another thrilling, see-saw encounter that required extra-time, but in retrospect it was one of the most important matches in the history of the national team, and its impact resounded down the decades.

"... these Germans are never finished. So often they seem able to pull something special out when their backs are to the wall"

ENGLAND 2
WEST GERMANY 3

AFTER EXTRA TIME

WORLD CUP QUARTER-FINAL
14 JUNE 1970
GUANAJUATO STADIUM, LEON

BY GEOFFREY GREEN,
FOOTBALL CORRESPONDENT
15 June

The World Cup drifted away from England in the Guanajuato Stadium here today and now they are left with a private sense of emptiness and a desolate sadness. Two goals up with only 20 minutes left, and Bell and Hunter substituted for Charlton and Peters at that point, they had both feet, so it seemed, in the semi-final of this ninth global football championship.

It looked all over. But it is never so against these Germans. The day of settlement for that 1966 final had to come some time and it came now, dramatically and in extra time as indeed there had been at Wembley four years ago.

In an admirable resurgence of spirit, stamina and skill the Germans earned a win that seemed at one point far beyond their reach. Drawing level at the end of normal time it was an old-fashioned move that finally drove the last blade in for victory, five minutes into the start of the second period of the extra half hour.

Grabowski, beating Cooper for speed on the outside, moved to the by-line and centred deep to the left. Up went Lohr to head back square and there was Muller to grab his ace goal of these championships as he volleyed home from close range. Never perhaps will he or his side treasure a goal more deeply.

That was it, the end of a remarkable battle royal in the midday sun which was finally a cruelty to man. England's guns were covered then, though they fought to the last inch and the last seconds to rescue their cause with shots by Mullery and Newton which dipped just over the German bar and a miscue by Ball as Hurst headed down to his feet.

Yet the better side won in the end. And they won because, once Beckenbauer had put the Germans back into the match when it was three-quarters gone, England wrongly proceeded to pull in their horns, pack the perimeter of their penalty area and concede the central areas to the twin German generals, Beckenbauer and Overath, supported by that wise old owl, Seeler. That was the heart and core of this extraordinary upheaval when all seemed done.

Meanwhile the future holds every germ of possibility. The semi-finals next Wednesday will be between Germany and Italy on the one hand and Brazil and Uruguay on the other. It was a neat division of world power: Europe against South America. It will be a struggle between different ways of life and playing football.

At the end Helmut Schoen, the German manager, said: "I never gave up hope of my side even when they were two down and once we had pulled one of those back and raised our game I did not think we would lose. But it was a magnificent match."

If Sir Alf Ramsey, in his disappointment followed with the words: "I have never seen England give away two such goals," I would not know which ones he meant. This may seem cruelly ungracious to anyone who had to suffer out there in the sun. But I do feel that Gordon Banks, had he been under England's crossbar would not have come off his line to let Seeler's header loop over him and that he would have cut out Lohr's cross header that led to the winner by Muller. But all that is now in the past.

Having travelled 170 miles by road yesterday from the turbulent concrete jungle of a million-strong city of Guadalajara, England moved to this charming little provincial centre, a place by comparison drowsy and closely wrapped. Already, in a week, the Germans, champions of their eliminating group, had made it their temporary home. With their black, red and yellow banners and their song of "Deutschland Uber Alles" they were now challenged by the invading English clans. But, all told, it was quieter, more inviting.

When the teams came out, England in red and Germany in white, there was an echo of that sunny Wembley final of July 1966. England now, sadly, were without Banks their master goalkeeper, sick overnight. In his place stood Chelsea's Bonetti. On the field were five men on each side who had contested the last World Cup final, but now there was something special. This was Bobby Charlton's 106th cap for England, to beat Billy Wright's record set up 12 years ago.

The English and the German games are alike in character. Both are full of control and this we saw as the first half hour unwound, with England 4–4–2 against Germany 4–3–3. In spite of that supposed mathematical superiority in midfield by Moore and his men, it was, in fact, Germany, through the offices of the great Beckenbauer, Overath and Seeler, who began to dominate no-man's-land.

It was a fascinating duel in the sun, spiced by firm, hard tackling and a physical challenge wedded to ball control. It was not the Brazilian game and within the opening 20 minutes both Lee – for the second time in three appearances – and Muller were booked by the Argentine referee.

England, by their quick breaks and concentration of numbers in the important places at the right time, held these Germans, with Moore marshalling superbly as usual and Charlton, Ball, Mullery and Peters breaking with the tide.

At the 31st minute one of these breaks paid off handsomely as England took the lead with a

magnificent goal. Mullery began the move in midfield with, a long cross pass to Newton, left to right, and then was up to glide through a crowded German goalmouth to hook home a rasping shot to the top corner from some eight yards. It was unstoppable. Mullery, the creator, was also the executioner – Alpha and Omega.

Germany began the second half with Schultz in their defence in place of Hottges. By the quarter hour, too, they had replaced Libuda, on the right flank of attack, with Grabowski. By then England had played both Germany's old-fashioned wingers out of the game, but, more important, by that moment England were two up.

Their second goal came after only four minutes into the second period. Again it was a quick break from defence into attack, a spring being uncoiled. At one end there was the monumental Moore to rob Seeler and start the move.

From Moore the ball sped between Ball and Hurst and there again was Newton, gliding in on the blind side from the right, to pitch his cross towards the far post, where Peters, also an unsuspected ghost, floated in to strike the ball home. At that the old chant of "You'll never walk alone" split the skies from the English sectors on the packed banks. It might have been home again.

But these Germans are never finished, as we have learnt before. So often they seem able to pull something special out when their backs are to the wall. Now it took an individual effort by Beckenbauer, the elegant ball player who seldom seems to change his pace, to rekindle Germany's flagging hopes. With 20 minutes to go he picked up a rebound from Lee, nosed his way past Cooper and, with a cross shot from the right hand edge of the penalty area, beat Bonetti's dive to the far corner. That was 2–1.

Now perhaps came one of the turning points. With 12 minutes left a fine move between Peters and Ball saw Bell cross to the near post and there was Hurst's diving, glancing header to roll a mere inch past the far post, with Maier stranded.

Yet Germany were not yet finished. With the clock showing only eight minutes to go Fichtel crossed from the left diagonally and there was little Seeler, who seems to live on spring heels, to get behind Labone and plant a looping header to the far top corner, catching Bonetti off his line. Like Wembley four years ago, it was extra time once more.

MATCH FACTS

England 2
Mullery 31, Peters 49

After extra time

West Germany 3
Beckenbauer 68, Seeler 82,
Muller 108

England: P. Bonetti, K. Newton, T. Cooper, A. Mullery, B. Labone, R. Moore, F. Lee, A. Ball, R. Charlton (sub: C. Bell, 70), G. Hurst, M. Peters (sub: N. Hunter, 81)
West Germany: S. Maier, B. Vogts, H.-D. Hottges (sub: W. Schutz, HT), K.-H. Schnellinger, K. Fichtel, F. Beckenbauer, W. Overath, R. Libuda (sub: J. Grabowski, 55), U. Seeler, G. Muller, H. Lohr
Referee: N. Coerezzo (Argentina)
Attendance: 23,357

21

HEREFORD UNITED v NEWCASTLE UNITED

FA CUP THIRD-ROUND REPLAY, 1972

Southern League Hereford United pulled off a notable shock in the third round of the FA Cup in 1972 by drawing 2–2 with first division Newcastle United at St James' Park. The replay at Hereford's Edgar Street was delayed by bad weather and did not take place until the Saturday of the fourth round. With a mud-heap pitch and BBC cameras in attendance, the stage was set for an upset.

"Balls are said often to fly like arrows, or bullets or shooting stars: this one just went like hell"

HEREFORD UNITED 2
NEWCASTLE UNITED 1
AFTER EXTRA TIME

FA CUP THIRD-ROUND REPLAY
5 FEBRUARY 1972
EDGAR STREET
....

BY JOHN WOODCOCK
7 February

Absurd though it may seem, Hereford United of the Southern League beat Newcastle United of the First Division by 2–1 after extra time, entirely on merit in their third round FA Cup replay at Hereford on Saturday. From half-time onwards Hereford played a brand of football that would have been a match for anyone.

Poor Newcastle! After kicking their heels in Worcester for a week, waiting for the rain to stop, they had an horrific experience. Twice in the first half they hit the Hereford crossbar and they forced the first six corners of the game. Yet by the end they were being beaten for pace and taught lessons of control. Even so, with eight minutes left and much against the run of play Macdonald looked to have won the game for Newcastle when be headed in a centre from Busby.

Hereford had had their chances and failed to take them, and that, it seemed, was that. Instead, what followed added a little to the history of an ancient city. When it was all over Colin Addison, formerly of Arsenal, Nottingham Forest and Sheffield United, and now Hereford's player-manager, described it as the greatest day in his life. From the scenes of wild delight many of the crowd, which numbered 15,000, must have felt the same.

While Macdonald was being gratefully mobbed by the Newcastle players for getting his goal, the actions of one of the Hereford side caught my attention. Radford was dashing around, shaking his fists and clapping his hands as though trying desperately to convince Hereford that the match could still be won. All afternoon he had been chasing the ball about the ground and now, with only four minutes left, he fired in such a shot as he can only have dreamt about – or seen from Bobby Charlton. From the moment that he kicked the ball, from a full 40 yards out, McFaul in the Newcastle goal had not the slightest chance.

Balls are said often to fly like arrows, or bullets or shooting stars: this one just went like hell into the top left hand corner of the net. In 67 matches for Newport County, Radford scored seven goals, and this was only his third for Hereford since they signed him last summer. Now, in an ecstatic moment, he had made the shot of a lifetime.

Thankfully reprieved and suitably inspired, Hereford looked, not only the better, but the fitter side in extra time. Addison by his conscious calm composed the others. He had a fine game. McLaughlin kept his hold on Macdonald, Mallender and Gough brought their experience to bear. Potter in goal could do no wrong, Tyler showed glimpses of exceptional promise. And in the 12th minute of the first period of extra time George, substituting for Griffiths, scored the deciding goal.

With the chance of a shot from a short pass by Radford, George slithered the ball just inside the far post from a range of 20 yards. Even the Newcastle giants of other years would have been hard put to it to save themselves after that. It may give an idea of just how improbable Hereford's performance was, to say that on the previous Saturday they lost at home to Telford United.

On Saturday Hereford were uplifted, Newcastle downcast, and when Hereford come to apply for election to the Football League in June they can be assured of a vote from St James' Park. Just as West Ham on Wednesday can he assured of a hot reception at Edgar Road.

MATCH FACTS

After extra time

Hereford United 2	Newcastle United 1
Radford 85 George 103	*Macdonald 82*

Hereford United: F. Potter, R. Griffiths (sub: R. George, 83), K. Mallender, A. Jones, M. McLaughlin, C. Addison, A. Gough, D. Tyler, W. Meadows, B. Owen, R. Radford

Newcastle United: I. McFaul, D. Craig, F. Clark, I. Nattrass, P. Howard, R. Moncur, V. Busby, A. Green, M. Macdonald, J. Tudor, T. Hibbitt

Referee: D. Turner (Cannock)

Attendance: 14,313

22

LEEDS UNITED v SUNDERLAND

FA CUP FINAL, 1973

For a decade from the mid 1960s, Leeds United were a dominant force, with a team packed with outstanding players. Yet it was a curiosity of their great era that they fell at the final hurdle as often than they won trophies. They approached the 1973 FA Cup final as holders and red-hot favourites against second division Sunderland – this time, surely, nothing could go wrong.

"With nothing to lose, Sunderland, keeping the ball on the ground handsomely, actually seemed to enjoy themselves in the way football should be enjoyed"

LEEDS UNITED 0
SUNDERLAND 1

FA CUP FINAL
5 MAY 1973
WEMBLEY STADIUM

BY GEOFFREY GREEN,
FOOTBALL CORRESPONDENT
7 May

In spite of all the myriad words written and spoken in advance, Wembley on Saturday in the end provided an emotional FA Cup final of live theatre with no script. It was played from the heart and it was Sunderland with a goal by Porterfield, just after the half hour, whose heart finally proved the bigger as they knocked down the giant of Leeds United, the holders and odds-on favourites.

Not since 1928 when Blackburn Rovers, struggling against relegation, beat Huddersfield Town, their own eyes on the double, has there been such a jumbo-sized upset in a final. Some of course might prefer to point to Portsmouth's defeat of the heavily fancied Wolverhampton Wanderers in 1939. But that is a mere academic point.

The real point was that here we had a triumph for the game itself, for the underdog, and for all the unashamed romantics all on a grey, wet afternoon when Wembley's fiftieth birthday was celebrated in champion fashion. So Sunderland became the

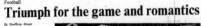

Football

Triumph for the game and romantics

By Geoffrey Green
Football Correspondent

The party is over. Sunderland's players and wives leave their hotel in London yesterday. Tonight the FA Cup winners return to League football with a match at Cardiff.

Rangers hungry enough to end years of famine

By John Davies

Liverpool out of Charity Shield game

Weekend results

European results

Today's fixtures

"Liverpool, Burnley, Bolton and Southport!"
"Champions of the four divisions of the football league, aren't they?"
"And all teams from the North West, old boy! That reminds me, Snoggins. Flange and Co are getting transfer to the North West."
"Good grounds, I suppose?"
"The best, old boy. Some of the finest sites for industrial relocation in the land. New Towns, ready-built factory units, Government grants, superb communications, and lower rents. A very sound proposition altogether."
"What about the supporters up there?"
"Oh, salt of the earth. The North West has a higher proportion of skilled workers than the average for England and Wales as a whole. And there's a pretty good record of labour relations."
"Good teamwork, eh? It's a bit 'Coronation Street' for old Snoggins though isn't it?"
"Oh, no! The quality of life is actually better up there. Some of the finest countryside in Britain. Wife loves it."
"Sounds as though he's put himself on the winning side?"
"He's positively gloating, old boy. Came across him the other day singing... We are the Champions!"

Clifford Chapman, at the North West Industrial Development Association, heads a great team offering a free information service to ambitious businessmen.

---

first second division side to lift the prize in 42 years and the voice of the north-east was raised over the nation's capital. As well it might, for not once in seven visits to the stadium by Newcastle and Sunderland has the north-east been left empty handed.

Once again, logic was put to flight, and Leeds cannot complain. They had their chances for victory but on the day – jaded perhaps after all their strenuous efforts in the League and in Europe – they were not big enough to grasp them. Even Bremner and Giles, frustrated and short of ideas the longer the battle went, made the mistake of lobbing high passes into the Sunderland penalty area where they were firmly despatched by the tall head of Watson, an impossible giant of a centre-half and on my card the man of the match with Madeley.

Any post mortem, however, might question that judgement and point instead to Montgomery, the Sunderland goalkeeper. Certainly it was he who provided the final turning point with an unbelievable save from Lorimer quite the equal of Banks's famous effort against Pele in the World Cup.

In fact, there were two saves in one, as it were and it all happened at the psychological moment midway through the second half. At that point, Leeds, with ten men on the hunt, were turning the screw tighter and tighter as Sunderland's resistance at last seemed to be draining away.

Giles began the move: Reaney took up the pattern, crossed deep from the right and there was Cherry catapulting in from the left to plant a fierce header to the far corner. Somehow Montgomery palmed it out but straight into the path of the oncoming Lorimer. All the Leeds man needed to do was push the ball home calmly for the equaliser. Instead he blasted it from six yards range but somehow Montgomery, still flat on the ground, put up an arm in reflex action like a man trying to ward off a blow, to divert the ball on to the crossbar and away. In that moment Leeds died. It was the final act and Sunderland were home, almost scoring again in the last seconds when Harvey magnificently pushed away a shot by Halom after Tueart and Kerr had ripped open the stretched Leeds defence.

Yorkshire, too, might feel aggrieved about one other moment some ten minutes after the interval when Watson hooked up Bremner inside the area. It looked all over a penalty but perhaps Bremner's own past told against him instinctively as the referee dismissed the swift passage with an imperious wave of the arm.

Certainly it would have been cruel if all Sunderland's spirited, talented offering had been brought to nothing from the penalty spot. Much of their football was gay and full of unexpected angles which had even Hunter and Madeley going the wrong way at times.

Hughes and Tueart were the mobile sharp prongs up front: Kerr, inexhaustible and a leader by example, ran himself into the ground as he hunted midfield and dropped back also to help eliminate Gray, the expected danger man, later substituted by Yorath. Horswill nagged Giles like a terrier from first to last: Bremner was similarly harried and hurried by Porterfield to break the Leeds rhythm.

It was an all-round team effort, skilful, spirited and free from fear. With nothing to lose, Sunderland, keeping the ball on the ground handsomely, actually seemed to enjoy themselves in the way football should be enjoyed. But at the heart of it all was Watson, the pillar of authority, and behind him Montgomery, a goalkeeper of instinct. Each earned an extra medal.

It was Watson's tall challenge in the air, assisted by Halom, to Hughes's corner from the left that actually opened up the goal. As the ball came down to Porterfield, he killed the bounce with his left thigh and swivelled elegantly to crash in his shot with his right.

Harvey's net puffed, the west bank of the stadium exploded into a canvas of red and stayed that way to the end. The voice of the north-east provided a wall of noise and there at the finish was Bob Stokoe, the Sunderland manager, first joyfully embracing his goalkeeper and then finding himself chaired by his team as the Cup headed for Wearside again after a lapse of 36 years.

It was Sunderland's hour after hour after hour. As for Leeds, tired but unbowed, they move on to another final in the European Cup Winners' Cup feeling perhaps that nine times out of ten they could have kept the trophy won last spring. But this was the tenth time and it is good for the game that these things should happen.

MATCH FACTS

Leeds United 0	Sunderland 1
	Porterfield 30

Leeds United: D. Harvey, P. Reaney, T. Cherry, W. Bremner, P. Madeley, N. Hunter, P. Lorimer, A. Clarke, M. Jones, J. Giles, E. Gray (sub: T. Yorath, 75)
Sunderland: J. Montgomery, R. Malone, R. Guthrie, M. Horswill, D. Watson, R. Pitt, R. Kerr, W. Hughes, V. Halom, I. Porterfield, D. Tueart
Referee: K. Burns (Stourbridge)
Attendance: 100,000

23

ENGLAND v POLAND

WORLD CUP QUALIFIER, 1973

England's campaign to qualify for the 1974 World Cup was unconvincing, but they arrived at the final group match with a simple equation: beat Poland at Wembley to reach the finals in West Germany. It was to be a match with consequences more far reaching than could have been foreseen for the national team and – more immediately – for manager Sir Alf Ramsey.

"So the night wore its jagged path away amidst a wall of sound rising in layers from the 100,000 crowd while nervous cigarettes darted like fireflies in the night"

ENGLAND 1
POLAND 1

WORLD CUP QUALIFIER
17 OCTOBER 1973
WEMBLEY STADIUM

BY GEOFFREY GREEN,
FOOTBALL CORRESPONDENT
18 October

England are out of the World Cup, being unable to do any more than draw 1-1 with Poland at Wembley last night. Now it is the Poles, after a tense and passionate finish to a passionate night, who can now take a first-class ticket towards Munich as winners of qualifying group five. How England failed to win will always remain one of those mysteries, hard to explain in a hundred years.

By the end there were few whole fingernails left and few larynxes that were not strained. Poland on a palpitating night plundered the draw they needed as England, pressing minute after minute from beginning to end, finally failed to keep cool and patient as chance after chance either spun away into the night or was denied by some last-ditch rescue on the goal line. Every Englishman gave everything he had to the last second, but they just could not achieve the final kill.

So Poland, the reigning Olympic champions, have reached the final stages of the World Cup for the first time since 1938 and this, sadly, is the first time that England have failed to qualify since entering the championship in 1950. Two major points remain.

First comes the managership of Sir Alf Ramsey. As the minutes unwound, seemingly faster and faster, there he sat with his substitutes on the sidelines. What fires were burning inside him, one will perhaps never know. But he sat there immobile while his men out on the field drained themselves of their last ounce of energy. Yet not until two minutes from the end did Sir Alf bring on Hector as substitute for Chivers, who had done virtually nothing all night and might well have been replaced a whole hour or more from the end.

The fact that little Hector in those last seconds had his header to a corner by Currie blocked on the very Polish goal-line is neither here nor there. This decision, or lack of it, is as difficult to explain as England's failure to win, when on the balance of play they could claim 22 corners in their favour against Poland's two and a whole sheaf of shots aimed all around the Polish goalposts.

When they were on the target there was Tomaszewski, at times like a windmill caught in a gale as he flapped his arms and feet in every direction. But with it all he produced four dazzling saves which clearly made him the Polish hero of the occasion. Tomaszewski indeed could be given as one reason for England's failure not to score just one more goal.

For Sir Alf I can find no excuse. England for 90 minutes gave their spirit and their hearts to the battle. Yet for all Currie's variety of approach and service from midfield this England side basically was short of brain. Football – the best football that is – is played in the mind and what England truly lacked this night was some guiding star.

Their failure will bring a dark shadow across the English game in the months ahead. But it need not be calamitous. We now have four years in which to re-examine our methods and rethink our whole attacking approach. If we can do that and do it under intelligent direction there may yet be a rebirth before 1978 as came after the historic Hungarian defeat which shook English football to its foundations precisely 20 years ago.

The goals when they came both arrived after the interval. With half an hour left, the score still blank and England still attacking, a quick break from the massed Polish defence saw Hunter miss his tackle on a long pass to Gadocha down the left wing. The England defence, caught extended, was outnumbered now three to one, and as Gadocha drew his last man, McFarland, there on his right were both Lato and Domarski. He chose Domarski for his pass and in went the low shot beyond Shilton's dive.

Yet within six minutes England had not only had a shot by Clarke into the Polish net disallowed, but had equalised when Peters was blatantly pushed over by Musial on the edges of the penalty area as England's captain was about to break through. It was a penalty. In spite of the responsibility and the tension that must have been within him Clarke took it finely on the goalkeeper's left-hand side.

With 26 minutes to go England were still in with a chance. But no need to go into the cascade of shots and near misses and escapes that finally saw Poland to their harbour. Indeed it was little but a chapter of accidents and negatives. Some things are better said without words.

In this case they are reflected with the agony of the English side as they finally left the field with the roar of the 100,000 crowd still chanting "England! England!"

The author of Poland's success, no doubt, was their windmill Tomaszewski but out in midfield Deyna, with his subtle control of a rearguard action, was the man who probably more than any other fertilised their escape. England used a hammer when they should have used a gimlet and there is no need any more to embellish the facts. All one need say is that every Englishman with Currie, Channon, Bell and Hughes outstanding, burnt themselves down to the wick.

Four moments, however, must be mentioned – Channon hitting the foot of the post after only 19 minutes; a wonderful save at full length from Currie just before half-time; Currie again striking the crossbar midway through the second half; and then, finally, three remarkable saves by Tomaszewski in the final stages – one with his feet – from Clarke, Channon and Currie.

What one can say thankfully is that this was no violent battle where the steel blade was unsheathed, though once in the first half Bulzacki was booked for a tackle on Channon eight minutes from the end in one of Poland's dangerous breaks out of defence.

McFarland, too, found his name in the referee's bad book when he caught Lato by the neck of his shirt when the winger was clean through on one of Deyna's clever, long passes from defence. Seldom have I seen a match so dominated in one half of the field. That indeed was much of the trouble for England. The whole company was too compressed into an area inside and around the Polish penalty area. It resembled Piccadilly Circus in the rush hour and there was nobody to entice the Poles out of their lair.

So the night wore its jagged path away amidst a wall of sound rising in layers from the 100,000 crowd while nervous cigarettes darted like fire-flies in the night. The whole Polish defence did a man-sized job. How they withstood so long a barrage is impossible to explain basically. One more shot surely should have got past, but it did not.

The Poles still have much intelligence and attacking skill in them when their backs are so heavily pressed against the wall. The fact that they survived such an onslaught and at the same time in passing moments showed their basic skills suggests that they may still have much to say for themselves in West Germany next summer. England somehow looked like a moth caught on a pin as they fought for one tiny last opening. But it did not come.

MATCH FACTS

England 1	Poland 1
Clarke 63 pen	*Domarski 57*

England: P. Shilton, P. Madeley, E. Hughes, C. Bell, R. McFarland, N. Hunter, A. Currie, M. Channon, M. Chivers (sub: K. Hector, 88), A. Clarke, M. Peters
Poland: J. Tomaszewski, J. Gorgon, A. Szymanowski, M. Bulzacki, A. Musial, H. Kasperczak, K. Deyna, L. Cmikiewicz, G. Lato, J. Domarski, R. Gadocha
Referee: V. Loraux (Belgium)
Attendance: 90,587

Jubilation for Arsenal's 'Invincibles' after they clinch the 2003–04 Premiership title on enemy soil at White Hart Lane.

Wayne Rooney reflects on the gulf between Barcelona and Manchester United in the 2011 Champions League final at Wembley.

Ecstasy is mixed with disbelief as David Beckham and Michael Owen revel in England's 5-1 demolition of Germany in 2001.

In a season of personal redemption, David Beckham is carried off Villa Park after Manchester United's FA Cup semi-final replay win over Arsenal in 1999.

Sealed with a kiss: Steven Gerrard plants a kiss on the European Cup after inspiring 'the Miracle of Istanbul' in the 2005 Champions League final.

The final whistle blows in Nice, and Iceland have inflicted a national humiliation on England at the 2016 European Championship.

A man apart: Lionel Messi established a claim to be considered the greatest footballer of all time.

Lionel Messi makes the most of the celebrations after Barcelona's exhilarating victory over Manchester United in the 2011 Champions League final at Wembley.

In an extraordinary climax to the season, Sergio Aguero clinches the 2011–12 Premier League title for Manchester City after an injury-time winner in the final moments of the campaign.

Manchester United lift the European Cup after completing a unique treble in 1998–99 with a breathless finish to the final against Bayern Munich.

Manchester United had trailed Bayern Munich since the early minutes of the 1999 Champions League final, until Teddy Sheringham grabbed a late equaliser.

Ole Gunnar Solskjaer stabs home Manchester United's winning goal to complete a fairytale comeback and secure United's second European Cup.

Ryan Giggs ends a brilliant run with an emphatic finish to take Manchester United through to the 1999 FA Cup final after a thrilling replay against Arsenal at Villa Park.

Arsenal's French striker Thierry Henry became one of the game's modern-day greats, and the club's all-time leading scorer.

There's no mistaking the Jules Rimet trophy as England's newly crowned world champions show the fans what all the fuss has been about.

Treble 20: Geoff Hurst, Bobby Moore and Nobby Stiles lead the celebrations on England's ecstatic lap of honour.

Moore, impressively in command of the situation as always, snuffs out another West German attack in the 1966 World Cup final.

His place in history assured, Bobby Moore appears to be realising the magnitude of England's achievement in winning the World Cup.

Two different views of an iconic image as Bobby Moore is held aloft at the start of England's lap of honour.

Exhaustion as well as delight is etched on the faces of the England players as they celebrate a stirring triumph over West Germany.

Frustration for Colin Bell as another chance goes begging: England can only draw with Poland and so fail to qualify for the 1974 World Cup.

Martin Chivers fails to get the better of a heroic Polish defence.

Allan Clarke coolly beats Poland's Jan Tomaszewski from the penalty spot to bring England level, but they could not conjure up a winning goal.

Jan Tomaszewski looks in agony during the World Cup qualifier against
England at Wembley in 1973 – but he recovered to play a starring role.

Blackpool goalkeeper George Farm turns the ball over the bar during the
1953 FA Cup final against Bolton Wanderers at Wembley.

Desperate to get back into the match after going 3–1 down, Blackpool attack
constantly in the final stages of the game.

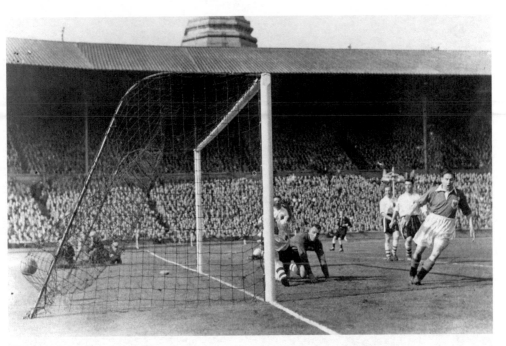

Stan Mortensen's free-kick rips into the net to complete his hat-trick and bring Blackpool level at 3–3 in the epic 1953 FA Cup final.

Blackpool captain Harry Johnston receives the FA Cup from the Queen after one of the greatest of all FA Cup finals.

Alan Sealey turns away triumphantly after scoring West Ham United's second goal in their European Cup Winners' Cup victory over TSV 1860 Munich at Wembley in 1965.

Bobby Moore exchanges pennants with TSV 1860 Munich captain Rudi Brunnenmeier before a magnificent match.

24

BORUSSIA MONCHENGLADBACH
v LIVERPOOL

EUROPEAN CUP FINAL, 1977

Manchester United's victory in 1968 stood as a lone beacon of English success in the European Cup, but by the mid-1970s an outstanding team had emerged at Liverpool under the unassuming management of Bob Paisley. After winning successive League titles, they were ready to lift the biggest prize in club football.

"In the end, after this extended and demanding season, the most valued prize of all came with a comfortable score"

BORUSSIA MONCHENGLADBACH 1
LIVERPOOL 3

EUROPEAN CUP FINAL
OLYMPIC STADIUM, ROME
25 MAY 1977

....

BY NORMAN FOX, FOOTBALL CORRESPONDENT
26 May

Ten years to the day since Celtic became the first British club to win the European Cup, Liverpool tonight became the third – also joining Manchester United who had beaten them at Wembley on Saturday, as one of a special little band to overcome the intense and wide continental challenge.

Here in the Olympic Stadium on a stifling night they added the final seal of satisfaction to their 13 years in amongst the finest teams of Europe. They dominated Borussia Monchengladbach, the West German champions, for all but a short period after half-time when the Danish international Simonson equalised. But, as if in a perfect fairy story, they were set on their way to victory by a goal from Tommy Smith, for whom this was the last game in the red shirt of the club he had served so stoutly for so long. In the end, after this extended and demanding season, the most valued prize of all came with a comfortable score, and though Liverpool did indeed defeat the Germans without a shadow of doubt, it was a thrilling and exacting night.

Throughout the sweltering day, too, Rome had been even more than usually colourful and alive with the banner waving, slogan chanting supporters from England and Germany, all carrying their noisy debate into the forum and reviving tired feet in the fountains. Here there was nothing but friendly greetings and all of football's problems seemed far away. It was later to become a night when British football could be proud of its champions, and of their followers.

The evening brought little respite from the breathless humidity that was even more oppressive in this stadium under the hills where Liverpool crowds outnumbered and out-voiced those from Germany.

Before the game Liverpool had chosen not to include Toshack who, they had originally said, might be brought back after eight weeks specifically to win the ball in the air. But in the early minutes that seemed irrelevant, and so it was to prove later, because Keegan was not seriously hindered by the close marking of Vogts and he even won many balls that floated high into the penalty area. Klinkhammer attached himself to Heighway though as soon as the two Liverpool strikers began to interchange positions both found promising space.

There was hesitation amongst the Borussia defenders from the beginning and even after two smart breakaways should have been their base for improving confidence. Neal blocked a firm shot from Heynckes and after 32 minutes, Bonhof ran unchallenged though the middle to hit the post from 25 yards. Liverpool, composed and uncharacteristically unhurried, controlled any nervousness and quickly recovered. Not long after Kennedy made Kneib, in the German goal, push his lone drive over the bar. Borussia were predictably caught without adequate cover as Callaghan took the ball away from Bonhof, who was strangely reluctant to chase him. Heighway took up the attack and played a fine pass into the penalty area for McDermott to follow and turn into a superb low shot that ended in the far corner of the German goal.

It could be argued that the element of good fortune that followed Liverpool when Bonhof's shot hit the post was crucial to their morale, particularly after the disappointment of Saturday's FA Cup final defeat by Manchester United, but they fully deserved to end the first half ahead and in control. Borussia lost Wimmer after 24 minutes yet it was Liverpool's whole approach, not the possible intervention of luck, that was so welcome. They played here as they had in earlier European matches in St Etienne and Zurich and it was not the tearaway football that generally satisfies the consumers at home. They cut their cloth for the occasion but, after 50 minutes, Borussia suddenly came back, leaving themselves plenty of time to play themselves back into the game.

Despite the trend of the first half there was a feeling, still, that a single mistake could destroy all of Liverpool's work, and sure enough Case, scorer of several of their important goals this season, allowed their advantage to slip away when he desperately tried to retrieve a German through pass but knocked the ball behind Neal. Simonsen, who had been injured in training, was quick enough to nip into the space and send a magnificent shot behind Clemence from wide on the left side.

For a few tense minutes Liverpool were troubled. Simonsen sent Stielike away through the middle and Clemence had to move out quickly to block the shot, allowing Liverpool

to regain their feel for the game. Yet it was hard to see who would pull them back. Keegan, tracked all the time by Vogts, was not often given room to see the goal, and the willowy Heighway made ground but not many chances for himself. How magnificent and how unexpected, then, that it should be Smith, hard as Italian marble, who should come surging into the penalty area to head Heighway's corner dramatically and unstoppably into the net.

Liverpool were again the masters of the night and in the end they assured themselves of a fitting climax to their season, and of their era, when Keegan was hit again heavily, and this time totally unfairly in the penalty area. He was sprinting when he fell and the referee could not refuse him the penalty. Neal, facing the giant German goalkeeper, could have nervously thrashed at the shot, but calmly scored with the inside of his foot.

MATCH FACTS

Borussia Monchengladbach 1
Simonsen 52

Liverpool 3
McDermott 28, Smith 64, Neal 82 pen

Borussia Monchengladbach: W. Kneib, B. Vogts, H. Klinkhammer, H.-J. Wittkamp, R. Bonhof, H. Wohlers (sub: W Hannes, 79), A. Simonsen, H. Wimmer (sub: C. Kulik, 24), U. Stielike, F. Schaffer, J. Heynckes
Liverpool: R. Clemence, P. Neal, J. Jones, T. Smith, R. Kennedy, E. Hughes, K. Keegan, J. Case, S. Heighway, I. Callaghan, T. McDermott
Referee: R. Wurtz (France)
Attendance: 52,078

25

HOLLAND v SCOTLAND

WORLD CUP GROUP MATCH, 1978

Scotland qualified for the 1978 World Cup in Argentina – England once again stayed at home – in a blaze of patriotic fervour and gung-ho optimism engendered by their manager Ally MacLeod. But their campaign quickly became a nightmare after a defeat by Peru and a draw with Iran left them needing to beat Holland by three goals to reach the second stage.

"... in the shadows of the Andes they lightened their own black depression."

HOLLAND 2
SCOTLAND 3

WORLD CUP GROUP MATCH
11 JUNE 1978
MENDOZA STADIUM,
ARGENTINA

....

BY NORMAN FOX, FOOTBALL CORRESPONDENT
12 June

Scotland's disastrous World Cup ended here today with a welcome touch of defiance and a token victory that came too late to erase all of the bad memories. Beaten by Peru, held by Iran, they were finally eliminated because they were unable to score the three clear goals that they needed against the Dutch. But there were times tonight when it seemed they might achieve an astonishing recovery.

With the adventurous Souness brought into the team to give purpose to the midfield section, the Scots played football of a quality that had it come earlier would undoubtedly have taken them into the second round with the Dutch. Now, they are out on goal difference. Nevertheless, they owed an apology and in the shadows of the Andes they lightened their own black depression.

This was a performance to leave the Scottish supporters saying "If only...", but at least some of them were singing again. Yet one had mixed feelings about the exact outlook of the Dutch. Once the lead had been stretched to two goals, they came out into the open and attacked with their first enterprise. Rep closed the gap again with a goal to vie with Gemmill's. Strolling through the centre of the field, he was allowed space and took an instant decision to shoot, and how.

His searing drive from 25 yards or more fairly whizzed past Rough, and it was as if to say that the Dutch, although quiet here, should not be underestimated or judged too seriously on this performance. In the minutes of Scotland's dying last hopes they showed fine attacking touches, and when Rene van der Kerkhof tore away down the left side, he was unfortunate that his final shot slid wide of the far post, after easily beating the Scottish goalkeeper. Scotland finished with Forsyth heading round the post and that, at least, showed they had found their spirit, but all too late.

The Dutch allowed Scotland to take the initiative. They used only three defenders because the Scots had chosen not to start with a winger, and, as always, they marked tightly, Rijsbergen hovering over Dalglish and Suurbier closing in on Jordan. Scotland's intention was to thrust men forward from midfield and almost from the start Rioch, Gemmill and, most important of all, Souness went forward to good purpose, with Rioch hitting the junction of post and bar after five minutes.

This tight marking quickly showed its ugly face and dangers as Rijsbergen hammered into Dalglish and Jordan was flattened. Free kicks on the edge of the Dutch penalty area gave the Scots encouragement and when Neeskens injured himself lunging at Gemmill, the cost of this emphasis on physical domination was seen. He was to take no further part, being carried off on a stretcher and replaced with Boskamp.

The Netherlands's casual attitude in the first half-hour gave Scotland their chance to give the remaining group of supporters some cheer, and indeed Dalglish had the ball in the net, but the goal was disallowed for an infringement that was not immediately obvious.

Dalglish followed up by driving a shot round the post and, with Rijsbergen also hurt in a tackle with Jordan, the chances of Scotland breaking through this weakened Dutch defence seemed reasonable, although in breakaways the Dutch were menacing. Rough once saved from Willy van der Kerkhof's feet yards outside the penalty area and there was some desperation in the air when a mistake by Kennedy allowed Rep through on the left side. Kennedy, chasing back to compensate, and Rough, charging out of goal, both tried to converge on him at the same moment, but succeeded only in bringing him down. Scotland complained, but the referee gave the penalty, and Rensenbrink scored.

The Dutch defence hampered by their injuries, looked increasingly frail and, with Souness always troubling them, it was not surprising that a minute before half-time his perfectly-placed lob to Jordan created the equaliser. Jordan headed down, and Dalglish lashed the ball in.

The attitude of the Dutch was difficult to assess. It had been said that they wanted to win the group in order to stay here in Mendoza, but some of their passing indicated that they would be happy to finish in second place in order to go to Cordoba to a pitch, they claimed, that was better.

Either way they were letting Scotland live a little, and after two more splendid headers from Dalglish and Jordan, Souness was bundled down as he again threatened the Dutch defence. Gemmill was having no nonsense with this penalty. Jongbloed chose one side of the goal to dive across and Gemmill, with his kick, the other.

At that moment Scotland summoned a little more of their faded pride and it carried them on with football that had it been seen earlier in the competition would surely have saved them much of their heartache. Suddenly, Gemmill was involved again – he was rarely out of the spotlight. Collecting the ball just outside the penalty area, he dodged and weaved inside and out of the apparently solid line of defenders and struck a marvellous shot past a thoroughly beaten goalkeeper. It was certainly among the finest goals of the competition, and so ironic.

MATCH FACTS

Holland 2	Scotland 3
Rensenbrink 34 pen, Rep 71	*Dalglish 44, Gemmill 46 pen 68*

Scotland: A. Rough, S. Kennedy, M. Buchan, T. Forsyth, W. Donachie, G. Souness, B. Rioch, A. Hartford, A. Gemmill, J. Jordan, K. Dalglish
Holland: J. Jongbloed, W. Suurbier, R. Krol, J. Poortvliet, W. Rijsbergen (sub: P. Wildschut, 44), J. Neeskens (sub: J. Boskamp, 10), W. Jansen, W. van der Kerkhof, R. van der Kerkhof, J. Rep, R. Rensenbrink
Referee: E. Linemayr (Austria)
Attendance: 35,130

26

NOTTINGHAM FOREST v SV HAMBURG

EUROPEAN CUP FINAL, 1980

There may be no greater managerial achievement in the history of British football than that of Brian Clough and Peter Taylor in turning unfashionable Nottingham Forest – with no previous history of success – into a European power. After winning the League championship in 1977–78 and the European Cup the following season, they reached a second final against SV Hamburg in 1980.

"This was an effort of rare collective responsibility"

NOTTINGHAM FOREST 1
SV HAMBURG 0

EUROPEAN CUP FINAL
28 MAY 1980
BERNABEU STADIUM, MADRID

....

BY NORMAN FOX, FOOTBALL CORRESPONDENT
29 May

Nottingham Forest tonight became the seventh in an illustrious line of football clubs to win the European Cup in two successive seasons. They join Liverpool, Bayern Munich, Ajax, Inter Milan, Benfica and, appropriately, Real Madrid, in whose Santiago Bernabeu Stadium they carried out the complete suppression of Hamburg.

They had to come through a final that was infinitely more difficult and totally different from last year's comparatively uneventful match against Malmo. Here they mixed remorseless attacks with organised defence. Their winning goal scorer was the enterprising Robertson, but this was an effort of rare collective responsibility – rare, that is, outside the teams that Brian Clough and Peter Taylor have made in the mould of no contemporary.

Tonight, once again, Forest pitted their concerted strength against individualism, here primarily contained in Hamburg's English exile, Keegan, who in the end bowed to their unfaltering defenders, who refused to fall to match-long pressure.

A disappointment befell Hamburg even before the start when Hrubesch,

Football

Forest cling on to the European Cup

From Norman Fox
Football Correspondent
Madrid, May 28

Nottingham F 1   SV Hamburg 0

Nottingham Forest tonight became the seventh in an illustrious line of football clubs to win the European Cup in two successive seasons. They join Liverpool, Bayern Munich, Ajax, Inter-Milan, Benfica and, appropriately, Real Madrid, in whose Santiago Bernabeu Stadium they carried out the complete suppression of Hamburg.

They had to come through a final that was infinitely more difficult and totally different from last year's comparatively uneventful match against Malmo. Here they mixed remorseless attacks with organized defence. Their winning goal scorer was the enterprising Robertson, but this was an effort of rare collective responsibility—rare, that is, outside the team that Brian Clough and Peter Taylor have made in the mould of no contemporary.

Tonight, once again, Forest pitted their concerted strength against individualism, here primarily contained in Hamburg's English exile, Keegan, who in the end bowed to their unfaltering defenders, who refused to fall to match-long pressure.

A disappointment befell Hamburg even before the start when Hrubesch, their imposing and tactically important centre forward, had to admit defeat to an ankle injury incurred last weekend and could play only in the second half. As a result, Keegan was for 45 minutes deployed at the nose of the German attack, perpetually trying to avoid the rugged attentions of Burns and Lloyd, who were quick to make a physical and psychological impact on his ambitions.

Predictably, Forest offered no aggressive early challenge in the Hamburg half, preferring to let the Germans move towards them on their broad deep-green pitch in the one-third-full stadium. Theirs was a policy of patient stealth; the spider trying to draw the prey into a dangerous web and then attack. Birtles was left as a lonely target for their occasional breakaways, one of which saw Gray swerve in from the wing as if wanting to go all the way on his own. But generally, Hamburg were the possessors.

Forest had weighed the risks inherent in their plans and certainly Keegan was kept under control; danger emanated from others. When Lloyd brought down Keegan, not for the first or the last time, the free kick, close to the penalty area, was tapped to one side and Magath's drive was deliberately punched round the post by Shilton, who was not always as confidently protected as he should have been when Hamburg penetrated deep into the penalty area. Otherwise the Forest defence played well to keep most attacks outside the danger area.

Full backs, it had been said, could decide the outcome of this final, and when Anderson fairly steamed out of defence to rob Nogly in midfield, he gave Birtles his first chance, but the shot went wide. It was all the same a taste of the opportunities that could be prised with good timing of breakaways.

The proof really came after 20 minutes when Robertson, collecting the ball from Mills, gloriously exposed the fundamental dangers of man-to-man marking by dodging past Kaltz and finding space opening like an inviting open road. He ran towards the penalty area and played a return pass with Birtles before slamming a low shot in off the post to give Forest a lead and great encouragement.

Although Hamburg immediately answered with Reiman shooting in after Shilton had parried an initial shot, the linesman stood by an offside decision. That successfully weathered, Forest went back to their business of destroying all of Keegan's lines of communication and blocking him as soon as he took possession. In fact, Burns treated him too harshly and had his name taken; but on the whole Keegan was unable to escape legitimate crowding and one could see why he was so sorry that Hrubesch was not there to afford some protection until his partner appeared for the second half.

Keegan did once leap high enough to expect something rewarding as he made to beat Shilton in the air, but this was yet another night of astonishingly brilliant saves by the goalkeeper who, just before half-time, cleverly diverted a drive from Milewski.

Having seen the strategy that Forest intended, the question for the second half, when the marching girls eventually allowed a continuation, was whether Hrubesch was fit enough to make a significant difference to the staunch defending of Burns, whose heading was superb, and Lloyd. Keegan was released to extemporize, dropping deep in attempts to intercept Forest's crucial breakaways and trying to counter.

Hrubesch soon discovered that the Forest penalty area was an uncomfortable place in which to win the ball in the air. Burns loomed over him but McGovern, concentrating unswervingly, was largely responsible for coordinating all of Forest's efforts as Hamburg gathered themselves for a final assault in which one enormous shot by Kaltz smacked against the goalpost.

Young Mills, who had been useful as a support in midfield, was given an honourable discharge in order to allow O'Hare to bring his experience to the last 20 minutes when Hamburg pummelled the Forest defence and brought Shilton's most spectacular save.

Afterwards Mr Clough said:

"They may have had the edge on us in technique but we beat them for application, determination and pride—all the things that portray our football. We weren't lucky. We were good and any good team would have no option but to defend, but if you have to defend you have to do it well. It is as important as attacking. At half-time I wondered how we would last. I saw knees buckling and Mills was one of only three players we could have taken off. In fact Birtles did not have the strength to remove his shin pads at the end of the game."

NOTTINGHAM FOREST: P. Shilton; V. Anderson, J. Lloyd, K. Burns, F. Gray, M. O'Neill, I. Bowyer, J. McGovern, G. Birtles, G. Mills, J. Robertson.

S.V. HAMBURG: R. Kargus; M. Kaltz, D. Jakobs, I. Bullan, P. Nogly, H. Hieronymus, F. Magath, W. Reiman, C. Memering, J. Milewski, K. Keegan.

Referee: A. Garrido (Portugal).

Clough's £100,000 Brian Clough, Forest manager, and his assistant, Peter Taylor, have agreed to sign better and longer contracts with the club. The chairman, Geoffrey Macpherson, announced their decision a few hours before the European Cup final in Madrid and said the two men would be staying at least until June 1983. Clough's new salary and bonuses are believed to make him the highest paid manager in the game and for the three year term could top £100,000. Taylor's new contract will be similarly rewarded.

Robertson takes the high road (and the low) past Kaltz to another Forest peak.

Kidd stunned at his release from Everton

Brian Kidd completed the final details of his transfer from Everton to Bolton yesterday for a fee of £150,000. Kidd said: "I've never played in the second division before and I don't intend to stay there too long, I am sure Bolton feel the same."

Kidd (31) was Everton's top scorer last season as he was in each of his two seasons with Arsenal and then Manchester City. He said "I am stunned that Everton have let me go with two years of my contract to run especially as I have scored a goal every two games. I have been top scorer at my last three clubs and I am going to do my best to keep that record with Bolton."

Mick Tait, Hull City's midfield player who was transfer listed at his own request, has joined the newly-promoted third division side, Portsmouth, for £100,000. He had made 29 appearances for Hull since moving from Carlisle for £150,000 last September.

Scotland given a lesson on importance of attack

Poznan, May 28.—Poland handed Scotland a lesson in attacking football with a 1—0 win in an international match here today. The Scots managed only two shots at goal in the entire 90 minutes and were lucky to escape a heavier defeat.

Poland, with four defeats and two draws in their last six matches, attacked at will and only the Aberdeen defender Miller and the Partick goalkeeper Rough kept Scotland on level terms. But even Rough was helpless when the 24-year-old Boniek, fired home a superb winner in the seventy-sixth minute. Collecting the ball in midfield he darted between two defenders and fired a great shot into the net.

The Scotland manager, Jock Stein, sent on Weir and Brazil to replace his strikers Jordan and Dalglish, who had tried unavailingly in the first half to pierce the Polish defence.

Weir could have scored the equalizer only a few minutes after he came on when he intercepted a pass and ran the length of the field unchallenged. But his final shot was weak. After the goalkeeper had saved from Strachan, Scotland's attacks petered out.

"We lost the second half not because the Polish team was better but because my players were tired," Mr Stein said.

"The Poles played well, particularly Boniek and the goalkeeper Mowlik who had little to do", he added.

The Polish manager Ryszard Kulesza said: "Obviously we still need to tidy up our game because we created many opportunities but only scored one goal. The victory could have been greater, but we deserved to win."

POLAND: P. Mowlik, M. Dziuba (sub: W. Ciolski), P. Janas, W. Zmuda, W. Barczak, L. Lipka, A. Nawalka, G. Lato, K. Kmiecik, A. Palasz, S. Terlecki.

SCOTLAND: A. Rough; G. Burley (sub: A. Dawson), D. McGrain, A. McLeish, W. Miller, G. Narey, G. Strachan, S. Aitken, K. Dalglish (sub: P. Weir), S. Archibald, J. Jordan (sub: A. Brazil).—Reuter.

NORTH AMERICAN LEAGUE: Edmonton Drillers 1, Memphis Rogues 0.

Europe blows the whistle on clubs and crowds

Berne, May 28.—European football authorities may have to impose more punitive sanctions on players and clubs to combat increasing field and crowd disturbances in international tournaments, Hans Bangerter, the European Football Union (UEFA) general secretary, said today. In a report covering 1978 and 1979, he said that trouble at UEFA club competition matches reached unprecedented levels at the start of the season just ended.

As well as emotional and irrational behaviour by a small section of supporters, whole teams were occasionally acting unsportingly, rather than just individual players, as in the past, Mr Bangerter said.

If such disturbances continued, UEFA, instead of imposing fines, would have to increase penalties on offending clubs to include deducting points won in competition, forfeiting of games, closing stadiums, playing matches behind closed doors or in neutral countries, or even expulsion from a competition.

their imposing and tactically important centre forward, had to admit defeat to an ankle injury incurred last weekend and could play only in the second half. As a result, Keegan was for 45 minutes deployed at the nose of the German attack, perpetually trying to avoid the rugged attentions of Burns and Lloyd, who were quick to make a physical and psychological impact on his ambitions.

Predictably, Forest offered no aggressive early challenge in the Hamburg half, preferring to let the Germans move towards them on this broad deep-green pitch in the one-third-full stadium. Theirs was a policy of patient stealth; the spider trying to draw the prey into a dangerous web and the attack. Birtles was left as a lonely target for their occasional breakaways, one of which saw Gray swerve in from the wing as if wanting to go all the way on his own. But generally, Hamburg were the possessors.

Forest had weighed the risks inherent in their plans and certainly Keegan was kept under control; danger emanated from others. When Lloyd brought down Keegan, not for the first or the last time, the free kick, close to to the penalty area, was tapped to one side and Magath's drive was deliberately punched round the post by Shilton, who was not always as confidently protected as he should have been when Hamburg penetrated deep into the penalty area. Otherwise

the Forest defence played well to keep most attacks outside the danger area.

Full backs, it had been said, could decide the outcome of this final, and when Anderson fairly steamed out of defence to rob Nogly in midfield, he gave Birtles his first chance, but the shot went wide. It was all the same a taste of the opportunities that could be prised with good timing of breakaways.

The proof really came after 20 minutes when Robertson, collecting the ball from Mills, gloriously exposed the fundamental dangers of man-to-man marking by dodging past Kaltz and finding space opening like an inviting open road. He ran towards the penalty area and played a return pass with Birtles before slamming a low shot in off the post to give Forest a lead and great encouragement.

Although Hamburg immediately answered with Reimann shooting in after Shilton had parried an initial shot, the linesman stood by an offside decision. That successfully weathered, Forest went back to their business of destroying all of Keegan's lines of communication and blocking him as soon as he took possession. In fact, Burns treated him too harshly and had his name taken but on the whole Keegan was unable to escape legitimate crowding and one could see why he was so sorry that Hrubesch was not there to afford some protection until his partner appeared for the second half.

Keegan did once leap high enough to expect something rewarding as he made to beat Shilton in the air, but this was yet another night of astonishingly brilliant saves by the goalkeeper who, just before half-time, cleverly diverted a drive from Milewski.

Having seen everything follow the strategy that Forest intended, the question for the second half, when the marching girls eventually allowed a continuation, was whether Hrubesch was fit enough to make a significant difference to the staunch defending of Burns, whose heading was superb, and Lloyd. Keegan was released to extemporise, dropping deep in attempts to intercept Forest's crucial breakaways and trying to counter.

Hrubesch soon discovered that the Forest penalty area was an uncomfortable place in which to win the ball in the air. Burns loomed over him but McGovern, concentrating unswervingly, was largely responsible for coordinating all of Forest's efforts as Hamburg gathered themselves for a final assault in which one enormous

shot by Kaltz smacked against the goalpost.

Young Mills, who had been useful as a support in midfield, was given an honourable discharge in order to allow O'Hare to bring his experience to the last 20 minutes when Hamburg pummelled the Forest defence and brought Shilton's most spectacular save.

Afterwards Mr Clough said: "They may have had the edge on us in technique but we beat them for application, determination and pride – all the things that portray our football. We weren't lucky. We were good and any good team would have no option but to defend, but if you have to defend you have to do it well. It is as important as attacking. At half-time I wondered how we would last. I saw knees buckling and Mills was one of only three players we could have taken off. In fact, Birtles did not have the strength to remove his shin pads at the end of the game."

MATCH FACTS

Nottingham Forest 1	SV Hamburg 0
Robertson 20	

Nottingham Forest: P. Shilton, V. Anderson, L. Lloyd, K. Burns, F. Gray (sub: B. Gunn, 78), M. O'Neill, I. Bowyer, J. McGovern, G. Birtles, G. Mills (sub: J. O'Hare, 67), J. Robertson
SV Hamburg: R. Kargus, M. Kaltz, D. Jakobs, I. Buljan, P. Nogly, H. Hieronymus (sub: H. Hrubesch, HT), K. Keegan, F. Magath, W. Reimann, C. Memering, J. Milewski
Referee: A. Garrido (Portugal)
Attendance: 51,000

27

BRAZIL v ITALY

WORLD CUP ROUND OF 12, 1982

At the 1982 World Cup in Spain, Brazil unveiled a team that appeared to be worthy heirs to the legends of 1970. They breezed through their first four matches playing breathtaking football and scoring dazzling goals. In their last game of the second group stage they needed merely to draw with the hitherto unimpressive Italians to reach the semi-finals and move closer to their inevitable destiny.

"...they had begun by trying to avoid Italian tackles with light-stepping, one-touch football but they were soon on their heels"

BRAZIL 2
ITALY 3

WORLD CUP ROUND OF 12
5 JULY 1982
SARRIA STADIUM,
BARCELONA

....

BY NORMAN FOX
6 July

Still attempting to play the elegant, eloquent football of their tradition, Brazil last night departed the World Cup. Italy beat them fairly and cleverly with three goals from the irresistible Paulo Rossi.

After criticism that had followed Italy's early performances, it is important that the fairness of their victory is emphasised. The World Cup will be the poorer for Brazil's failure to reach a semi-final match with Poland on Thursday but Italy, if they continue to concentrate on their skills rather than their unattractive strength, can still be a credit to the tournament.

Italy will be among the last four for the third time in four successive competitions. Yesterday, however, they were at a disadvantage. To reach the last four they had to win; Brazil required only a draw. The urgency of the situation brought them out of their defensive, abrasive inner character and they punished Brazil for a performance marginally less vivacious than before.

Brazil were no strangers to the situation they found themselves in after only five minutes. Against Scotland and Soviet Union they conceded early goals and recovered in style. Here they had begun by trying to avoid Italian tackles with light-stepping, one-touch football but they were soon on their heels.

Rossi had mistimed his first opportunity of the game but was soon offered a second. Conti swung a pass out to the line and Cabrini made ground before crossing for Rossi to enjoy vacant space and head strongly past Waldir Peres.

Creditably, Italy occupied themselves without the callousness of their performances against Argentina. Now they looked first for the ball rather than their opponent, but it was those illustrious opponents who immediately showed their pedigree.

Six minutes after Italy scored, Zico wafted into their penalty area with Serginho and this time it was the Italians who were caught sleeping despite the cacophony in the Sarria Stadium. Serginho snatched at his shot; but after 13 minutes a similar flowing movement ended successfully.

Zico, slight against the square-shouldered Italian defenders, smuggled himself into their penalty area. Socrates accelerated ahead of him. Zico gave the stronger Socrates possession and he avoided Scirea to place a stunning low shot between Zoff and the near post to equalise.

Of course, Italy could not resist the occasional brusque tackle but though Gentile was cautioned, and will miss the semi-final, the Brazilians themselves were not above a rough interception in their concerted efforts to control an Italian side exuding pace and character.

Italy's initiative and determination kept pace with Brazilian art, and in the twenty-fifth minute it brought them another goal. Lethargic reactions in the Brazilian defence contributed. An extraordinary, careless pass across his penalty area by Cerezo put Junior in a hopeless situation and Rossi was left unmarked. The Italian was still 15 yards out but struck a splendid shot to leave Brazil looking human in their annoyance and still slightly below their incomparable best.

Although they lost Collovati with a leg injury, Italy effectively reorganised their defence with Bergomi positioning himself close to Serginho. It was this uncompromising Italian defensive security which caused Brazil to fail in the enterprising things they were relying upon. Zoff played an important part, especially when plunging at the feet of Cerezo just inside the penalty area. He was also alert to the variations of Eder's free kicks.

Had Italy taken their most inviting chance from one of a series of rapid breakaways, they could probably have put the game beyond Brazil's recall but Rossi, of all people, sliced wide from five yards. He was easily forgiven; his speed and control when Italy broke away always worried the Brazilians, though, after sixty-eight minutes his mistake seemed costly indeed.

Junior made another advance down the left side and turned the ball into the centre for Falcao, who stepped aside from challenges and powered in an enormous low drive to equalise. There were 22 minutes left and Italy had to start all over again.

Rossi, whose fitness had been in doubt after a two-year suspension, still had the energy and skill to catch out Brazil when they risked allowing Leandro and Cerezo upfield, but when the winning goal came, after 74 minutes, it was from the formality of a corner by Conti.

Bergoni's first attempt to turn it into a goal was denied by Socrates and Rossi hit the rebounding ball accurately as he had throughout the game. This time it meant victory, despite Brazil's still admirably considered pressure over the last 10 minutes.

MATCH FACTS

Brazil 2	Italy 3
Socrates 12 Falcao 68	*Rossi 5 25 74*

Brazil: W. Peres, Leandro, Oscar, Luizinho, T. Cerezo, Junior, Socrates, Serginho (sub: P. Isidoro, 69), Zico, Eder, Falcao.
Italy: D. Zoff, A. Cabrini, F. Collovati (sub: G. Bergomi, 34), G. Scirea, C. Gentile, G. Antognoni, G. Orilai, M. Tardelli (sub: G. Marini, 75), B. Conti, F. Graziani, P. Rossi
Referee: A. Klein (Israel)
Attendance: 44,000

28

EVERTON v BAYERN MUNICH

EUROPEAN CUP WINNERS' CUP
SEMI-FINAL SECOND LEG, 1985

In the mid 1980s, seemingly out of nowhere, the latest challengers to Liverpool's hegemony emerged from just across Stanley Park. Everton won the FA Cup in 1984 and the following season were heading for the League title and another FA Cup final when they met Bayern Munich in the last four of the European Cup Winners' Cup at a febrile Goodison Park.

"It was an occasion to rival some of those memorable evenings across the way"

EVERTON 3
BAYERN MUNICH 1

EVERTON WIN 3-1 ON AGGREGATE

EUROPEAN CUP WINNERS'
CUP SEMI-FINAL SECOND LEG
GOODISON PARK
24 APRIL 1985

....

BY CLIVE WHITE
25 April

Three mountain peaks await the blue-and-white flag of the all-conquering Everton after they overcame the precarious ridge presented by this Cup Winners' Cup semi-final second leg at Goodison Park last night. Again they made their supporters suffer terribly before coming from behind to reach their first European final in their 107-year history.

They were drawing, and yet trailing by the away goal, with 17 minutes remaining when Gray, their guru and goal-getter, lashed in the deciding goal as Pfaff, the Bayern goalkeeper, was impeded by his own defenders. It was fitting justice after the cynical attitude of the West German team throughout this tie.

Everton meet Rapid Vienna in Rotterdam on May 15 by which time they almost certainly will have won the League championship and will be three days away from scaling the final summit at Wembley in the FA Cup final against Manchester United. This is the extent of Everton's Everest.

It was an occasion to rival some of those memorable evenings of high drama just across the way. A capacity audience of 49,476, Evertonians to the core, gave their boys in blue a rapturous welcome and unrelenting support.

Uncompromising German tackling began from the second minute with a bad foul on Reid and continued until matters reached a stormy head when Pflugler, who had declared open war on Sharp, tested Gray's patience. The Scot responded wildly to a particularly unsavoury tackle, lashing out with his boot, and both were booked and fortunate not to be sent off.

Southall had not had a shot to save until the 37th minute when he narrowed the angle intelligently to hold on to one by Matthaus. In the next minute, Southall was beaten as was the Everton defence for the first time in eight tries in this competition. Matthaus, a quality midfield player, put Kogel in behind an advanced Everton defence and though Southall again did superbly well to parry his shot Hoeness was on hand to steer the ball past two defenders on the goal-line.

Everton came out of the second half even more tightly sprung. They knew that they needed two goals to overtake Bayern, who were well equipped for the job with an extra midfield player, Nachtweih, for the discarded Michael Rummenigge. But within three minutes the task facing Everton had been halved. Gray backheaded a throw-in by Stevens and Sharp glanced another header past Pfaff for his 29th goal of the season.

The breakthrough Everton sought arrived after 73 minutes and was indirectly the result, fittingly, of a German foul of their own goalkeeper. Sharp challenged another Stevens throw-in, Pfluger impeded Pfaff allowing Gray to lash the ball into the unguarded net.

MATCH FACTS

Everton 3
Sharp 48, Gray 73, Steven 86

Bayern Munich 1
Hoeness 38

Everton: N. Southall, G. Stevens, P. van den Hauwe, K. Ratcliffe, D. Mountfield, P. Reid, T. Steven, G. Sharp, A. Gray, P. Bracewell, K. Sheedy
Bayern Munich: J.-M. Pfaff, W. Dremmler, H. Willmer (sub: B. Beierlorzer, 66), N. Eder (sub: M. Rummenigge, 73), K. Augenthaler, S. Lerby, H. Pflugler, L. Matthaus, D. Hoeness, N. Nachtweih, L. Kogl
Referee: E. Fredriksson (Sweden)
Attendance: 49,476

SPORT

England sent tumbling out by Maradona

From Stuart Jones
Football Correspondent
Mexico City

Argentina	2
England	1

England yesterday suffered at the hands of the best player in the world. After being nudged out of the quarter-finals in the Aztec Stadium here, Shilton led a possee of players who surrounded the Tunisian referee to complain angrily about the legitimacy of the crucial opening goal. The television cameras supported their claim.

A slow motion replay confirmed that Maradona had indeed used his forearm to put Argentina ahead in the 50th minute. It seemed impossible, anyway, that he could have extended his stocky frame that measures only 5ft 4in to outjump Shilton, complete his exchange with Valdano and shake the foundations of England's World Cup challenge.

Yet if justice was to play a cruel role in their eventual downfall, there can be little doubt that they were beaten by a superior side. It was only after Bobby Robson had been forced to resort to an attacking four-two-four formation by bringing on Waddle and Barnes that they threatened to unhinge the only South American representatives left in the competition.

As had been feared, Maradona, a dwarf by comparison to those around him, towered above the tie. England's defence and the whole stadium itself trembled in expectation whenever he was on the run, either twisting and weaving with the ball attached securely to his remarkable left foot or merely gliding smoothly into position.

Within a few seconds that were tucked inside the 55th minute, he scored a second goal of such dazzling beauty that it will be remembered forever by all those privileged enough to witness it. England in the end can have no complaints about effectively being knocked out by a moment of pure and irresistible genius.

Maradona, accelerating as swiftly as a bird on the wing, swayed and swerved his way past Sansom, Butcher, Fenwick and finally Shilton with effortless ease. With a nonchalant prod, he claimed not only the individual goal of the competition so far but he also ended England's journey towards the last four.

England had won a psychological battle before the start. Carlos Bilardo, fearing that his side might be outnumbered in midfield, omitted one of his forwards, Pasculli, in favour of the more defensive Enrique. Bobby Robson's lone alteration was to recall Fenwick in place of Martin.

But England lost the contest for the favourable weather conditions. The sharp black shadow cast by the ornate loudspeaker system suspended above the centre circle concerned that the sun, stationed directly overhead, was shining at its brightest. Even those grappling with the Spanish language were aware that it was "Muy Caliente". It was, in other words, "very hot".

So was the atmosphere. Horns blared like the humming of a thousand bees, chants of "Inglaterra" poured down the terraces from the throats of the Mexicans and the tension, stretched out in the unforgiving mid-day sun, crackled like strips of bacon in a huge frying pan.

Reid's recovery from his ankle injury was tested in an initial challenge with Brown and Fenwick was booked for his first assault on Maradona.

Nevertheless, Pumpido took an early gamble and almost paid for it. As Argentina's goalkeeper chased Hoddle's inaccurate through ball outside his area, he lost his footing and subsequently the race with Beardsley. As he struggled to retain his position, Beardsley spun away towards the touchline, turned and curled his shot into the side netting.

Maradona had already given several warnings, particularly from free kicks, of the threat that he was to present. Argentina's tall and comparatively immobile central defenders looked no more solid under pressure but, in spite of the ceaseless scurrying of Lineker and Beardsley, England were unable to shake their uncertain foundations before the interval. It was during it that the peace in the stands was disturbed.

Even though an estimated police force of some 20,000 had been assembled specifically for the potentially explosive occasion, none were to be seen when several skirmishes broke out between odd individuals rather than groups. Within ten minutes of the second half, their distant colleagues at the other end were capturing much more signficant events as Maradona stamped his indelible mark. Yet England, encouraged by the introduction of the two substitutes, were lifted even higher by Lineker in the 80th minute.

Barnes followed a pass to the byline and Lineker, who scored all but one of England's seven goals, stabbed home from close range. He almost repeated the feat in the dying minutes after Tapia had struck a post and Fenwick, fortunate not to be dismissed, had crudely halted another Argentine break by bringing down Valdano.

As Maradona, now the leader of South America's hopes, received his deserved acclaim from the crowd, England walked away to nurse their disappointment. Had the little man-mountain not chosen to give such an extravagant display of his wondrous talent, they might by now be preparing to fulfil the title of the World Cup favourites. As it is, their conquerors are expected to regain the crown they won in 1978.

ENGLAND: P Shilton (Southampton); G Stevens (Everton), K Sansom (Arsenal), T Fenwick (Queen's Park Rangers), T Butcher (Ipswich Town), T Steven (Everton) (sub: J Barnes, Watford), G Hoddle (Tottenham Hotspur), P Reid (Everton) (sub: C Waddle, Tottenham Hotspur), S Hodge (Aston Villa), P Beardsley (Newcastle United), G Lineker (Everton).
ARGENTINA: N Pumpido; J Cuciuffo, J Brown, O Ruggeri, J Olarticoechea, R Giusti, S Batista, J Burruchaga (sub: C Tapia), H Enrique, D Maradona, J Valdano.
Referee: A Bennacour (Tunisia).

Schumacher saves Germans

Monterrey (Reuter) – Harald Schumacher made two saves in the penalty shoot-out to salvage a scrappy, ill-tempered victory for West Germany over Mexico on Saturday.

The host nation made their exit under a cloud of eight players being booked and two – Berthold, of West Germany, and Aguirre, of Mexico – sent off. The football was largely incidental with no goals in 120 minutes of normal play.

The Germans won the shoot-out 4-1 after Schumacher saved the second and third Mexican penalties, stopping Quirarte's effort with his feet and Servin's diving to his right. Allofs, Brehme and Matthaeus were successful with the first three German penalties, despite howls of derision from the partisan crowd and then Littbarski, who came on as a late substitute in extra time, converted the fourth to seal Mexico's fate.

The West Germans now face France in Wednesday's semi-final – a repeat of the 1982 World Cup semi-final in Seville, Spain, another penalty drama won by the Germans.

Franz Beckenbauer, the West German manager, said: "It was a physical match. We were forced to play cautiously because Mexico only played with one forward.

"France are a very fine team and have been one of the best for the last three or four years, but we believe we will have a chance against them in our semi-final."

WEST GERMANY: H Schumacher; D Jakobs, T Berthold, K-H Förster, N Eder (sub: P Littbarski), H-P Briegel, L Matthaeus, F Magath, A Brehme, K-H Rummenigge (sub: D Hoeness), K Allofs.
MEXICO: P Larios; R Amador (sub: F Cruz), F Cruz, F Quirarte, R Servin, C Munoz, J Aguirre, M Negrete, M Espana, T Boy (sub: C de los Cobos), H Sanchez.
Referee: J Diaz (Colombia).

Reid on the receiving end: the England player loses out to Batista (Photograph: Ian Stewart)

Robson pays a heavy price for his timid tactics

It is a stain upon the World Cup when its arguably most dangerous performer is accused of being a cheat. I do not hold with the accusation. The fact that Maradona's first goal, five minutes into the second half, was knocked past Shilton with his forearm as they went up together for Hodge's sliced clearance is counter-balanced by his second goal: an incomparable, solo gem which personified his talent.

As an argument that, but for Maradona's first goal, England might otherwise be in the semi-final, the controversy holds little substance. On the run of the game, there was no doubt that the right team won. England must question not so much Maradona's fortuitous goal as their own tactical approach. If you are organized specifically to stifle a single opponent, it is unrealistic to complain if on one of many occasions when he has you on the ropes he is given the benefit of an unfair decision.

Arguments can rage forever whether Maradona's intention was to use his arm, but he is not the only player to benefit in this competition from something illegal. Some critics called him a cheat at half-time on account of his regular tumbles when tackled. They are deliberately blurring an argument in which Maradona possesses most of the advantages.

No cheat commands the efforts of three and sometimes four men to try to halt him. This was often England's calculated response to the threat which his ability poses for any team. They closed around him like a gang of farm hands gingerly trying to grapple with a bull which has slipped his pen.

It was no more disturbing that Maradona handled the ball than it was, say, to see Fenwick apparently elbow Maradona in the face only nine minutes after he has been booked for a foul on him. Cheating takes various forms.

England can blame only the unfortunate referee on that first goal, and, dependent on his position, any referee might have been unsighted on what was undeniably a bad decision. It was far easier to determine that Maradona used his arm from high in the stand than is sometimes possible on the pitch, though England's manager is quite emphatic that he saw the foul. Maradona's arm was raised, but no higher than his head. Yet, to become obsessed with the decision, is to overlook all the other evidence which is relevant to England's defeat.

The unavoidable verdict is that England, on the admission of their own tactics until the time they were two behind, had not the nerve nor the ability to risk attacking a suspect defence which by the finish was having its inadequacies exposed by England's belated rally. The possibility of levelling or winning the match in the last 20 minutes might have been substantially greater had England been more positive in the first 20 minutes.

COMMENTARY

David Miller

To keep nine men behind the ball, and achieve not a single co-ordinated penetration of the Argentinian penalty area in the first half, was as negative as Italy, a blatant policy of parking on a double yellow line. The risk is substantial, and requires defenders technically more nimble than those available to Bobby Robson. If he believed that stopping Argentina's attack was the first and essential priority, then such tactics are based on the admission that the opposition is more dangerous and skilful. To say that Argentina are nothing without Maradona is no more valid than to say that Australian cricket in the Thirties would have been nothing without Bradman. They exist: they must be accounted for.

England sought to do so with a system which was always stretched. An often square back four awaited Maradona's sorties like an Indian rural village not knowing when the tiger may strike next. Butcher, who is an acceptable defender in the context of the Football League, is out of his depth at the level of a World Cup quarter-final, an honest digger of potatoes. The England defence had extensive possession of the ball, yet seldom had any fluidity of positional change which might have opened up the Argentinian ranks.

The middle line was, frankly, little better. Reid was soon injured, again, and Hoddle never found his front runners. Steven and Hodge could not compete with Argentina's control. The flourish at the finish provided some hope when Lineker at last was able to start running at defenders and Barnes finally made his World Cup debut. That was one of many decisions which needs some analysis.

● The high price of match tickets has been blamed for the poor sales of World Cup souvenirs. Strict rules were laid down for the souvenir trade, with would-be sellers having to apply for a licence that was issued only shortly before the start of the games.

However, most fans brought the paraphernalia to support their teams with them, and sales of the tournament mascot, Pique, a manikin wearing a sombrero topped by a green chile, have been far from brisk.

A classic game opens way for French revenge

From David Miller, Guadalajara

It is doubtful if the first half-century of the World Cup saw a more eventful match than Saturday's quarter-final between France and Brazil. And the second half-century will be fortunate to see its equal. The two teams defied the ferocious temperature of 120 degrees in the Jalisco Stadium, and each other, to re-invigorate international football with a classic tussle which will be talked about for years.

Whether France can recover their mental and physical fibre in three days after such an epic to avenge the semi-final of 1982 when they meet West Germany again, keeps this competition in a state of fascinated anticipation.

Over two hours and a half, including the wretched necessity for the nevertheless spellbinding execution by penalty shoot-out, there were the dramatic qualities of many sports. No 15-round world title bout, nor match-play golf taken to the 19th nor five-set tennis final fluctuating on every

Supreme suspense for any sport

point, nor Olympic race decided in the last few strides, nor Test won in the last over could have had more suspense.

It was one of those rare occasions which makes my occupation uniquely pleasurable, yet how to recapture the emotions, skills and courage which flowed back and forth across the sunlit pitch? I have not seen a better match in eight finals, nor one played in such a marvellous spirit: only one single mean foul, sheer desperation by Carlos, the Brazil goalkeeper late in extra time, amid mutual generosity which put many teams here to shame. As in all great sporting moments, the quality of the losers contributed as much or more than that of the winners. How we grieve for Brazil: such a flourish, yet no reward other than admiration.

The match swung from end to end throughout, almost with the rapidity of ice hockey, and one knew not how the players sustained the momentum in their fifth match at altitude in three weeks. There were 16 scoring opportunities created by Brazil to 15 by France. In some matches there are none.

On Friday, Joao Saldanha, Brazil's former manager whose marvellous team of 1970 was taken over at the last moment by Mario Zagalo, insisted this team was better than four years ago. It was stronger defensively and more balanced, with Elzo, of Athletico Minas Gerais the foundation of the mid-field - "the man who carries the piano", Saldanha said evocatively. What heroics were performed by Elzo and Branco for Brazil; by Bossis, Amoros and Fernandez for France, in the shadow of more famous reputations.

Brazil developed with every successive match, and if France, who provided thrilling performances against the Soviet Union and Italy, were their first opponents of quality, they unleashed within minutes all the traditional, instinctive touches which make Brazilian football so appealing: the enticement and the acceleration clear of a tackle by Junior, Careca and Muller which puts the opponents momentarily out of the game, the half-vollied trap-come-pass by Julio Cesar at the back or Socrates as the fulcum of attack, which transforms apparent innocence into danger. Bossis, unexpectly swapping sweeper/marker-roles with Battiston, was for half an hour or so being pounded by Careca as Junior and Socrates ceaselessly primed the guns like powder-monkeys.

Suddenly France, the masters for four or five years of silken mid-field embroidery, were worried stiff by the shielded first-touch which was wrong-footing them. After 17 minutes, Brazil scored the most breath-taking goal of the finals yet, a ripple of passes between Socrates, Branco and Josimar, a first time exchange between Junior and Muller and a final thrust by Junior sending Careca through a stricken French rearguard.

It was the first time France had been behind since they played the Soviet Union, and it stung them into response.

At last, in the 46th minute, France's rhythm clicked: Giresse, the oldest of ten players in the match in their 30s, slipped another of them, Rocheteau, who was finding a new lease of speed, clear of on the right and his early low centre was deflected off Edinho. Stopyra's goalmouth dive confused Carlos, and the ball ran free as Platini stole through unnoticed, and with all the calm of a training stint in a deserted stadium tapped into the net.

The second half contained sufficient incidents for half a dozen matches. Zico replaced Muller with 17 minutes to go, and with almost his first touch sent Branco through on an overlap. Out rushed Bats, spread himself across Branco's path, missed the ball and hauled him down. Unwisely, Zico, not yet in tune, moved up to take the penalty. Behind Zico's back, Platini signalled to Bats's left and Bats took the hint to parry the shot. Brazil's chance to win in normal time had passed.

Extra time. We wilted in the shade in 90 degrees. On the touchline, the teams sank to the ground, grasping at ice pads and water. How could such a fight endure?

Somehow it did. Both sides continued to hurl themselves at each other, but their

Referee blunders at Carlos foul

legs were beginning to crumble. A last glorious pass by Platini, the most memorable of the match, sent Bellone clear, only for him to be manhandled off the ball a yard outside the area by Carlos. No foul given, no booking. A blunder by the sweat-soaked referee, Igna of Romania.

The whistle went. The unenvied penalty kickers assembled in the centre circle drained and blank-faced like actors being asked to audition after running a marathon. Socrates had the first kick saved by Bats, and France were 3-2 up when Bellone, with moral justice, scored with a rebound off the post and back off Carlos's head. Platini skied his shot, to level the situation, but Josimar slammed against a post, and Fernandez, stoic, dependable Fernandez atoned for Platini's miss.

So now France must meet the West Germans to claim the place in the final which they deserve. It will be a better final if they do: and France have a score to settle with Schumacher.

BRAZIL: Carlos; Josimar, Edinho, J Cesar, Branco, Elzo, Socrates, Junior (sub: Silas), Alemao; Muller (sub: Zico), Careca.
FRANCE: J Bats; M Amoros, M Bossis, P Battiston, T Tusseau, L Fernandez, M Platini, A Giresse (sub: J-M Ferreri), J Tigana, Y Stopyra, D Rocheteau (sub: B Bellone).
Referee: I Igna (Romania).

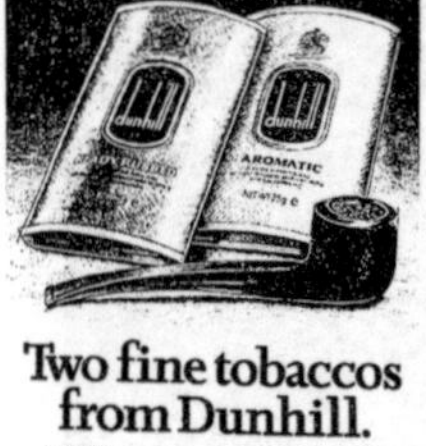

SPORT IN BRIEF

Hammer record

Yuri Sedykh, of the Soviet Union, bettered his own hammer world record yesterday when he threw a distance of 86.66 metres at an international athletics meeting between the Russians and East Germany in Tallinn. Sedykh's previous mark was 86.34 metres which he set in Cork, Ireland, in 1984.

Rider killed

Le Touquet (AP) – A 19-year-old Polish rider, Dariusz Soroka, was killed on Saturday when his horse fell on him during a jumping competition here. Soroka, a student from Drzonkow, near Zielona Gora in Silesia, was killed instantly.

Totten's job

Alec Totten, the former Rangers assistant manager, has been appointed the new manager of the Scottish first division club Dumbarton.

Totten, previously successful with Alloa and Falkirk, lost his job at Rangers along with the manager, Jock Wallace, when Graeme Souness was appointed player-manager.

Barry McGuigan is 9-1 on favourite to retain his featherweight boxing championship of the world when he meets Steve Cruz in Las Vegas in the early hours of tomorrow morning.

Preview, page 45

Cup draw

The draw for the Yorkshire county rugby league cup was made yesterday.

PRELIMINARY ROUND (ties to be completed by September 10): Halifax v Mansfield; Sheffield Eagles v Doncaster.
FIRST ROUND (to be played on September 14): Castleford v Halifax or Mansfield; Dewsbury v Sheffield or Doncaster; Batley v Wakefield Trinity; Hull v Bramley; Featherstone Rovers v York; Hull Kingston Rovers v Huddersfield; Hunslet v Bradford Northern; Leeds v Keighley.

Suzuki wins

Nishinomiya (Reuter) - Koichi Suzuki, of Japan, shot a final round of 69 to win a 50 million yen (£200,000) international golf tournament yesterday – his first major success in 11 years. He had five birdies to give him a four-round total of 273, 19 under par, and a two-shot win over the Australian Brian Jones.

Breathing fire

Hong Kong (AP) – China won Hong Kong's International Dragon Boat Race yesterday for the fourth consecutive year, capturing both the men's and women's championships. The defending men's champions, China's Shun De team from Guangdong province, completed the 640-metre course in 2 min 34.01 sec.

East and West

Plymouth Argyle, promoted to the second division last season, will play a pre-season match against Moscow Torpedoes, the Russian Cup holders, at Home Park on August 18. The Torpedoes have arranged a short tour of England, which also includes games against West Bromwich Albion and Nottingham Forest.

Santana resigns after defeat

Tele Santana, the Brazilian coach, resigned after his team's defeat by France in the World Cup quarter-final on Saturday. It is the second time he has given up the job – he also resigned in the 1982 competition after Brazil lost to Italy.

Santana was recalled in February, when his backers in the Brazilian football confederation won a battle to rename him coach. But in-fighting between Santana and Mario Zagalo, who was coach to the 1970 World Cup winning squad, kept the team's line up so uncertain that former superstar Pele, now 45, volunteered three weeks before the tournament to join the team. The offer was refused.

Santana said his last game as coach was "the best I've ever seen in a World Cup. It should have been the final."

● A "friendly" match between officials of FIFA and the Mexican World Cup organising committee turned into a brawl and two players, including a FIFA official, were sent off.

Spectators at the match, played in Mexico City's Centro de Capacitacion, the training ground used by Mexico's World Cup squad, said the two teams began taking the match a little too seriously and a brawl ensued after a series of bad fouls.

The referee, Mario Rubio, of Mexico, who officiated during matches at the last World Cup in Spain, sent off FIFA official Walter Gagg, of Switzerland, and one player from the Mexican organisers.

● An estimated 12 billion viewers in 108 countries watched the World Cup quarter-final matches at the weekend – 20 per cent more than tuned in at the corresponding stage in Spain four years ago – according to a market survey. Next Sunday's final, in the Azteca Stadium in Mexico City, is expected to attract 500 million viwers, 80 per cent of them from Europe and Latin America.

● Eight players have been sent off and 104 shown the yellow card after 46 of the scheduled 52 matches in the World Cup finals. Saturday's quarter-final between West Germany and Mexico saw two players sent off and another seven cautioned. Yellow cards are now running almost neck-and-neck with goals, which now total just 112, a record low average of 2.435 a game.

● Brazilian goalkeeper Carlos missed setting a World Cup record as well as winning a place in the semi-finals in Saturday's game against France, which ended with the French winning on penalties after the teams had been deadlocked at 1-1. Carlos, who went into the match without conceding a goal in four games, a total of 360 minutes, had his eye on the record of England's Gordon Banks, who kept a clean sheet for 442 minutes before conceding an 82nd minute goal to Portugal's Eusebio in the semi-finals of the 1966 World Cup. Carlos was on target until Michel Platini's 41st-minute equalizer, which left him 41 minutes short of the record.

● Leading the World Cup goalscoring list seems to carry something of a jinx. When Carecas scored Brazil's goal against France he boosted his total to five, joining England's Gary Lineker and Spain's Emilio Butragueno, but Brazil's elimination left him unable to add to his score, a fate earlier suffered by Denmark's Preben Elkjaer and the Soviet forward, Oleg Belonov.

Results

Saturday

Brazil	(1) 1	France	(1) 1
Careca		Platini	
		65,777	

France won 4-3 on penalties.

W Germany	(0) 0	Mexico	(0) 0
		41,700	

West Germany won 4-2 on penalties.

29

ARGENTINA v ENGLAND

WORLD CUP QUARTER-FINAL, 1986

The 1986 World Cup quarter-final between England and Argentina in Mexico City bristled with sub-texts. It was their first meeting on such a grand stage since the quarter-final of 1966 that had ended in Alf Ramsey calling the South Americans "animals". And it came just four years after the two countries had gone to war in the south Atlantic over the sovereignty of the Falkland Islands.

"... he scored a second goal of such dazzling beauty that it will be remembered forever by all those privileged enough to witness it"

ARGENTINA 2
ENGLAND 1

WORLD CUP QUARTER-FINAL
22 JUNE 1986
AZTEC STADIUM, MEXICO CITY

BY STUART JONES, FOOTBALL CORRESPONDENT
23 June

England yesterday suffered at the hands of the best player in the world. After being nudged out of the quarter-finals in the Aztec Stadium here, Shilton led a posse of players who surrounded the Tunisian referee to complain angrily about the legitimacy of the crucial opening goal. The television cameras supported their claim.

A slow-motion replay confirmed that Maradona had indeed used his forearm to put Argentina ahead in the 50th minute. It seemed impossible, anyway, that he could have extended his stocky frame that measures only 5ft 4in to outjump Shilton, complete his exchange with Valdano and shake the foundations of England's World Cup challenge.

Yet if justice was to play a cruel role in their eventual downfall, there can be little doubt that they were beaten by a superior side. It was only after Bobby Robson had been forced to resort to an attacking four-two-four formation by bringing on Waddle and Barnes that they threatened to unhinge the only South American representatives left in the competition.

As had been feared, Maradona, a dwarf by comparison to those around him, towered above the tie. England's defence and the whole stadium itself trembled in expectation whenever he was on the run, either twisting and weaving with the ball attached securely to his remarkable left foot or merely gliding smoothly into position.

Within a few seconds that were tucked inside the 55th minute, he scored a second goal of such dazzling beauty that it will be remembered forever by all those privileged enough to witness it. England in the end can have no complaints about effectively being knocked out by a moment of pure and irresistible genius.

Maradona, accelerating as swiftly as a bird on the wing, swayed and swerved his way past Sansom, Butcher, Fenwick and finally Shilton with effortless ease. With a nonchalant prod, he claimed not only the individual goal of the competition so far but he also ended England's journey towards the last four.

England had won a psychological battle before the start. Carlos Bilardo, fearing that his side might be outnumbered in midfield, omitted one of his forwards, Pasculli, in favour of the more defensive Enrique. Bobby Robson's lone alteration was to recall Fenwick in place of Martin.

But England lost the contest for the favourable weather conditions.

The sharp black shadow cast by the ornate loudspeaker system suspended above the centre circle confirmed that the sun, stationed directly overhead, was shining at its brightest. Even those grappling with the Spanish language were aware that it was "Muy Caliente". It was, in other words, "very hot".

So was the atmosphere. Horns blared like the humming of a thousand bees, chants of "Inglaterra" poured down the terraces from the throats of the Mexicans and the tension, stretched out in the unforgiving mid-day sun, crackled like strips of bacon in a huge frying pan.

Reid's recovery from his ankle injury was tested in an initial challenge with Brown and Fenwick was booked for his first assault on Maradona.

Nevertheless, Pumpido took an early gamble and almost paid for it. As Argentina's goalkeeper chased Hoddle's inaccurate through ball outside his area, he lost his footing and subsequently the race with Beardsley. As he struggled to retain his position, Beardsley spun away towards the touchline, turned and curled his shot into the side netting.

Maradona had already given several warnings, particularly from free kicks, of the threat that he was to present. Argentina's tall and comparatively immobile central defenders looked no more solid under pressure but, in spite of the ceaseless scurrying of Lineker and Beardsley, England were unable to shake their uncertain foundations before the interval. It was during it that the peace in the stands was disturbed.

Even though an estimated police force of some 20,000 had been assembled specifically for the potentially explosive occasion, none were to be seen when several skirmishes broke out between odd individuals rather than groups. Within ten minutes of the second half, their distant colleagues at the other end were capturing much more significant events as Maradona stamped his indelible mark. Yet England, encouraged by the introduction of the two substitutes, were lifted even higher by Lineker in the 80th minute.

Barnes followed a pass to the byline and Lineker, who scored all but one of England's seven goals, stabbed home from close range. He almost repeated the feat in the dying minutes after Tapia had struck a post and Fenwick, fortunate not to be dismissed, had crudely halted another Argentine break by bringing down Valdano.

As Maradona, now the leader of South America's hopes, received his deserved acclaim from the crowd, England walked away to nurse their disappointment. Had the little man-mountain not chosen to give such an extravagant display of his wondrous talent, they might by now be preparing to fulfil the title of the World Cup favourites. As it is, their conquerors are expected to regain the crown they won in 1978.

MATCH FACTS

Argentina 2	England 1
Maradona 51 55	*Lineker 81*

England: P. Shilton, G. Stevens, K. Sansom, T. Fenwick, T. Butcher, T. Steven (sub: J. Barnes, 74), G. Hoddle, P. Reid (sub: C. Waddle, 69), S. Hodge, P. Beardsley, G. Lineker
Argentina: N. Pumpido, J.-L. Cuciuffo, J.-L. Brown, O. Ruggeri, J. Olarticoechea, R. Giusti, S. Batista, J. Burruchaga (sub: C.-D. Tapia, 75), H. Enrique, D. Maradona, J. Valdano
Referee: Ali Bin Nasser (Tunisia)
Attendance: 114,580

30

LIVERPOOL v NOTTINGHAM FOREST

FOOTBALL LEAGUE FIRST DIVISION, 1988

In the first half of the 1980s, Liverpool were often functional rather than thrilling. But after a season without a trophy in 1986–87, manager Kenny Dalglish recalibrated his team with the addition of the dazzling talents of John Barnes and Peter Beardsley. What followed was a season of some of the best football Anfield has ever seen.

"Once they blazed the sight was breathtaking"

**LIVERPOOL 5
NOTTINGHAM FOREST 0**

BARCLAYS LEAGUE,
FIRST DIVISION
13 APRIL 1988
ANFIELD
....

**BY STUART JONES, FOOTBALL
CORRESPONDENT**
14 April

Last night at Anfield was unforgettable. Liverpool, with their most emphatic victory of the season, lifted themselves mathematically to within two points of collecting their tenth English crown in 15 years. But statistics are irrelevant. It was, instead, an occasion that provoked myriad superlatives.

The Kop expected a party. Over the weekend the team had won a place in the FA Cup final and four of its individuals had been recognised by their fellow professionals.

One way and another there were a few reasons to celebrate, and Liverpool are nowadays not in the habit of disappointing their customers. Yet no one could realistically have expected that the evening would embrace such sweeping beauty and five goals, all of them memorable, especially after a typically subdued opening.

Liverpool were merely stoking their embers. Once they blazed, the sight was as breathtaking, as colourful, as enchanting and as riveting as watching the most lavish firework display. The dazzling explosion was to entertain an audience of almost

40,000 from the seventeenth to the closing minute.

Nottingham Forest may be young, and they were hampered by a recurrence of Walker's ankle injury, but Liverpool were not simply ruthlessly punishing a weakened and inexperienced opposition. They were also relishing the joy of a simple, instinctive game.

Had it not been for Sutton, some of whose reactions were astonishing, Forest would have been humiliated. Having beaten Liverpool at their own City Ground 10 days ago and dared to attack Liverpool in the FA Cup semifinal at Hillsborough on Saturday, they did not merit such a cruel fate. Yet Liverpool so outclassed their potentially closest challengers that Maurice Roworth, the Forest chairman, was prompted to say that "no one could have competed against them."

He cannot be accused of exaggeration. He added: "They are the best team in Europe, which is why they are not in Europe. They are too good."

Liverpool's opening goal, which cut through the middle of the Forest defence, was irresistible. Hansen, starting the move with a customary neat interception, invited Houghton to accelerate into the area. There he exchanged delightfully with Barnes and rolled in the return. Aldridge nonchalantly chipped in the second before a ferocious drive from Beardsley was tipped onto the bar by Sutton.

Gillespie, with an emphatic volley on the hour, claimed the third and Beardsley, with the most subtle assistance from Barnes, the players' player of the year, added the fourth 10 minutes from the end.

Aldridge kept the party going with his 24th goal of the season to complete a performance that was hailed by the Liverpool captain, Hansen, as "the best since I've been here".

MATCH FACTS

Liverpool 5
Houghton 18, Aldridge 37 88, Gillespie 58, Beardsley 79

Nottingham Forest 0

Liverpool: B. Grobbelaar, G. Gillespie, G. Ablett, S. Nicol, N. Spackman, A. Hansen, P. Beardsley, J. Aldridge, R. Houghton (sub: C. Johnston, 85), J. Barnes. S. McMahon (sub: J. Molby, 78)
Nottingham Forest: S. Sutton, S. Chettle, S. Pearce, D. Walker (sub: D. Wassall, HT), C. Foster, T. Wilson, G. Crosby, N. Webb, N. Clough, L. Glover, B. Rice
Referee: R. Milford (Bristol)
Attendance: 39,535

★ ★ ★ SL

● CRICKET 46, 47
● SPORTS BOOK 48
● GRAND PRIX 49
● POINT TO POINT 50

THE TIMES

SPORT | TRAVEL & LEISURE

SECTION 4

SATURDAY MAY 27 1989

45

Arsenal champions at last

IAN STEWART

Finishing touch: Thomas prods the ball past Grobbelaar for the goal which completed Arsenal's 2-0 victory against Liverpool at Anfield last night and took the championship to Highbury for the first time since 1971

Graham marvels at fairy tale end

Arsenal's manager, George Graham, was at first speechless but recovered to say: "Nobody outside Highbury expected us to do it, but when you lose belief you might as well get out of football. No words can really describe how I feel. But we have laid a foundation at Highbury, a way to handle ourselves both on and off the pitch, and this is our reward.

"Sometimes the way we play doesn't go down too well among other teams, but tonight is a fairy tale for football and that's why the game is so popular and why we love it so much.

"There is no doubt we had a mountain to climb to come here and win 2-0. A lot of people expected we would get carried away and try to play gung-ho football, but in actual fact we were very controlled and were content to be at 0-0 at half-time, still hoping for the goals in the second half."

Graham gave credit to his players. "I feel particularly pleased for somebody like Tony Adams, who has suffered an awful lot of stick which has given football very little dignity. But there are good things in the game, plenty of them, and I think we proved that tonight."

Graham believes Arsenal can go on from this dramatic success. "In the end I still think Liverpool play magnificent football and that's what we want to emulate. We can do it in spasms, but it will get better and better.

"At the end of the day it's the players who have to go out on the pitch and do it and I am delighted for them. It was nice to see Michael Thomas getting the winner. In the first half of this season he was probably the most effective midfield player in the country. He has had a lapse, but exceptional players don't go bad overnight and he has soldiered on, staying in the side because of Paul Davis's injury, and has got his just reward."

Kenny Dalglish said: "At Liverpool, we never accept second best. But I'm still very proud of the players and their achievements this season considering all they have been through."

He refused to blame his team's hectic end-of-season schedule for their defeat, adding: "It just wasn't to be."

Thomas has final word

By Stuart Jones
Football Correspondent

Final table

	P	W	D	L	F	A	Pts
Arsenal	38	22	10	6	73	36	76
Liverpool	38	22	10	6	65	28	76
Notts For	38	17	13	8	64	43	64
Norwich	38	17	11	10	48	45	62
Derby	38	17	7	14	40	38	58
Tottenham	38	15	12	11	60	46	57
Coventry	38	14	13	11	47	42	55
Everton	38	14	12	12	50	45	54
QPR	38	14	11	13	43	37	53
Millwall	38	14	11	13	47	52	53
Man Utd	38	13	12	13	45	35	51
Wimbledon	38	14	9	15	50	46	51
Southampton	38	10	15	13	52	66	45
Charlton	38	10	12	16	44	58	42
Sheff Wed	38	10	12	16	34	51	42
Luton	38	10	11	17	42	52	41
Aston Villa	38	9	13	16	45	56	40
Middlesbrough	38	9	12	17	44	61	39
West Ham	38	10	8	20	37	62	38
Newcastle	38	7	10	21	32	63	31

Arsenal's youngsters last night came of age and were crowned as champions in the most astonishingly dramatic fashion. In the closing seconds of a season which had lasted for nine months, and amid almost unbearable tension, Michael Thomas changed the destiny of the title with a deceptively simple prod.

His majestic goal, worthy of the occasion, defied belief, logic and all expectation. So did Arsenal's performance as a whole. The result leaves both teams on 76 points with the same goal difference, but Arsenal become champions because they have scored more goals.

Liverpool were heavily favoured to extend to 25 their prolonged unbeaten sequence stretching back to New Year's Day and to create a notable piece of history. No other club

had won the double twice.

At the close, the Liverpool players sank to their knees, unable to comprehend the defeat and its dispiriting consequences. But they and their followers, though equally stunned, picked themselves up and magnanimously offered their congratulations before leaving the stage to the side which had earned its unforeseen glory.

A silken red banner proclaimed: "You name it, we've won it." Liverpool have in-

deed won the FA Cup, the Professional Footballers' Association fair play award and Nicol was voted the player of the year, but the principal honour belongs to George Graham, the strongest candidate for the manager of the year, and his side.

Graham controversially disrupted an apparently successful formation at the beginning of last month and introduced a sweeper system. With hindsight, the move might have been designed to complete the script which unfolded in front of the television cameras last night. The ploy worked to perfection.

In confirming that the tactic should not be regarded necessarily as negative, Arsenal turned predictions upside down. Their most experienced individual, O'Leary, had admitted that Anfield is "the hardest place in the world to win by one goal, let alone by two". The possibility became genuine in the 53rd minute.

Before the kick-off, delayed by 10 minutes to allow the

capacity crowd to take their places, Arsenal threw bouquets of red roses to the spectators. Their charming gesture of generosity added abruptly and they subjected their hosts to undisguised ferocity.

No one was more committed than Adams nor more influential than Thomas, two comparative youths, whose England international careers have been suspended. The contribution of Winterburn suggested again that his should soon begin.

Arsenal restricted Liverpool to two long-range attempts in the first half (Rush struck the first with such force that he pulled a groin muscle and had to be withdrawn) and had threatened twice themselves. Nicol cleared Bould's header off the line and Smith glanced a free kick, curled in by Winterburn, narrowly wide. The two combined more precisely after the interval. After Smith had stooped to nod in his 23rd League goal, the outcome of the game and potentially of the championship hung in the balance. The referee, surrounded by Liverpool complaints, asked for a second opinion and a linesman supported his original verdict.

Thereafter, the legs and the concentration of Liverpool began to buckle. Sensing that they were losing control of their own fate, their touches became uncharacteristically edgy and their followers grew increasingly anxious. Never more so, seemingly, than a quarter of an hour from the end.

Then Thomas, pierced by Richardson, had Liverpool at his mercy, but he snatched at the possibility and Grobbelaar, who had never finished on the losing side in 28 previous appearances this season, collected the half-hit shot.

After Houghton and Aldridge had scored opportunities, the ball was swept from one end of the pitch to the other, where Thomas brought the season to a thrilling climax.

After the unseemly behaviour of the spectators at Wembley last Saturday it was heartening to witness the conduct of the crowd of 41,718 inside the arena which shuddered with noise throughout the extraordinary evening. In elation and in despair, everybody restrained themselves.

LIVERPOOL: B Grobbelaar; G Abiett, S Nicol, S McMahon, A Hansen, R Whelan, R Houghton, J Aldridge, I Rush (sub: J Barnes), P Beardsley, J Barnes.

ARSENAL: J Lukic; L Dixon, N Winterburn, M Thomas, D O'Leary, T Adams, D Rocastle, K Richardson, A Smith, P Merson (sub: M Hayes), B Marwood (sub: P Groves).

Referee: D Hutchinson.

Anfield magnanimous in applauding victors

David Miller

The loyal public came out of Merseyside's mean streets and bleak apartment blocks as the sun disappeared and poured into Anfield for the last game of the season: to share that beautiful illusion that exists inside the stadium, to enjoy that aura of reflected fame and glory which lifts them out of the ordinariness of everyday life. And the illusion was broken.

It would have been informative for Jacques Georges and his UEFA committee to have been there last night to witness the exemplary character of a full house during a match of the utmost intensity.

In spite of the crushing disappointment for the home faithful, they applauded Arsenal, the new champions, without reservation as they paraded the trophy before a crowd, many of whom must have had relations who perished at Hillsborough, yet who could now still recognize the achievement of their rivals.

There were no fences save in Anfield, and everyone stayed in his place. But there was applause from the Liverpool public as Michael Thomas, the scorer of the goal that robbed Liverpool of the double, ran alone round the pitch before the trophy had been presented, to applaud the Liverpool crowd. Arsenal's

owe their first title for 18 years.

Whether Graham can now develop his team so that they have more flair and less physical expediency, whether they can eliminate those elements of ill-temper that were evident at times last night, remains to be seen. It is not good to see members of the champion team repeatedly arguing with and gesticulating against the referee. These characteristics need to go before Arsenal can begin to compare themselves with Liverpool.

It is ironic that Liverpool, their supporters renowned for their sense of humour and appreciation of the good football of visitors, which they so amply demonstrated again last night, should have been involved in two appalling incidents — Heysel and Hillsborough.

Maybe the trauma of Hillsborough has taught even the more aggressive of Anfield supporters the value of restraint. It is difficult to imagine such a scene as we saw last night, in a stadium without moats or wire or fences, where the favourites and the leaders were beaten at home and managed to retain their equanimity and magnanimity, for all their passion so held of their defeated heroes.

several thousand in the opposite corner of the ground responded with "You'll Never Walk Alone".

It was an astonishing winning goal on which to determine the championship in the final moments of the final match during almost unbearable suspense as Liverpool vainly tried to play out time.

It was poignant that the kick-off should have been delayed 10 minutes to allow latecomers to gain admission, and for almost an hour it seemed that Liverpool would sustain the remarkable streak that had brought them back to within reach of the title since they last lost, on New Year's Day to Manchester United.

During that spell Arsenal had several times allowed their control at the top of the table to waver, and now it required exceptional character to come and win at a ground where so few are successful.

They did so because in Thomas, Rocastle and Richardson, they have a midfield line that is both imaginative and competitive. And on their final night it is primarily to those three that Arsenal

Distinguished by intelligence

By David Miller, Chief Sports Correspondent

Don Revie, who died yesterday, aged 61, in the Murrayfield private hospital, Edinburgh, was distinguished throughout more than 30 years as a player and manager by the intelligent thought which he attempted to bring to football.

He was at the forefront of the tactical developments of the English game in the mid-1950s when with Manchester City he attempted to emulate the Hungarian rôle of the deep-lying, creative centre forward; with him, City won the FA Cup in 1956.

He carried six England caps, although he was never able to establish a regular position. As a player, he always had something of a reputation as a dressing-room lawyer, and it was no surprise when he quickly established a standing as a manager and coach.

Revie paid quite remarkable attention to detail in his planning, and in his search for and care of youngsters, in a style set by Matt Busby, his mentor. Yet he was always dominated by an overriding pessimism, and it was this that introduced a cynicism into his approach to management.

I witnessed the exceptional way, behind the scenes, in which he lifted Leeds from an impoverished second division team and carried them to peaks of the League championship in 1969 and 1974, the FA Cup in 1972, and the UEFA Cup in 1972 and 1974. He produced teams of the utmost co-ordination and skill, and he also permitted some of the worst excesses in gamesmanship.

For all the concern about the mannerisms of Revie

teams, he was in many ways the obvious choice as successor to Sir Alf Ramsey as England manager, and he tried to bring to the management of the national team the same immense thoroughness the dossiers on opposition, a compulsive team spirit.

Yet the fears were still there, and his selections over a three-year period were characterized by multiple changes which bred an uncertainty among the players, led to poor results and his eventual expediency in opting for financial rewards in the United Arab Emirates.

As a journalist, I found him to be one of the most honest managers I ever dealt with. Those that worked with him had a similar kind of respect to that which had been built in those who had been associated with Busby.

Revie's players praise a manager and friend

Billy Bremner, Allan Clarke and Trevor Cherry, who between them played more than 1,000 times for Don Revie, the former Leeds United and England manager, rated the man who joined the Yorkshire club in 1961: "The greatest manager I played for" (Martin Searby writes).

Bremner, the footballer of the year in 1970 when the team was runner-up for the first division championship and later succeeded Revie as manager at Elland Road, said: "We had some marvellous times and a few disappointments, but that was only his soccer. To know the man as I did, as much as anyone could know him, was tremendous. He showed his players a fierce

loyalty and if you were a friend of his you were a friend for life."

Clarke, who signed for Revie from Leicester City in 1968, said: "Without doubt he was the best manager I ever played for. My thoughts at the moment are very much with his family but it is a sad day for everyone."

Trevor Cherry, another player bought by Revie, said: "It is sad news but I have been expecting it for some time. He was such a fit fellow and so much loved that his long illness has been upsetting throughout. I had total respect for him. He was a man manager second to none."

Obituary, page 12

Simon Barnes's Sporting Diary, page 10

George Graham
He said when Arsenal appointed him in May 1986 that it would take three years to make them champions

Chart shows the positions for the top four clubs after each first division match

31

LIVERPOOL v ARSENAL

FOOTBALL LEAGUE FIRST DIVISION, 1989

Still numbed by the Hillsborough tragedy, Liverpool resumed the 1988–89 season with the prospect of a second Double in three years. They won the FA Cup final against Everton and arrived at the final league game of the extended season in touching distance of the championship. By serendipity, their opponents were Arsenal, the only team who could overtake them. But the Gunners had the unlikely task of winning by two clear goals.

"... the ball was swept from one end of the pitch to the other, where Thomas brought the season to a thrilling climax."

LIVERPOOL 0
ARSENAL 2

BARCLAYS LEAGUE,
FIRST DIVISION
26 MAY 1989
ANFIELD
....

BY STUART JONES, FOOTBALL CORRESPONDENT
27 May

Arsenal's youngsters last night came of age and were crowned as champions in the most astonishingly dramatic fashion. In the closing seconds of a season which had lasted for nine months, and amid almost unbearable tension, Michael Thomas changed the destiny of the title with a deceptively simple prod.

His majestic goal, worthy of the occasion, defied belief, logic and all expectation. So did Arsenal's performance as a whole. The result leaves both teams on 76 points with the same goal difference, but Arsenal become champions because they have scored more goals.

Liverpool were heavily favoured to extend to 25 their prolonged unbeaten sequence stretching back to New Year's Day and to create a notable piece of history. No other club had won the double twice.

At the close, the Liverpool players sank to their knees, unable to comprehend the defeat and its dispiriting consequences. But they and their followers, though equally stunned, picked themselves up and magnanimously offered their congratulations before leaving the stage to the side which had earned its unforeseen glory.

A silken red banner proclaimed: "You name it, we've won it." Liverpool have indeed won the FA Cup, the Professional Footballers' Association fair play award and Nicol was voted the player of the year, but the principal honour belongs to George Graham, the strongest candidate for the manager of the year, and his side.

Graham controversially disrupted an apparently successful formation at the beginning of last month and introduced a sweeper system. With hindsight, the move might have been designed to complete the script which unfolded in front of the television cameras last night. The ploy worked to perfection.

In confirming that the tactic should not be regarded necessarily as negative, Arsenal turned predictions upside down. Their most experienced individual, O'Leary, had admitted that Anfield is "the hardest place in the world to win by one goal, let alone by two". The possibility became genuine in the 53rd minute.

Before the kick-off, delayed by 10 minutes to allow the capacity crowd to take their places, Arsenal threw bouquets of red roses to the spectators. Their charming gesture of generosity ended abruptly and they subjected their hosts to undisguised ferocity. No one was more committed than Adams nor more influential than Thomas, two comparative youths, whose England international careers have been suspended. The contribution of Winterburn suggested again that his should soon begin.

Arsenal restricted Liverpool to two long-range attempts in the first half (Rush struck the first with such force that he pulled a groin muscle and had to be withdrawn) and had threatened twice themselves. Nicol cleared Bould's header off the line and Smith glanced a free kick, curled in by Winterburn, narrowly wide. The two combined more precisely after the interval. After Smith had stooped to nod in his 23rd League goal, the outcome of the game and potentially of the championship hung in the balance. The referee, surrounded by Liverpudlian complaints, asked for a second opinion and a linesman supported his original verdict.

Thereafter, the legs and the concentration of Liverpool began to buckle. Sensing that they were losing control of their own fate, their touches became uncharacteristically edgy and their followers grew increasingly anxious. Never more so, seemingly, than a quarter of an hour from the end.

Then Thomas, released by Richardson, had Liverpool at his mercy, but he snatched at the possibility and

Grobbelaar, who had never finished on the losing side in 28 previous appearances this season, collected the half-hit shot.

After Houghton and Aldridge had scorned opportunities, the ball was swept from one end of the pitch to the other, where Thomas brought the season to a thrilling climax.

After the unseemly behaviour of the spectators at Wembley last Saturday it was heartening to witness the conduct of the crowd of 41,718 inside the arena which shuddered with noise throughout the extraordinary evening. In elation and in despair, everybody restrained themselves.

MATCH FACTS

Liverpool 0	Arsenal 2
	Smith 52, Thomas 90

Liverpool: B. Grobbelaar, G. Ablett, S. Staunton, S. Nicol, R. Whelan, A. Hansen, R. Houghton, J. Aldridge, I. Rush (sub: P. Beardsley, 32), J. Barnes, S. McMahon

Arsenal: J. Lukic, L. Dixon, N. Winterburn, M. Thomas, D. O'Leary, T. Adams, D. Rocastle, K. Richardson, A. Smith, S. Bould, P. Merson

Referee: D. Hutchinson (Oxfordshire)

Attendance: 41,718

THE TIMES

No 63,750 — THURSDAY JULY 5 1990 — 30p

£2.5bn but no new capping powers

Patten wins cabinet battle on poll tax

By NICHOLAS WOOD, POLITICAL CORRESPONDENT

CHRIS Patten has secured an extra £2.5 billion to hold down poll tax bills next year and won his battle within the cabinet against the introduction of extensive new legislation on the community charge in the run-up to the next election.

The environment secretary has persuaded Margaret Thatcher and John Major that the government's powers to curb council spending are powerful enough to rule out the need for a draconian new bill. This also means that about three-quarters of all local authorities will continue to be exempt from capping because their budgets are below the £15 million qualifying mark.

The extra £2.5 billion in central government grants to local authorities will help to cushion next year's rises in bills to charge-payers. On top of this, additional money will probably be made available to pay for more generous transitional relief to individuals particularly hard hit by the switch from rates to the community charge.

Environment department sources said yesterday that the internal cabinet wrangling had been "rough" over the past three months, but that the atmosphere had improved in recent days as the outlines of a settlement became clearer.

Their main concern is that the package may be regarded as unsatisfactory by the many backbench Tory critics of the poll tax who, in the words of one insider, are "just waiting to sink their claws into it".

Mr Patten's package of measures aimed at easing the political pain inflicted on the Conservatives by the introduction of the poll tax in April was approved in principle at a Downing Street meeting yesterday afternoon. The talks, chaired by Mrs Thatcher, lasted nearly two hours. Among the cabinet ministers present were Mr Major and Kenneth Baker, the party chairman.

Mr Patten is now close to obtaining final approval of the full cabinet for his proposals. He is expected to make a Commons statement on his package and the level of revenue support grant to councils the week after next.

Mr Patten has been supported by Mr Baker and Malcolm Rifkind, the Scottish secretary, in arguing that his existing powers to cap council spending do not need to be strengthened. With the support of Timothy Renton, the government chief whip, they have given warning that a capping bill in the next session of parliament would be used by dissident Tory backbenchers as a vehicle for further damaging rebellions over the principles underpinning the community charge. There will probably be a small, tightly drawn piece of legislation dealing with "technical" matters such as the position of caravan owners.

Mrs Thatcher has been determined to find a way of curbing council spending, running at £36.6 billion this year, almost £4 billion above Whitehall targets. She was attracted by the idea of subjecting councils to local referendums if they breach spending ceilings, but has been persuaded to delay such a step, at least until the next Tory manifesto.

The two court rulings upholding Mr Patten's action in capping 21 councils for "excessive" spending this year have proved crucial to the debate within the group of ministers reviewing the community charge. Mr Patten has been able to reassure Mrs Thatcher by pointing to his vindication in the courts as evidence that the existing legislation will enable him to cap far more widely next year if councils fail to heed ministerial warnings about spending. Only the law lords, who are due to rule on an appeal by the capped councils later this month, can upset these calculations.

The extent of the government's existing capping powers was drummed home last week by Michael Portillo, the local government minister, who said that next year ministers would be able to cap on the basis of year-on-year increases in budgets as well as spending levels judged to be "substantially excessive".

Mrs Thatcher will demand that when Mr Patten makes his statement to MPs, about a week before they rise for the summer recess, he leaves local authorities in no doubt about his determination to take a tough line with high spenders and, if necessary, to cap more councils than the 21 singled out this year.

Environment sources said that the extra cash agreed between Mr Patten and Mr Major at a meeting last week would steer a course midway between backbenchers and council leaders calling for a huge cash injection, and those opposed to throwing money at it. They remain apprehensive about how it will be received by Tory MPs, many of whom are worried that another round of big increases in bills next spring could scupper their chances of holding their seats in a general election later in the year.

It will not be enough to satisfy council leaders, who meet Mr Patten today to press their case for an extra £5-£8 billion. The Association of Metropolitan Authorities said yesterday that the average poll tax would rise to £501 from £360 this year if government funding remained the same.

Sir Rhodes Boyson, a former junior environment minister, said last night that he would oppose Mr Patten's package because it meant a further shift of power to the centre. He said that there must be a bill allowing for local referendums if councils overstep the mark.

Payment survey, page 2

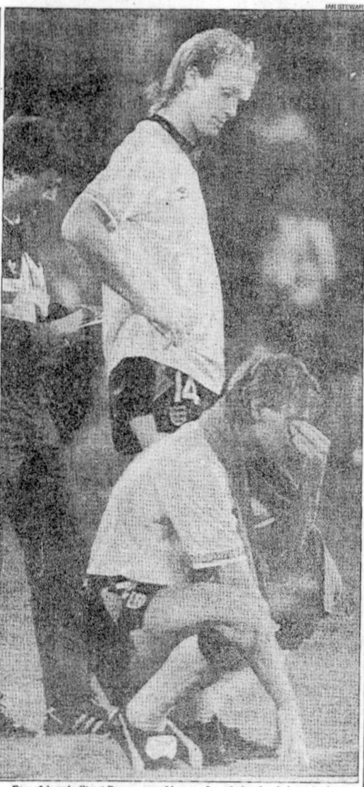

Face of despair: Stuart Pearce covers his eyes after missing the vital penalty for England last night as his team-mate Mark Wright looks on sympathetically

England fail at the last in penalty shoot-out

From JOHN GOODBODY IN TURIN

IN THE cruellest fashion, England went out of the World Cup last night by losing in a penalty shoot-out to West Germany in the semi-final at the Stadio Delle Alpi in Turin.

Before 80,000 spectators and with almost half the population of Britain watching the match on television, Chris Waddle drove the final kick high into the stand to end England's hopes of reaching the final for only the second time. There were tears in the dressing room after a match of constant tension and drama had ended with Stuart Pearce and Waddle failing to convert their penalties.

West Germany, who won the shoot-out 4-3 after the teams had finished extra time level at 1-1, will play Argentina, the holders, in the final in Rome on Sunday, in a re-match of the 1986 final. England will play Italy in Bari on Saturday for third place in what will be Bobby Robson's last game as England manager.

Robson said after the match last night that the England players had nothing of which to be ashamed. "There were tears in the dressing room tonight. I had a job keeping mine back. We graced a World Cup semi-final which we did not consider we lost. You have to accept the penalties rule.

"I wish West Germany success in the final. They are a very good team but we matched them. We reached the last four of a major tournament and we can go home feeling very proud."

Three of England's six games went to extra time, including last night's match in which Andreas Brehme gave West Germany the lead in the 61st minute only for Gary Lineker to equalise in the 82nd minute.

On a day when there was so much for which English football could be proud, there were also violent incidents. Clashes erupted after the match at the main railway station when German and English fans arrived at the same time and firecrackers were thrown at the English. There was also violence earlier when Germans and Italians attacked English supporters.

● **Patriotic silence:** England's roads and places of entertainment were virtually deserted during the match (Lin Jenkins writes). Even the Commons fell silent for the penalty shoot-out. As it began, an MP rushed into the chamber, placed an imaginary ball at the bar of the House, feinted a penalty shot towards the Speaker and disappeared to watch the television.

England mourns, page 3
Letters, page 13
Penalty alternatives, page 37
World Cup, pages 36, 37, 42

Nato may send envoy to support Gorbachev

By PETER STOTHARD AND MICHAEL EVANS

THE United States is to ask Nato to send a special envoy to Moscow, to present what it hopes will be the "reassuring" results of the London summit which begins at Lancaster House today.

The summit envoy, who could be Manfred Worner, Nato secretary-general, or James Baker, the American Secretary of State, would fly to the Soviet capital on Sunday. The Communist party congress, in which President Gorbachev has been criticised for "losing" Eastern Europe and permitting the resurgence of German power, would not be in progress that day.

President Bush and the other Nato leaders were arriving in London overnight to face two days of what may be fierce debate on the final summit declaration. Disagreements are likely about the role of the Conference on Security and Co-operation in Europe and arms control strategies.

American officials believe that Moscow is ready to drop its opposition to a united Germany joining Nato, if the Western allies can make the move appear less threatening to the Soviet Union.

They argue that a dramatic delivery of the plan may be more significant than further concessions. The handing over of "a piece of paper" to Eduard Shevardnadze, the Soviet foreign minister, would be a potential propaganda coup which would not only help Mr Gorbachev to face his critics at home, but would also reassure the West about the prospect of peace and its financial dividends.

Early indications yesterday suggested, however, that some of the smaller members of Nato want a more substantial change in the alliance's long-standing strategy. One Nato diplomat said: "The US and Britain want to make Nato appear more of a political than a military force. Others want it to be only a political force."

Rift on future role, page 10
Soviet congress, page 11
Leading article, page 13

Two-year deadline for perestroika

From REUTER IN MOSCOW

PRESIDENT Gorbachev said yesterday that he and the rest of the leaders would quit if perestroika did not bring changes within two years. "If there are no changes in two years, then this leadership will go of its own accord," he told journalists on the third day of the 28th party congress.

But from a Soviet television recording of his comments, he seemed to be referring only to his post as party leader and not that of state president.

Conservative delegates denounced radicals at the congress yesterday but Mr Gorbachev appeared secure despite the rift. The president, who must stand for re-election as party chief next week, sought to play down the division in the congress, which could decide the future of Soviet communism itself.

"No one at the congress has called into doubt the political course of perestroika," he said. "That is the main thing."

Passionate support, page 10

Hospitals apply for trust status

By PHILIP WEBSTER

TWELVE health service units, including Europe's largest teaching hospital, have applied to become self-governing in the five days since the government's reforms became law, Kenneth Clarke said yesterday.

The health secretary announced in the Commons that a further 25 had promised early applications. The requests received so far include St James's University Hospital, Leeds, the largest teaching hospital in Europe, the Royal Liverpool Children's Hospital, and the Royal National Orthopaedic Hospital.

Mr Clarke said applications had also been received from Bradford acute services; Leeds General Infirmary and associated hospitals; Central Middlesex and North Middlesex hospitals; Southend district services; Crewe acute services; Liverpool regional adult cardio-thoracic unit; East Gloucestershire services; and the Mid-Surrey general unit.

Bart's decision, page 7

INSIDE

Scargill faces new enquiry

Arthur Scargill, president of the National Union of Mineworkers, is to face a fresh enquiry into what became of £1 million donated by Soviet miners to help their British counterparts during the year-long strike.

The union's national executive committee has decided to ask a lawyer specialising in international cases to conduct further investigations into the affair........Page 22

Fewer jobs

The number of vacancies offered by employers to graduates since last November has fallen by 12 per cent, it was disclosed yesterday......Page 3

Press curbs

Louis Blom-Cooper, chairman of the Press Council, replies for the first time to the Calcutt committee's proposals on curbing the press..Page 12

Rail loss

Losses from last year's rail strikes combined with a decline in leisure travel to give British Rail an operating loss for the first time in five years, Sir Robert Reid, the chairman, said............Pages 5, 22

Albania move

Ramiz Alia, the Albanian president, will attempt to head off popular revolution with changes in political and state security leadership, it was reported yesterday. Large crowds gathered again yesterday in Tirana........Page 11

Wet start

Rain diluted the Pimm's on the first day of Henley Royal Regatta yesterday and delayed play at Wimbledon, where the men's first three seeds, Lendl, Becker and Edberg, all won their matchesPages 38, 41, 42

INDEX

18 pages of top jobs in today's appointments section

★★★ SL

Thatcher-Mandela meeting 'cordial'

By ANDREW MCEWEN AND MICHAEL KNIPE

NELSON Mandela acknowledged yesterday that Margaret Thatcher was sincere in opposing apartheid even if they disagreed over the best way to end it.

After three hours with the prime minister at Downing Street, the deputy president of the African National Congress told journalists: "There is no doubt that she is an enemy of apartheid ... we have our differences in the methods of dismantling (it)."

Neither Mrs Thatcher nor Mr Mandela gave ground on the key issues of sanctions against Pretoria and the ANC's continued use of violence, but both appeared to be playing down the importance of their differences.

Whitehall sources said the differences between the two were not important, and that the main object was to get rid of apartheid. The two leaders had had a very good exchange of views and agreed to keep in touch and to build on the rapport they had established.

Mrs Thatcher reported that, as Mr Mandela left, he had told her: "I hope a time will come when Mr de Klerk (the South African president) and myself can see you together."

Mr Mandela left Mrs Thatcher in no doubt that he wanted peace and a negotiated outcome in South Africa. For her part the prime minister emphasised the importance of flexibility in the management of the South African economy

Continued on page 22, col 6

Photograph, page 5
Petrol bombs, page 9
Speech to CBI, page 23
City comment, page 25

Soviet troops storm Bundesbank for marks

From ANNE MCELVOY IN EAST BERLIN

A DOZEN sirens screamed, 30 officers dismounted from military buses brandishing their Kalashnikovs and a cavalcade of police and Soviet army vehicles with lights flashing sped through the heart of East Berlin. The soldiers had business at the bank.

Two officers presented their credentials at the Bundesbank's new East Berlin headquarters yesterday and announced to the cashier: "We would like to cash a cheque." They then picked up what a Bundesbank spokesman would confirm only as a "two-figure million-mark sum" to pay the Soviet army's 360,000 troops stationed in East Germany their first allowance in German marks.

The money was withdrawn from the East German state budget after an agreement last week that East Berlin would supply the soldiers' living allowance in hard currency in return for raw materials from the Soviet Union. The deal which effectively means a preferential exchange rate for the Soviet Union is worth 1.24 billion marks (£428 million) and was reached after Moscow said that it was unable to meet the cost of supporting its troops after currency union with the West.

The Bundesbank has moved into the former Communist party headquarters and now bears the incongruous address Marx-Engels Platz on its headed notepaper. Until 1945 the building housed the Reichsbank, the financial centre of the Nazi regime. The four-storey vaults are now being used to store German marks.

A spokesman for the bank said that the Soviet army "simply turned up with a cheque for the amount", probably enough to cover payments for a month. "They obviously took the security aspect very seriously indeed, although I don't think anyone here would mess with them."

Soviet soldiers stationed for two years in East Germany received a meagre allowance of between 15 and 25 old marks monthly but were still envied because they had access to the wider range of goods available in East German shops than at home.

The amount has remained the same in German marks to the chagrin of the troops. The army newspaper, *Krasnaya Swesdna*, commented yesterday that the changeover did not mean "paradisical times" ahead for the soldiers as prices for basic goods, including the popular East German beer, have doubled since the disappearance of the old currency on Sunday.

● **Jobless protests:** Thousands of East German workers, alarmed by soaring unemployment, staged unofficial strikes all over the country yesterday to back demands for more pay, job security and shorter working hours (Reuter reports).

The walkouts, which in many areas turned into protest marches, coincided with labour ministry data showing 142,000 jobless in June, a rise of 47,000 or almost 50 per cent over the previous month. Economists believe that up to two million of the country's nine million workers will be unemployed by January.

Election date agreed, page 10
Unemployment fears, page 23

32

ENGLAND v WEST GERMANY

WORLD CUP SEMI-FINAL, 1990

After the dark years of the 1980s, English football was reborn at the 1990 World Cup. Under Bobby Robson's management England progressed – somewhat fortuitously – to their first appearance in the last four since 1966. There they again faced their perennial foes West Germany. It was another titanic encounter.

"With a touch of fortune, England could have featured in the main event in Rome on Sunday and sought revenge for Maradona's infamous handled goal"

ENGLAND 1
WEST GERMANY 1

AFTER EXTRA TIME: WEST GERMANY
WIN 4-3 ON PENALTIES

WORLD CUP, SEMI-FINAL
4 JULY 1990
STADIO DELLE ALPI, TURIN

BY STUART JONES, FOOTBALL CORRESPONDENT
5 July

A dream which almost became reality last night turned into a personal nightmare for Stuart Pearce and Chris Waddle. The unfortunate pair will forever be haunted by the dreadful moment they missed the penalties which condemned England to the role of runners-up in a dazzling and ultimately cruel World Cup semi-final here. They and their colleagues deserved a kinder fate.

They had outplayed "the most impressive team in the tournament", as Bobby Robson had justifiably described West Germany, to an astonishing degree in the first 40 minutes. They had recovered from Brehme's goal, the result of a wicked deflection, to equalise through Lineker with only ten minutes left in normal time.

Pushed into extra time for the third successive match, they called on the spirit which had lifted them beyond reasonable expectations and struck a post through Waddle. The Germans also struck an upright through Buchwald before the second semi-final, like the first in Naples on Tuesday night, became a game of Russian roulette.

Lineker, Beardsley, and, less convincingly, Platt all scored but Pearce's penalty cannoned off the legs of the German goalkeeper, Illgner, and Waddle, with the destiny of the tie at his trembling feet, hit his high over the bar. Thus, the Germans go into their third successive World Cup final and against Argentina, their conquerors in Mexico City four years ago.

With a touch of fortune, England could have featured in the main event in Rome on Sunday and sought revenge for Maradona's infamous handled goal. Instead, they will finish the competition in a meaningless sideshow for third place with the hosts in Bari the previous night. It promises to be a dispiriting anti-climax.

England's performance here was anything but. The Germans were appearing in their 67th tie and their ninth semi-final, both of which are records, but they were never the masters of the evening. Nor were they even in control of it until Pearce turned round to complete the loneliest walk in the world back to the centre circle and the consolation of his colleagues

No one could have predicted that the Germans, the highest scorers in the competition, would be kept so subdued for so long. England rose to an occasion which was a new experience for all of them, including their 40-year-old goalkeeper, who in the end could do nothing more to carry the nation even further.

It was indisputably their finest display since they opened their challenge in the comparatively tedious domestic affair against the Republic of Ireland almost a month ago. Indeed, many observers hailed the two hours as the most enthralling of the World Cup. As Bobby Robson claimed later: "We graced the semi-final."

He kept his faith in the system which has transformed his team but he changed the roles to protect Wright, who was playing with half a dozen stitches in his left eyebrow, from further facial damage. Instead of acting as the sweeper, he was instructed to mark Klinsmann.

Walker shadowed Voller, until he departed with a leg injury after half an hour, and Butcher was left free. Parker contained the threat of Brehme, the most constructive of defenders, and Parker and Gascoigne worked industriously to stifle their foes in midfield. Initially, therefore, the Germany strike force was negligible.

Waddle, who tormented Belgium in the second round, was at his elusive best. Floating behind Lineker and Beardsley, whose partnership was renewed because of the enforced absence of Barnes, he curled passes behind, beyond and through a German rearguard which, early on, was extended to an unforeseen degree.

But Illgner was not stretched except when Waddle outrageously tried to chip him from 40 yards. His impudence would not have been rewarded anyway, since the whistle had already been blown. Apart from a crisp volley from Gascoigne, the product of England's domination was disproportionately meagre.

The Germans closed the first half and opened the second in ominous fashion. As the balance shifted and the game followed a more expected course, Shilton was forced to tip over Augenthaler's drive before he was beaten in the 59th minute. Brehme's free kick from the edge of the area veered off Parker and looped over him.

That might effectively have been the end but the goal lifted the semi-final on to an even higher plane and it stirred the imagination of Gascoigne in particular. Within five minutes, he had fashioned three openings which might have produced an instant equaliser. In turn, Beardsley, Wright and Waddle were all a bootlace or strand of hair away from doing so.

But all was not lost. Robson again withdrew his captain, Butcher, to design a more attacking formation. Steven was brought on to augment the midfield. No one was protecting the flat back four, but one member of the defence was to be the source of England's belated ray of hope.

Parker's cross caused confusion in the German defence and especially in the mind of Kohler. He miscued his clearance and before he could recover, Lineker had found a gap between Illgner and the far post. It was his fourth goal in the World Cup and his 35th for his country, and it earned England an additional half hour.

There were anxious moments for both sides in extra time. Shilton parried a header from Klinsmann, who almost immediately wasted an opportunity provided by Augenthaler's cheeky lob. Later, the England goalkeeper dived to catch Thon's shot and was startled when Buchwalds shuddered a post.

England also had their moments, and never more exciting than when Waddle's drive rebounded off an upright so sharply that Lineker had no time to turn in the rebound. Platt headed in Waddle's free-kick but his effort was disallowed for offside.

In spite of three cautions, the conduct matched the quality, but one of the bookings was to be sadly significant. Gascoigne, who has done as much as any individual to promote England's unlikely ambitions of being crowned as the world champions, will miss the third place play-off because of suspension.

MATCH FACTS

England 1
Lineker 80

`After extra time`

West Germany 1
Brehme 60

Penalties: England – Lineker scored, Beardsley scored, Platt scored, Pearce saved, Waddle missed. West Germany – Brehme scored, Matthaus scored, Riedle scored, Thon scored.

England: P. Shilton, D. Walker, M. Wright, T. Butcher (sub: T. Steven, 70), P. Parker, P. Gascoigne, D. Platt, S. Pearce, C. Waddle, G. Lineker, P. Beardsley
West Germany: B. Illgner, J. Kohler, K. Augenthaler, T. Berthold, G. Buchwald, O. Thon, L. Matthaus, T. Haessler (sub: S. Reuter, 67), A. Brehme, J. Klinsmann, R. Voller (sub: K. Riedle, 38)
Referee: J. Ramiz Wright (Brazil)
Attendance: 62,628

33

ITALY v REPUBLIC OF IRELAND

WORLD CUP GROUP MATCH, 1994

England failed to qualify for the 1994 World Cup in the United States, but the appearance of the Republic of Ireland – under the management of Jack Charlton and full of familiar players from English football – in their second successive finals generated huge interest. Their opening match could hardly have been more mouth-watering – Italy in the Giants Stadium, New York.

"The stadium was awash with green as the Irish gave New York a stunning introduction to the World Cup"

ITALY 0
REPUBLIC OF IRELAND 1

WORLD CUP GROUP MATCH
18 JUNE 1994
GIANTS STADIUM, NEW YORK

....

BY PETER BALL
20 June

On Saturday, in the cauldron of the Giants Stadium here, Ireland won the most notable victory in their history. With McGrath a towering figure in the centre of their defence, they kept an Italian team, which had begun the match as one of the favourites to win the World Cup, at arm's length in a throbbing, pulsating game.

It was Ireland's first victory over Italy in eight attempts. By the end, they had won it with some comfort, if such a phrase can be used about a day on which the temperature soared in a packed stadium to well over 90°F. They had the measure of a disappointing Italy in almost every way.

Even the prediction that Italians would flood the stadium proved false. Instead, it was awash with green as the Irish gave New York a stunning introduction to the World Cup. If the early chants of "Are You Watching, England?" suggested an insecure upstart, by the end "You'll Never Beat the Irish" rang out with conviction rather than defiance. Ireland have now beaten Holland, Germany and Italy in the last two months, but this was far and away the most significant victory. In an open World Cup, Ireland gave notice that their claims should be taken seriously. How far they can go remains to be seen but they have no reason to fear any of the European teams. The heat in Orlando next week may be a more serious problem, with the supply of water on Saturday far from adequate.

It was the only blot on a riveting afternoon as Ireland announced their arrival in the big league. The days are gone when only their spirit is praiseworthy, as Andy Townsend, an inspiration as midfield leader, suggested afterwards. "When are you going to start saying how good our football is?" he inquired when someone fell into the cliché trap.

After Saturday, there is no excuse, as they outplayed Italy as well as outfought them. Coyne's ceaseless, unselfish running in the remorseless sun won the plaudits of his colleagues but Keane, Babb, Townsend, Irwin and Phelan all had outstanding games. So did the bubbling McAteer, who had the temerity to nutmeg the disappointing Roberto Baggio. "I suppose it was a bit cheeky," McAteer said, "but I looked at him after I'd done it and thought, 'Does that mean I'm worth his money?'"

That confidence was reflected in Ireland's display, much of it stemming from the authority of McGrath, whose stature as one of the world's great defenders is unchallengeable. Six weeks ago, the player's place in the squad was in doubt as his shoulder injury produced a general deterioration in his physical condition, to the displeasure of Jack Charlton, the manager.

Even at the beginning of the week, Charlton was uncertain about his readiness. On Saturday, there was no question. He was simply immense, from the minutes after Houghton's goal, when he beat the dangerous Signori to Roberto Baggio's pass, to the time late in the game, when he rose for the umpteenth time to head clear in spite of being charged down by two desperate attackers as he did so.

Alongside him, Babb was almost as impressive in his first competitive international, taking to the scene without a trace of nerves. "I was only nervous at the start when I looked up and saw the whole of the end of the ground was just a sea of green," Babb said, "but I got a firm header in almost immediately and the nerves disappeared. I thought I did well, but it is easy playing with Paul McGrath."

But it was not just a great defensive performance. They began as they meant to go on, Keane and Townsend rattling firmly into tackles to disrupt the Italian rhythm, and it was no surprise when they scored. The Italian defence had looked suspect as soon as it was put under pressure and, in the twelfth minute, Houghton, racing in from the right, pounced on Baresi's weak header, the second in succession, to breast the ball down and hit a left-foot shot looping over Pagliuca.

"He tries that shot every day in training and I've never seen him score before," Charlton said. One-nil to the Irish, and one up to Charlton, whose decision to recall Houghton was so promptly justified. That inevitably sparked growing Italian retaliation, but with Coyne an ever-willing target, and the midfield players passing the ball securely, they came under less pressure than they expected. By half-time, Bonner had not had a shot to save.

He did afterwards, denying Signori as Italy regrouped with Massaro on, and for a time Ireland came under serious pressure as Dino Baggio gave them far more trouble with his runs from deep than Roberto. But the storm abated and, by the end, Ireland could have increased their lead as Pagliuca saved well from Houghton and Townsend, and Sheridan hit the bar after a strong run by Keane.

MATCH FACTS

Italy 0	Republic of Ireland 1
	Houghton 12

Ireland: P. Bonner, D. Irwin, P. McGrath, P. Babb, T. Phelan, R. Houghton (sub: J. McAteer, 67), J. Sheridan, R. Keane, A. Townsend, S. Staunton, T. Coyne (sub: J. Aldridge, 89)
Italy: G. Pagliuca, M. Tassorti, A. Costacurta, F. Baresi, P. Maldini, R. Donadoni, D. Baggio, D. Albertini, A. Eyani (sub: D. Massaro, HT), R. Baggio, G. Signori (sub: N. Berti, 83)
Referee: M. van der Ende (Holland)
Attendance: 75,338

34

LIVERPOOL v BLACKBURN ROVERS

FA CARLING PREMIERSHIP, 1995

Jack Walker, a Blackburn businessman who made his millions in steel, used his fortune to take his beloved home-town football club back to the top of English football. He recruited Kenny Dalglish as manager and funded a string of high-profile signings. They reached the last game of 1994–95 – by remarkable coincidence, away to Liverpool – in touching distance of the title but knowing that they could be overtaken by Manchester United, who were playing West Ham United at the same time.

"There have been two world wars and an industrial revolution since 1914 when Rovers were last champions"

**LIVERPOOL 2
BLACKBURN ROVERS 1**

FA CARLING PREMIERSHIP
14 MAY 1995
ANFIELD

....

**BY ROB HUGHES, FOOTBALL
CORRESPONDENT**
15 May

In the end, there was dignity and honour on the final day and in the final tense moments of the FA Carling Premiership. There was a full house of 40,014, bathed in sunshine at Anfield, to see that Liverpool's much depleted side still had the integrity and the anger to prove, in their manager's words, that it was "absolute rubbish" to suggest that they would lie down and allow Kenny Dalglish and his Rovers to take the championship from Manchester United.

Lie down? Liverpool outplayed the new champions. They came from behind to beat them with a goal struck in time added for injuries. And then, in the instant that the ball hit the Blackburn net, at the moment that sheer devastation etched itself into the faces of the 11 Blackburn players, a mighty roar spread from the Kop, spread all around the ground and told Blackburn that in defeat they had won the ultimate victory of a ten-month season.

The roar came because there was hardly a soul in the ground who wanted United to establish a third consecutive crown. This was partly the animosity between Liverpool and Manchester, but more it was the deep affection that still unites Liverpudlians to "King Kenny".

He, the winner of eight championships while a player and manager here, a man who had left active participation in football four years ago, was described by Bob Paisley as the greatest player he had seen in half a century at this famous stadium. And now Dalglish is in select company as a manager too, joining Herbert Chapman (Huddersfield Town and Arsenal) and Brian Clough (Derby County and Nottingham Forest) as the only men in England to win league championships with different clubs.

And yet, much as Dalglish himself tried so hard, and as the Liverpool choir sang *You'll Never Walk Alone*, their anthem to the team in blue and white, there was a more emotional figure in the ground. Jack Walker, the multimillionaire of steel, sat in the directors' box and suffered – and thought that the goal struck after the ninetieth minute by Jamie Redknapp had taken the trophy to Manchester. "When Liverpool scored that second goal my heart stopped," the man whose £50 million bequest relaunched Blackburn from obscurity to a force vibrant enough to finish the season one point ahead of United, said.

"I couldn't believe what was happening. Then reporters behind me told me United had only drawn at West Ham. It's a miracle." And Walker, publicity-shy as he is, had no option but to carry the trophy out to the field, to the supporters who, strange as it may seem, had chanted throughout not the name of a player, nor that of an idol, but of the benefactor. As Walker returned, climbing the steps beneath the sign reading "This is Anfield", a mixture of emotion and the heaviness of the silver trophy (the Premier League guessed correctly that it was needed in the North) overcame Walker.

He put the cup laboriously down on a step. He gasped for breath. A police officer helped him and, recovered, he revealed that the title had come a year ahead of schedule. "We didn't plan on winning it this year," Walker said.

More practised at speaking into microphones than their paymaster, the players and Dalglish were uninhibited. It was as if they represented a town which had not won the biggest prize in the land in living memory... which, considering that there have been two world wars and an industrial revolution since 1914, when the Rovers were last champions, is about right.

Yet they did it in a fog of mental and physical fatigue, the style that demands so much running of so many players quite crucially slowing them in the second half of games during the past weeks. Thank goodness, then, for Shearer. He, almost inevitably, gave the team hope and purpose with the opening goal in the twentieth minute. It had come from his own prompting, for he delivered a pass out to the wing to Ripley, and then, with instinct that is uncanny, found three yards of space around the penalty spot. Ripley delivered, Shearer delivered; the pass was low and direct, the shot with the right foot angled, also low and unstoppably accurate against the far stanchion. That equalled the 34 goals that Andy Cole had scored for Newcastle in setting the Premier League record; but, more important, it was Shearer's 21st goal in the past 24 games.

By now, the atmosphere was surreal. Large ripples of applause, not in any way polite, were coming from the stands as the plight of Manchester United in London was being relayed by radio. But then Liverpool, whose passing had commanded 64 percent of the possession in the first half, translated that into potency. In the 64th minute, they equalised when young Mark Kennedy swung the ball in from the left and Barnes calmly guided it beyond the right hand of Flowers.

Now, the tension began to bite, and, though Shearer and Sutton were to miss opportunities that they would ordinarily have scored, the clock was running away when McManaman was fouled 25 yards out. Wearily, Blackburn lined up; almost casually, Redknapp struck the ball right-footed, dipped and curled it inside the near post of Flowers.

Blackburn turned, their faces like schoolboys who had lost the prize – but they turned straight into the welcoming arms of the Liverpool players who, more aware than they, had heard the final score from Upton Park. McManaman cradled the head of Ripley, and congratulated him... and all around the Liverpool supporters were singing, gleefully: "Always look on the bright side of life ... Are you listening, Manchester?"

MATCH FACTS

Liverpool 2	Blackburn Rovers 1
Barnes 64, Redknapp 90	*Shearer 20*

Liverpool: D. James, J. Scales (sub: D. Matteo, 81), S. Harkness, P. Babb, M. Thomas, J. Redknapp, J. Barnes, M. Kennedy, S. McManaman, R. Fowler, N. Clough

Blackburn Rovers: T. Flowers, H. Berg, I. Pearce, C. Hendry, G. Le Saux, S. Ripley, D. Batty, T. Sherwood, J. Kenna, C. Sutton, A. Shearer

Referee: D. Elleray (Harrow on the Hill)

Attendance: 40,014

35

LIVERPOOL v NEWCASTLE UNITED

FA CARLING PREMIERSHIP, 1996

After Blackburn faded, the next challenge to Manchester United's dominance came from Newcastle United. Under Kevin Keegan, they played an intoxicating brand of attacking football with apparently little regard for the niceties of defending. For much of 1995–96 it seemed destined to bring them the title, but in the home straight they began to feel United's breath on their shoulders.

"Newcastle are winning the championship at one end of the field and relinquishing it at the other"

LIVERPOOL 4
NEWCASTLE UNITED 3

FA CARLING PREMIERSHIP
3 APRIL 1996
ANFIELD

. . . .

BY DAVID MILLER
4 April

Newcastle United's addiction to glorious football is a gift to the game, but too often for comfort is their own handicap. So it was last night, when Stan Collymore won for Liverpool a truly fabulous encounter between two fine teams in the fragments of injury time.

When Kevin Keegan and his team reflect on this defeat, and its setback to their challenge for the FA Carling Premiership title, they will be obliged to recognise that, for the last quarter of an hour, the tide was in Liverpool's favour because McManaman, running like an antelope from the right of midfield, was repeatedly shredding the left flank of their defence.

Newcastle are winning the championship at one end of the field and relinquishing it at the other. Yet Keegan remains unrepentant. It was, he said, "a classic", and nothing would change his or the team's attitude. "It was a terrific game, and we shall go on playing the same way, because that's what we believe in. Either we go on, or I go."

A match of seven goals and at least three dozen other attempts – two to one in Liverpool's favour – left hardened professional observers, never mind a full house at Anfield, breathlessly open-mouthed in admiration. Roy Evans, unlike Keegan, acknowledged the spectacle, but suggested soberly that reality demanded better defending by both teams.

The Liverpool manager smilingly referred to this epic as "kamikaze", while paying tribute to his team for their recovery after twice being behind. One suspects that Evans's managerial career may bring more trophies than Keegan's. Idealism so often deserves better than it receives.

This was the most electric encounter I have seen since a cup-tie two seasons ago against Tottenham Hotspur at Anfield, and Newcastle's mood now, the turbulence of their attacking – and their tackling – from the first whistle was a tribute to them and their manager. "I've never managed a team that played so well and got nothing," Keegan said, but Liverpool's performance in the final phase reminded him, he said, of the Liverpool of 20 years ago. "Watch out," was in effect his message.

Newcastle thus remain three points behind Manchester United, now with one game in hand. Liverpool are five points behind the leaders from the same number of games. Alex Ferguson, of Manchester United, will probably be the happiest of the three managers for the moment, but all football

should be celebrating this morning a match of such exceptional action and entertainment.

Liverpool all but floundered in the middle of the first half because Asprilla, Ferdinand and Ginola mesmerised them with their scintillating footwork, to the point where Liverpool's rearguard of Wright, Scales and Ruddock shuddered like the beams of a house caught in an earthquake. At the same time, the ageing Barnes was being swamped in midfield, McManaman had yet to find his touch, and in the eagerly awaited duel between McAteer and Ginola, McAteer, initially, was embarrassingly overrun. His contribution would come later, as would McManaman's.

There could not have been a more volcanic opening, Liverpool taking the lead inside two minutes with a move that ran from one end of the pitch to the other. Wright, who had an unhappy time before injury forced his replacement by Harkness at half-time, put Fowler away down the right with a 40-yard pass. Fowler cut inside, was thinking about what to do next, but had the decision removed by Redknapp's high cross to the left flank. Jones deflected the ball first time down the line to Collymore, who went round Howey on the outside. From close to the byline, Collymore's cross dropped at the far post, where Fowler, unmarked, headed sharply down beyond Srnicek.

Liverpool were on cloud nine, barely able to credit that it could be so easy. It could not. Newcastle's onslaught was about to explode, the first sign coming when Ferdinand twisted his way clear of three men and let fly straight at James. With 11 minutes gone, Newcastle were level. Asprilla, as elusive as an eel yet oddly managing to look like, at times, a schoolboy wearing his father's pyjamas, tormented Ruddock on the right, playing the ball between his legs, then pulling it back from near the line into the path of Ferdinand seven yards out. With one controlling touch, Ferdinand hooked a shot upwards, the ball flashing between James's hands. A potential international goalkeeper should have done better.

Now Newcastle were in flood. Asprilla and Ferdinand were making their rivals look like relegation candidates for a while, and four minutes later they went ahead. Ferdinand sent a raking pass, made on the turn in the centre circle, into the path of Ginola, going flat out ahead of McAteer. Drawing James, Ginola swept the ball home.

A lesser team than Liverpool might have crumpled, but not they. McManaman began to sing, Fowler twice went close, and there was clearly all to play for, though Barnes, having put Ginola clear with a faulty pass, was fortunate not to concede a penalty when sending him headlong from behind as he attempted to retrieve the error.

Only a superb save by James prevented Lee, on a solo run, putting Newcastle two up early in the second half, but by now Liverpool were in the groove. Fowler levelled the scores with a low shot from 14 yards, taken as coolly as Greaves of old, when McManaman put the ball to his feet from square on the right.

Newcastle, true to style, were ahead again inside two minutes as Lee sent Asprilla clear for the Colombian to clip the ball wide of James. Liverpool's response was not long arriving: McManaman to McAteer down the right, a curling low cross, a stab from Collymore, with Newcastle again in disarray. Scenting victory, Liverpool's pressure mounted. When Ferdinand threatened another goal, James was his equal, and with Rush having come on in the 86th minute for Jones, he and Barnes set up the opening for Collymore to crash home the winner. It was an ecstatic or cruel moment, depending on how one looked at it.

MATCH FACTS

Liverpool 4	Newcastle United 3
Fowler 2 65, Collymore 68 90+2	*Ferdinand 10, Ginola 14, Asprilla 57*

Liverpool: D. James, M. Wright (sub: S. Harkness, HT), J. Scales, N. Ruddock, J. McAteer, J. Redknapp, J. Barnes, S. McManaman, R. Jones (sub: I. Rush, 86), R. Fowler, S. Collymore
Newcastle United: P. Srnicek, S. Watson, S. Howey (sub: D. Peacock, 82), P. Albert, J. Beresford, P. Beardsley, R. Lee, D. Batty, D. Ginola, L. Ferdinand, F. Asprilla
Referee: M. Reed (Birmingham)
Attendance: 40,702

36

ENGLAND v HOLLAND

EUROPEAN CHAMPIONSHIP GROUP MATCH, 1996

Nothing demonstrated the extent of football's cultural revolution in England in the 1990s more thoroughly than the hosting of the 1996 European Championship. It felt overpoweringly like a different game watched by a new audience. It helped that England appeared to have a chance of winning the tournament, never more so than after their final group game against Holland.

"The lions were rampant, Holland were wilting"

ENGLAND 4
HOLLAND 1

EUROPEAN CHAMPIONSHIP,
GROUP MATCH
18 JUNE 1996
WEMBLEY STADIUM
....

**BY ROB HUGHES, FOOTBALL
CORRESPONDENT**
19 June

With a display of pace, passion and power, England trounced Holland at Wembley last night, earning them the right to play Spain in the stadium in the quarter-finals on Saturday afternoon. It was such a performance, beating Holland for the first time for 14 years, that it left even the most sober among the 76,798 crowd feeling high on victory.

Holland recovered from a four-goal deficit to score a consolation goal that keeps them in the competition at the expense of poor Scotland. It is Holland who now travel north to Anfield to face an impressive France.

Paul Gascoigne sauntered through the first half, awoke to tease the Dutchmen in the second, and Shearer and Sheringham each capitalised with a brace of goals. When England took the lead midway through the first half, the stadium erupted. It was a strange but pleasing sight, a ground where segregation had completely broken down, where the orange shirts dotted among English white defied the efforts of the organisers and the law to separate human beings by their colours.

England had lurked deep, following defensive instincts, with Gascoigne again, and now also Sheringham, often hanging back, one knows not with what purpose, patrolling as deep as Ince, the allotted anchor in front of the back four.

Yet it was Sheringham, creating out of this repose, who sparked England's opening goal. Halfway in English territory, he controlled the ball, held it at his feet, turned and released it as if out of a catapult into the inside right channel for McManaman. The Liverpool forward, at last liberated on the side of the field that suits him, advanced at pace towards the penalty area. He showed the patience to wait for support and, when Ince produced a darting run, he passed precisely into his path.

Ince, revealing a trick of great virtuosity, used his instep to flick the ball on, and induced from Blind, the Holland captain, a late trip which brought a penalty and a yellow card. Up strode Shearer, now confident of scoring for England again, and with unremitting force plus fine accuracy his penalty defeated the long stretch of Van der Sar, the lean Dutch goalkeeper. Three goals in three games for Shearer, his 21-month England drought now a distant memory.

Early on, Dutch fluidity had threatened England, thrown them back on their heels, and with Anderton, among others, augmenting the defence, England were reduced to hopeful breakaways. Yet,

in the seventh minute, an Anderton corner found Shearer, surprisingly free of Bogarde, his marker, and free also to take aim at goal from 14 yards. His right-foot shot was true, but Witschge deflected the ball with his heel on the goal line. England had to rely on Seaman's athleticism when Bergkamp anticipated a poor back-header from Southgate. The goalkeeper came off his line and stood tall, forcing Bergkamp to shoot, and then he jackknifed to the ground to deflect the ball with his feet.

Just before half-time England broke again. A McManaman throw-in was hooked on by Gascoigne and Sheringham, the goal at his mercy, sliced the ball across the face, bouncing beyond the far post. The bad news for England came with a yellow card for Ince, for his second crude and spiteful tackle, which rules him out of the quarter-final.

Gascoigne was saving his irrepressible self, but, from a corner six minutes into the second half, he delivered an accurate ball, swinging high towards the penalty spot, and there Sheringham, producing a tremendous leap above Winter and turning in mid-air, found the power with his header to defeat Van der Sar.

The lions were rampant, Holland were wilting, and the best night that English football has known for many years was developing. It took another six minutes, and another piece of Gascoigne inspiration, to invent goal number three. He rolled the ball impudently away from Seedorf, turned and sprinted into the penalty area and, when McManaman returned it to him, Gascoigne had the power and the momentum to sweep away Winter's challenge.

When Gascoigne then laid the ball on a plate for Sheringham, the Tottenham man feinted to shoot and cleverly diverted it to a player who would not miss: Shearer, again with awesome force, drove past Van der Sar.

Another five minutes and, when Anderton struck a shot that deflected off Blind, the goalkeeper could only push it to Sheringham, who this time poached the fourth goal from eight yards.

The Dutch disarray was near complete, although in the 77th minute Bergkamp looped the ball over England's square defence and Kluivert, just on as a substitute, stole three yards off Pearce and struck a vital goal.

Guus Hiddink, as honest as ever, finished the night with words that must be sweet music to English ears. "We must recognise that they taught us a lesson in every sense of the game," the Holland coach said. "It's a credit to the English team."

MATCH FACTS

England 4
Shearer 23 pen 57, Sheringham 51 62

Holland 1
Kluivert 78

England: D. Seaman, G. Neville, T. Adams, G. Southgate, S. Pearce, S. McManaman, P. Ince (sub: D. Platt, 67), P. Gascoigne, D. Anderton, E. Sheringham (sub: N. Barmby, 76), A. Shearer (sub: R. Fowler, 76)
Holland: E. Van der Sar, M. Reiziger, D. Blind, W. Bogarde, A. Winter, R. de Boer (sub: P. Kluivert, 72), C. Seedorf, R. Witschge (sub; J. de Koch, HT), Jordi, D. Bergkamp, P. Hoekstra (sub: P. Cocu, 72)
Referee: G. Grabher (Austria)
Attendance: 76,798

37

CHARLTON ATHLETIC v SUNDERLAND

FOOTBALL LEAGUE FIRST DIVISION PLAY-OFF FINAL, 1998

When promotion play-offs were first introduced in the 1980s, they were denounced as a gimmick and, worse, grossly unfair to teams who had finished higher in the table. But it was soon obvious that they were here to stay and, with the stakes sky high, a number of the Wembley finals produced epic battles.

"There was never going to be a fair way to separate these two sides after such an epic duel"

CHARLTON ATHLETIC 4
SUNDERLAND 4

AFTER EXTRA TIME: CHARLTON
WIN 7-6 ON PENALTIES

NATIONWIDE LEAGUE
FIRST DIVISION
PLAY-OFF FINAL
25 MAY 1998
WEMBLEY STADIUM

BY MATT DICKINSON
26 May

THEY went to cheer but their throats were hoarse. They went to cry but the tanks were empty. If ever a football match squeezed the emotions dry it was this, an afternoon of unparalleled drama – football, glorious football at its best.

One wished it would never end, and, as they matched each other penalty for penalty, it appeared it might not. But after nine months, 48 games and a day of breathless excitement in the Nationwide League first division play-offs at Wembley, a winner had to be found and when Michael Gray scuffed his hopelessly weak penalty into Sasa Ilic's arms, the life drained out of Sunderland's fans and Charlton Athletic's exploded with delirium.

"It must be one of the best games anyone has ever seen," Alan Curbishley, the Charlton manager, said and if he meant for sheer drama he was right. "It would be doing the players a dishonour if I even mentioned next season. Let them just enjoy this. They deserve to."

There will indeed be plenty of time to savour the fact that top flight football is back at The Valley, once an abandoned shell, for the first time since 1957. There will be time enough for the Charlton board to work out how best to spend the £8 million that will transform their meagre budget.

Yesterday evening was, as Peter Reid, the Sunderland manager, rightly said, a time to drink. For Charlton champagne, for Sunderland bitter. In some cases very bitter.

As Clive Mendonca dragged his shattered legs from the field, his marvellous hat-trick for Charlton almost forgotten amid the frenzy, two North East supporters could contain their fury no longer. Not only had they been beaten but by a player who had once stood among them on the terraces of Roker Park and who had played for Sunderland schoolboys. "They threatened to slit my throat if I came back to Wearside," Mendonca revealed.

"It's upsetting because I am the biggest Sunderland fan in the world

Ilic is buried beneath a pile of Charlton players after making the penalty save from Gray that took the London club into the FA Carling Premiership. Photograph: Hugh Routledge

and I am genuinely gutted at the way it has worked out. I moved there when I was 2 and lived there till I was 16 so I really wish it could have come out differently. I really feel for poor Michael Gray. I went to the same school as him and I can't imagine how he felt. It's terrible that there is that kind of pressure on one guy. The whole season has come down to one kick."

It was cruel indeed but there was never going to be a fair way to separate these two sides after such an epic duel. As Reid pointed out, Sunderland might have finished two points ahead in the first division but they paid yesterday for a weakness – the inability to defend a lead – that has plagued them all season. Too inexperienced, too bullish and too gung-ho, if they did not learn their lesson yesterday they never will.

Three times they allowed Charlton to claw back the lead, but then Curbishley has been battling against the odds ever since he took over as Charlton manager. Organisation has been his touchstone, creating a side greater than its parts, and it appeared enough to subdue Sunderland in a first half that went perfectly to Curbishley's plan. Mendonca had given them the lead after 24 minutes with a mesmerising turn past Craddock and Sunderland were reduced to frenetic punts towards Niall Quinn.

It was inevitable that Reid – whose half-time team talk must have contained more swear words than the entire series of *Premier Passions* – would rouse more from his team after the interval and they emerged with a renewed sense of purpose.

Level after 50 minutes thanks to a stooping header by Quinn from Summerbee's corner, they were ahead for the first time eight minutes later when Kevin Phillips beat the offside trap for his 35th goal of the season.

Thereafter the goals became a blur as Charlton equalised through Mendonca, only for Quinn to strike again, and then Richard Rufus to send the game into extra-time in the 85th minute with his first goal for the club after Lionel Perez came for, but never reached, a Robinson corner.

One imagined there was no way that extra time could match the excitement but, as players staggered round the field like drunks on their way home, they managed to strike another two blows, Nicky Summerbee putting Sunderland back ahead at 4-3 before Mendonca struck for his hat-trick in the 103rd minute with the finish of a player who believes there will be plenty more where they came from in the FA Carling Premiership.

On they lurched to penalties and Gray's unfortunate miss. "I had not saved anything all afternoon," Ilic said, "so I thought I had better start now.

I actually found a 2p coin on the pitch at the start of the shoot-out and was tossing it between the kicks to keep me busy. I threw it away before the last one because it was not working."

Moments later, Charlton were in the Premiership, where they will have a lot more than tuppence to throw around. For now, though, just enjoy the day. Football, glorious football.

MATCH FACTS

Charlton Athletic 4   `After extra time`   **Sunderland 4**
Mendonca 23 71 103, Rufus 85   *Quinn 50 73, Phillips 58, Summerbee 99*

Penalties: Charlton – Mendonca scored, Brown scored, S. Jones scored, Kinsella scored, Bowen scored, Robinson scored, Newton scored. Sunderland – Summerbee scored, Johnston scored, Ball scored, Makin scored, Rae scored, Quinn scored, Gray saved.

Charlton Athletic: S. Ilic, D. Mills (sub: J. Robinson, 76), R. Rufus, E. Youds, M. Bowen, S. Newton, K. Jones, M. Kinsella, N. Heaney (sub: S. Jones, 64), C. Mendonca, M. Bright (sub: S. Brown, 93)
Sunderland: L. Perez, D. Holloway (sub: C. Makin, HT), J. Craddock, D. Williams, M. Gray, N. Summerbee, K. Ball, L. Clark (sub: A. Rae, 99), A. Johnston, N. Quinn, K. Phillips (sub: D. Dichio, 73)
Referee: E. Wolstenholme (Preston)
Attendance: 77,739

38

ARSENAL v MANCHESTER UNITED

FA CUP SEMI-FINAL REPLAY, 1999

The intense rivalry between Arsenal and Manchester United – and their respective managers Alex Ferguson and Arsene Wenger – provided a compelling soap opera over several seasons at the end of the twentieth century and the beginning of the twenty-first. None of their encounters was more thrilling than the FA Cup semi-final replay of 1999: United were in pursuit of a unique Treble of FA Carling Premiership, FA Cup and Champions League, Arsenal a mere second successive Double.

"United's players were carried from the pitch on the shoulders of their supporters in a spontaneous outpouring of joy and celebration"

ARSENAL 1
MANCHESTER UNITED 2

AFTER EXTRA TIME

FA CUP SEMI-FINAL REPLAY
14 APRIL 1999
VILLA PARK
....

**BY OLIVER HOLT, FOOTBALL
CORRESPONDENT**
15 April

A goal of breathtaking skill from Ryan Giggs in the second half of extra time, one that recalled all the uninhibited brilliance of his youth, propelled ten-man Manchester United into the FA Cup final last night and dashed Arsenal's dreams of emulating their feats of last season by winning the Double.

Amid scenes of chaotic jubilation rarely witnessed in recent years, United's players were carried from the pitch on the shoulders of their supporters in a spontaneous outpouring of joy and celebration. It took David Beckham fully 15 minutes to reach the sanctuary of the tunnel. He was still dancing and punching his fists into the air in delight when he disappeared.

It had seemed that the tie was beyond United, their season perhaps on the brink of falling apart, when Roy Keane, their captain, was sent off late in the second half of a semi-final replay that turned into a classic, an epic of passion and resilience. Somehow, though, the heroics of Peter Schmeichel, their goalkeeper, including a brilliant injury-time penalty save from Dennis Bergkamp that took the match into extra time, kept their hopes alive, allowing Giggs to conjure an improbable victory after Bergkamp had equalised Beckham's opening goal.

There seemed to be little danger when Giggs picked the ball up midway inside the Arsenal half in the 108th minute, but he dribbled past five players, leaving a trail of the best defenders in the country prostrate in his wake, before lashing his shot high into the roof of the net.

It might just be the goal that turns United's season. The pursuit of the European Cup, the FA Carling Premiership and the FA Cup seemed to be taking its toll at last, but at Villa Park last night they broke the hold that Arsenal seemed to have established over them by beating the North London side for the first time in seven attempts.

To gild their night, Chelsea could only draw with Middlesbrough at the Riverside Stadium and so failed to leapfrog United at the top of the table.

United have also given themselves a crucial psychological advantage for the title run-in and a boost for their return match against Juventus in Turin next week. More than that,

they rediscovered the joy of the sight of one of their most gifted players at his peak.

Giggs, once the brightest star in United's firmament, has been overshadowed in recent years by the emergence of Beckham and, more recently, the goals of Dwight Yorke and Andy Cole. He reclaimed his birthright last night, leading Alex Ferguson, the United manager, to acclaim his "genius". But Giggs's night of glory was marred slightly by an ankle injury sustained in a tackle by Lee Dixon at the end of extra time that could keep him out of United's Premiership game against Sheffield Wednesday on Saturday.

Ferguson said: "I think over the two ties we deserved to go through. We were hanging on for grim death, but you cannot beat that kind of courage. We needed something out of this world, something special. It was a truly remarkable goal. We are delighted."

It was all achieved with a team lacking four of United's starting players. Yorke was on the bench, Cole was rested because of an ankle injury and Denis Irwin and Paul Scholes were substitutes.

In the first half, Teddy Sheringham proved a more than able deputy in attack. Even the Arsenal back four, so imperious on Sunday and on the brink of what would have been a record eighth successive clean sheet, succumbed to his guile as he defied their attempts to mark him by dropping into his familiar role, playing just off the main striker, in this case Ole Gunnar Solskjaer.

In the space of ten minutes, he caused Tony Adams, Martin Keown and company more discomfort than they had endured for the duration of the first tie and his prompting in the seventeenth minute led to United taking the lead.

Beckham began the move, nipping in ahead of Petit to steal the ball midway inside the Arsenal half. He played a short ball forward to Sheringham, who shielded it from Adams and laid it back to his colleague. Beckham looked up and curled a fierce drive towards the bottom right-hand corner, across David Seaman. The goalkeeper seemed to have it covered but, somehow, as if he had misjudged his angles, it eluded his dive and nestled in the back of the net.

Sheringham, though, kept driving United on. First, a one-two with Nicky Butt allowed the United midfield player to hit a rasping drive that surely would have put United further ahead had it not knocked the wind out of Keown. A minute later, Sheringham volleyed a pass out to Jesper Blomqvist on the United left and then drifted away from Keown to receive the return, which he lashed into the side-netting.

The match slipped into a bad-tempered blitz of bookings, flailing arms, raised feet and anguished exhortations, particularly from Bergkamp, who was becoming increasingly irate with Jaap Stam.

When the smoke cleared, Arsenal attempted to force their way back into the game. Schmeichel saved well from Petit and, three minutes before the interval, Anelka made his first worthwhile contribution when he went past Johnsen but hit his left-foot shot just wide of the post.

United should have extended their lead at the start of the second half when Keane, who had won his own battle with Vieira and Petit, played Solskjaer in on Seaman, but the Norway forward dragged his shot hopelessly wide.

The opportunities were coming thick and fast now, but after Anelka lifted a cross from Parlour high over the bar, the introduction of Overmars changed the course of the game and forced United on to the defensive for the first time.

In the 68th minute, five minutes after the substitute had risen from the bench, Bergkamp collected a pass from Winterburn with his back to goal. He turned and advanced towards goal before unleashing a right-foot shot that Schmeichel had covered – but the ball deflected off Stam's left leg and bounced beyond the goalkeeper into the corner of the net.

Arsenal, suddenly rampant, thought they had scored again in the 72nd minute when Bergkamp's shot squirmed out of Schmeichel's grasp and Anelka rounded the goalkeeper and slid the ball home, but the Frenchman was offside.

Two minutes after that, Keane, who had already been booked for a foul on Bergkamp, scythed down Overmars as he hurtled along the left flank and was shown the red card. It seemed then that the game had swung irrevocably towards Arsenal and that impression appeared to be confirmed when Phil Neville tripped Parlour in the box deep into injury time.

Bergkamp, so desperate to reach Wembley after missing out on the Cup Final through injury last season, took the penalty but Schmeichel flung himself to his left and pushed the kick round the post.

Schmeichel rescued United again early in extra time when he beat out a shot from Bergkamp at full stretch and then produced an astonishing reaction save to beat out Ronny Johnsen's inadvertent touch to Petit's corner, which seemed destined to be an own goal. The stage was set for Giggs.

MATCH FACTS

Arsenal 1   After extra time   **Manchester United 2**
Bergkamp 68   *Beckham 17, Giggs 108*

Arsenal: D. Seaman, L. Dixon, M. Keown, T. Adams, N. Winterburn, R. Parlour (sub: Kanu, 105), P. Vieira, E. Petit (sub: S. Bould, 120), F. Ljungberg (sub: M. Overmars, 63), N. Anelka, D. Bergkamp
Manchester United: P. Schmeichel, G. Neville, R. Johnsen, J. Stam, P. Neville, D. Beckham, R. Keane, N. Butt, J. Blomqvist (sub: R. Giggs, 62), O.G. Solskjaer (sub: D. Yorke, 91), E. Sheringham (sub: P Scholes, 76)
Referee: D. Elleray (Harrow)
Attendance: 30,223

1 2 3

TIMES SP🏆RT
10 PAGES

United seize glory in photo finish

Up for the cup: United's players scale the peaks of delight as Ferguson and Schmeichel show off the trophy last night. Photograph: Sergio Perez

A THOUSAND flashbulbs recorded the moment. When the final whistle went last night, they lit up the Nou Camp as though it was noonday in the Barcelona sun and froze the Manchester United players with their arms in the air. It was the instant they passed into legend.

In two astonishing, almost surreal, minutes at the end of the last European Cup final of the 20th century, the gilded youth of the most famous of clubs left excellence behind them and toured the greatness they have been searching for.

The treble is theirs now, as well, something unprecedented, something that even the great English sides of the past have always fallen short of. It is unlikely that it will ever be repeated.

By coming from behind to beat Bayern Munich with two goals in the final minutes, by transforming what seemed like certain defeat into glorious, glorious victory, this United side escaped once and for all from the shadow of Sir Matt Busby and the team that won the trophy in 1968.

The problem for future United teams, for future teams of all nations for that matter, will not lie in trying to recreate the magic of George Best and Bobby Charlton, it will lie in the impossible task of trying to surpass the unsurpassable, of bettering a finish that could not be imagined.

The game had already entered injury time when the comeback began. It had seemed that United had fallen to a tame defeat courtesy of a sixth-minute free kick from Mario Basler. They have developed a reputation for conjuring comebacks in Europe this season, but this time, against the resilience of the Germans, the match seemed to be out of reach.

Instead, Teddy Sheringham, who had been ridiculed this season for being a loser, snatched an equaliser, just as he had scored in the FA Cup Final last Saturday. As Bayern were trying to adjust to that, Sheringham nodded on a Beckham corner and Ole Gunnar Solskjaer, who had only been on the pitch for eight minutes, hooked it into the roof of the net.

A few seconds later, the final whistle went and the Germans threw themselves to the floor

Oliver Holt on the moment Alex Ferguson's team passed into footballing legend

as if they had the falling sickness. Carsten Jancker, who had hit the bar for Bayern ten minutes from the end, sobbed uncontrollably. Most of his team-mates looked stunned.

United were, of course, the souls of jubilation and solid celebration. As they stood in front of their supporters, Sheringham mimicked the action of sweeping as his equaliser and Dwight Yorke and Andy Cole danced a samba of delight in the centre circle. If there was any poignancy among the English, it was sympathy for Roy Keane and Paul Scholes, the men who had missed out because of suspension.

Yet the triumph was perhaps sweetest for Alex Ferguson, the United manager. He has suffered in Busby's shadow more than most, but now he can retire in three years knowing he has found the

fulfilment that he deserves. It was he who took the gamble of playing Beckham in central midfield, he who risked everything by throwing on Sheringham and Solskjaer. It was his triumph more than anyone's and he admitted afterwards that he could hardly take it in.

"You cannot deny the most important fact of all," Ferguson said, "and that is the spirit and the will to win that exists at this club. That is what won the trophy for us tonight.

"It is the greatest night of my life. I was prepared to risk and if you risk in a game of football you deserve to succeed. Sheringham and Solskjaer are goalscorers and they are good at their job. They are terrific substitutes.

"I am proud of my heritage tonight. I am proud of my family. I was starting to adjust to defeat near the end. I kept saying in myself. 'Keep your dignity and accept it is not your year.'

"It is a fairytale; it would have been Sir Matt Busby's birthday today and I think he was doing a bit of kicking up there in the last couple of minutes. I suppose you could say we have come out of his shadow now but, with all the team has achieved this year, they could not have had any question marks against them.

"This team plays the right way. They embrace every concept of football that I like. What they have achieved is unprecedented. Nobody has ever done it. They deserve it."

When Ferguson had finished, he got up to leave. The room erupted in applause and the flashbulbs started flashing again.

Last gasp: Solskjaer scores the winner from Sheringham's header to complete United's comeback in Barcelona

39

BAYERN MUNICH v MANCHESTER UNITED

CHAMPIONS LEAGUE FINAL, 1999

Having won the title and the FA Cup, United's date with destiny in the Champions League came in Barcelona's Nou Camp Stadium against Bayern Munich. It was not a classic match – nor even a good performance – but its sensational denouement came to define the character of Ferguson's indomitable United teams.

"...they have gone from excellence to greatness, they will be feted as the most resilient, adventurous English side of all time"

BAYERN MUNICH 1
MANCHESTER UNITED 2

CHAMPIONS LEAGUE FINAL
26 MAY 1999
NOU CAMP STADIUM,
BARCELONA
....

BY OLIVER HOLT, FOOTBALL
CORRESPONDENT
27 May

Manchester United last night sated the magnificent obsession that has inspired their strivings these past 31 years when they pulled off one of the most astonishing victories in the history of the European Cup and finally emulated the great team of Sir Matt Busby.

In the end, it hardly seemed to matter that they had won the treble. That was almost forgotten in the incredible drama of a match that seemed to have been lost, of a triumph so sudden and shocking that it almost defied belief.

It had seemed that United's attempt to win the trophy for the first time in 31 years had slipped to an anticlimactic failure, that they had fallen to a sixth-minute free kick from Mario Basler, that Bayern Munich had maintained the hold that German football seemed to have established over its English counterpart.

But as the red digital clocks at either end of the Nou Camp here showed that 90 minutes were up and Alex Ferguson began to prepare for the misery of defeat and the brave words of congratulation for the Germans, the unbelievable, the unthinkable, began to unfold before his eyes.

United's desperation had already forced them to rely on a huge chunk of good fortune as they saw shots from Carsten Jancker and Mehmet Scholl rebound off the woodwork. With injury time beckoning, Peter Schmeichel joined the rest of the United team in the penalty area as David Beckham prepared to take a corner.

It was cleared only to the edge of the box and when Ryan Giggs volleyed it back in, Teddy Sheringham, a second-half substitute, side footed it into the corner of the net. United went wild; Bayern could not believe it.

Yet two minutes later, events took a surreal turn. Beckham took another corner, Sheringham flicked it on and Ole Gunnar Solskjaer, who had been on the pitch for only eight minutes, hooked it into the roof of the net.

The Bayern players stood disbelieving as United fell into ecstasy. A few seconds later, the final whistle went, the Germans flung themselves to the floor in utter despair and the victory was complete.

Even United could scarcely believe it, but, when they wake this morning, they will know that they are the first English team for 15 years to lift the European Cup and that they have finally dragged themselves out of the shadow of Busby, George Best and Sir Bobby Charlton.

They are their own men now, they have gone from excellence to greatness, they will be feted as the most resilient, adventurous English side of all time. They have developed a reputation for coming back from the dead, but this was beyond anything we could have expected.

Now, we will talk about the moment when Sheringham scored, about the disbelief at Solskjaer's strike in the same breath as we talk about Best's goal against Benfica at Wembley all those years ago. Nothing could equal the drama of what United achieved here.

From before the start, the atmosphere surrounding the game had been laden with the weight of history and expectation. Eric Cantona sauntered around the white marquees that ringed the stadium, Charlton sat nervously in the stands with the rest of the United directors.

In the opening minutes, in particular, it all seemed like a crushing burden on Ferguson's players. They looked as though they were frozen with tension, with the realisation of how close they suddenly were to the prize that they had sought for so long. Schmeichel, playing in his last game for the club, appeared to be particularly badly affected. Twice he fell into the grip of hesitation before his team had had time to settle and was forced into hasty, inelegant clearances that hinted at panic.

The United goalkeeper was also partly to blame when Bayern took the lead in the sixth minute. Passes from Jens Jeremies and Michael Tarnat had split the United defence and forced Ronny Johnsen into making a clumsy foul on Carsten Jancker, but Schmeichel arranged a long wall of red shirts on the edge of the area that should have been unbreachable.

Basler took the kick. He did not do anything fancy or attempt to bend the ball over the wall and under the crossbar. Instead, as Markus Babbel dragged Nicky Butt out of the way, he clipped it round the side of the United players so that it arrowed straight into the right-hand corner of the net. Schmeichel stood rooted to the spot.

It was then that attention began to focus on Ferguson's bold experiment of playing Beckham in the centre of midfield, with Giggs switched to the right wing and Jesper Blomqvist stationed on the left. In the first half, it simply did not work. It was not Beckham's fault. When he did get possession, he used it wisely, and well, spraying passes right and left towards Andy Cole, Giggs and Blomqvist, but far from being discomfited by the sight of Beckham occupying his unfamiliar role, Bayern seemed to be encouraged by it.

When United had possession, Bayern pushed Lothar Matthaus forward into midfield, where Beckham was already facing the formidable twin obstacle of Stefan Effenberg and Jeremies.

It was simple enough, but it had the effect of swamping Butt and Beckham and denying them the time or space to operate. When the German champions chose to counter-attack, United missed the doggedness of the suspended Roy Keane and Paul Scholes and Bayern sliced through them.

Oliver Kahn was forced to make a save for the first time midway through the half, when he punched Yorke's flick away at the near post, and Beckham nearly created a chance for Cole with a raking 50-yard pass that split the Bayern defence.

Still Bayern seemed the more dangerous side, though, still it was their counter attacks that carried the most penetration. From one of these on the half-hour, Jeremies burst into space, but, when Jancker back-heeled his pass to Zickler on the edge of the box, Zickler dragged it wide.

The start of the second half did not bring any change of fortune or incisiveness for United. Nine minutes after the interval, Babbel could have put Bayern farther ahead, but, under pressure from Johnsen, he glanced his header wide.

Two minutes later, Blomqvist wasted an excellent chance when he scooped a cross from Giggs over the bar from six yards. Nothing was working for United. Giggs tried to sell a dummy to Basler and saw it intercepted, Cole tried an audacious overhead kick and almost missed it completely. The Germans were proving far more resilient than other opponents this season.

Midway through the half, Ferguson bowed to the inevitable and introduced Sheringham for Blomqvist. Yet that did not turn the tide immediately, either. The more they pressed forward, the more desperate and vulnerable United became. In the 73rd minute, Schmeichel made an outstanding save from Effenberg after Jancker's first-time pass had put him clear. A few minutes later, after Basler's run had turned Johnsen inside out, Schmeichel was powerless as he watched Mehmet Scholl's delicate chip float over him. To the relief of the United section of the crowd, the ball rebounded off the post.

United had another lucky escape a few minutes later, when Jancker's overhead kick crashed off the underside of the crossbar. They forced a couple of opportunities of their own through Solskjaer and Sheringham, but the Germans remained defiant and resolute – until United's desperate last assault.

MATCH FACTS

Bayern Munich 1	Manchester United 2
Basler 6	*Sheringham 90+1, Solskjaer 90+3*

Bayern Munich: O. Kahn, T. Linke, L. Matthaus (sub: T. Fink, 80), S. Kuffour, M. Babbel, J. Jeremies, S. Effenberg, M. Basler (sub: H. Salihamidzic, 87), M. Tamat, C. Jancker, A. Zickler (sub: M. Scholl, 70)
Manchester United: P. Schmeichel, G. Neville, R. Johnsen, J. Stam, D. Irwin, R. Giggs, D. Beckham, N. Butt, J. Blomqvist (sub: E. Sheringham, 67), A. Cole (sub: O.G. Solskjaer, 81), D. Yorke
Referee: P. Collina (Italy)
Attendance: 90,245

40

GERMANY v ENGLAND

WORLD CUP QUALIFIER, 2001

Ever since the shocking World Cup quarter-final reverse in Leon in 1970, England had appeared to live in the shadow of successive German teams. All that changed in a World Cup qualifier in Munich in 2001 when England – under their first foreign manager, Sven-Goran Eriksson – administered nothing less than a thrashing.

"Owen's opponents dithered between tight marking and terrified retreat"

GERMANY 1
ENGLAND 5

WORLD CUP QUALIFIER
1 SEPTEMBER 2001
OLYMPIC STADIUM, MUNICH

BY MATT DICKINSON, FOOTBALL CORRESPONDENT

3 September

There were 17 match balls in the Olympic Stadium on Saturday evening but, as far as Michael Owen was concerned, the one inside his black bin-liner was definitely, conclusively and undoubtedly the real thing. "Do you want to touch it?" he asked, like a priest offering up a holy relic. One man stretched his arm out to feel the healing power of the most celebrated English hat-trick since 1966.

And, unlike Geoff Hurst, Owen did not need the help of a Russian linesman. "Supergau," was how Oliver Kahn – or Kahnt as he is now known – described the impact of the Liverpool wunderkind and, for the English listeners, it was quickly translated as the explosion of a nuclear bomb. "The scars will last for life," Kahn added, and it was possible to believe that, 30 years from now, Owen will still be scorching through the goalkeeper's restless dreams.

The striker was not the only difference between the two sides on Saturday but, for Germany, he offered the only way of making sense of an otherwise bewildering defeat. While a group of England players

World Cup Special
SPORTS DAILY
MONDAY SEPTEMBER 3 2001

8
PAGE
FOOTBALL
SOUVENIR
PLUS
8 MORE PAGES
OF SPORT
www.thetimes.co.uk/sport

Perfect ten: Owen, left, is congratulated by Beckham, the captain, on his hat-trick during England's momentous win in Munich. The result gives England a good chance of reaching the World Cup finals outright. Photograph: Marc Aspland

New world beckons England

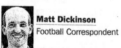

Matt Dickinson
Football Correspondent

IT WAS easy to spot the Englishmen in Munich's Marienplatz on Saturday evening. Instead of hurling bricks through windows, they were the ones whose faces were set in a quizzical and permanent grin. "As the third, fourth and fifth goals went in, the lads were looking at each other and saying 'what the hell is happening?'" David Beckham said. What hope the rest of us when even the players were struck with joyous disbelief?

Better than the 4-1 victory over Holland in Euro 96? More significant than reaching the World Cup semi-finals in 1990? Perspective is not easy when victories on this scale are so few and far between.

Comparisons are inevitable to fill the void left by decades of underachievement, but the true measure of England's 5-1 triumph in Munich on Saturday evening was that, in postwar history, it was wonderfully, deliriously, unforgettably unique.

Like Tim Henman at Wimbledon or the England cricket team in Australia, Englishmen had long accepted the certainty that our football teams go to Germany

and come back chastened by defeat. This was the first victory on German soil since the maximum wage for footballers became a healthy minimum and, after 34 years without a win in a competitive fixture, England have now beaten their old foe twice in a year.

"Winning was amazing but to do it in style was what really mattered," Gary Neville said and, aside from Michael Owen's hat-trick, the everlasting memory will be of England scouring victory with an arrogance that is said to be the preserve of the Germany team. Steven Gerrard twice twisted away from Dietmar Hamann with a matador's

flourish before thrusting in the dagger with a wave to the sidelines.

"Olé!" shouted the England supporters. Thousands of Germany fans instantly left their seats.

Not long after, a visitor entered the England dressing-room but, instead of triumphant pandemonium, he found the players sitting silently amid a sea of muddied boots and sweat-stained kit. Their eyes were all fixed to one corner where a television screen was replaying the highlights. It was as if they had never seen the goals before as they greeted each of the famous quintet with a spontaneous leap from their seats.

So what now? A knighthood for Sven-Göran Eriksson? World Cup victory in Japan and South Korea next year? The Swede was quick last night to remind the country that two victories are still required before his team even secures its passage to the Far East. "What is important is that it is now in our own hands," Adam Crozier, the Football Association's chief executive, said yesterday. "Who could have hoped that when we were beneath Albania last year?"

In the glow of Saturday night's triumph, the passing of Kevin Keegan and Wembley Stadium seemed to come from a sepia age. Humiliated under a biblical downpour, it was only 11 months ago that the national team was brought to its knees.

It has taken a Swede to rescue our football side and, far beyond the pitch, he leads the team with a quiet dignity that is winning this country back some respect. Informed that Rudi Völler, his German counterpart, had rushed away from the stadium because his father had suffered a heart attack during the game, Eriksson

quickly tempered his joy with human sincerity. "That tells you that there are more important things than football," he said. "It is a great evening for England but I always tell the players it is just a game."

One that has persuaded the country that England at last has a football team to be proud of, although the youth of Saturday's starting XI would indicate that this team might not peak until 2006. France and the other leading countries will have noticed the scale of England's victory with a raised eyebrow, but it will take considerably more to turn that into fear.

"It is always difficult to play a match after a victory like this," Eriksson said, and, when England play Albania at St James' Park in Newcastle on Wednesday, there is the possibility of a "small disaster" if a famous win is followed up with an equally memorable defeat.

"We have not even qualified for the World Cup yet, so I do not think people should talk about winning it," Eriksson said. They think it is all over, but this campaign isn't. Not yet.

Your World Cup paper

How Eriksson transformed England
Page W2
"We couldn't believe what had happened"
Gary Neville, page W2
Matt Dickinson's match report
Page W3
Beckham's command performance
Page W4
"The best result in England's history"
Bobby Robson, page W5
Ireland's glory; Scotland flirt the straw
Pages W6-W7
Germans scorned for life
Page W8

had gathered before kick-off and been lightened by the ordinariness of the German line-up, the opposition dressing-room was heavy with memories of what Owen had done to Bayern Munich in the European Super Cup. Paralysed by indecision, his opponents dithered between tight marking and terrified retreat.

On Thursday, Owen had reacted with irritation to a question about his 1998 slalom through the Argentina defence and now he has fixed a new milestone on the road to greatness in his young career. He will have to score a hat-trick in a World Cup final to equal Hurst's feat but, for those looking for parallels, it did not go unnoticed that he scored his third after 66 minutes. "He is very cold and very, very quick and that combination is a killer," Sven-Goran Eriksson said. It is his pace that makes Owen a special footballer but it should not be forgotten that two of Saturday's goals relied mostly on mental speed.

They helped to take his tally to ten goals in six games this season for club and country and, in this form, it is impossible to see what can stop him apart from his own hamstrings. Owen had brought relief just when England had needed it most against Finland and Albania in previous qualifiers and his opening goal in the thirteenth minute on Saturday was a mercifully quick response to Germany's hasty grasping of the lead.

Eriksson later remarked on how often his team begin matches slowly and they responded sluggishly to the early threat. Sol Campbell had left Rio Ferdinand isolated and the Leeds United defender was the helpless pig-in-the middle when Oliver Neuville nodded Sebastien Deisler's chip to Carsten Jancker to slide past David Seaman.

"The real reason we came back from a goal down was that the players believed we have a great team," Eriksson, the England head coach, said. A certainty that, in Owen, David Beckham, Paul Scholes and Steven Gerrard, they had all of the match's world-class players, is just part of the explanation. A team is only as good as its weakest link and Eriksson has built his side so it can hold firm under stress.

Against a side with wing backs, a 4-4-2 team always runs the risk of being outmanned in midfield but Eriksson solved that problem by convincing Ashley Cole and Gary Neville that they could play like Roberto Carlos and Cafu. Full of overlapping runs, the pair enjoyed their best games for their country and Neville was instrumental in the opening goal as he nodded back into the penalty area, where Barmby headed for Owen to hook the ball in.

Glitches remain. There is still a vacancy on the left wing, where Nick Barmby is a willing worker but not even good enough for

Liverpool's first team. At the back, Campbell needs more fine-tuning by Arsene Wenger. England's weakest defender, he will have been relieved to see Deisler's horrible miskick in the 22nd minute with the score at 1-1 and he was absent again in the second half when, with the score delicately balanced at 3-1, Jancker opted to head back across goal when he had a simple route past Seaman.

There is room for improvement but it seems almost treasonable to quibble after such a memorable, thrilling victory and it must be remembered that Barmby was the oldest outfield player at 27. While a reason for optimism, it is also a sign that England have a soft, youthful underbelly. The generation of Alan Smith and Michael Carrick may have to grow up quicker than they think.

One fears for Eriksson if any of his midfield succumb to injury but he knows that he has courageous men in Gerrard and Beckham, who was an heroic figure as he ignored his groin strain to take control of the game. Gerrard was magnificent alongside him after some early wobbles, and it was his thunderous volley with almost the last kick of the first half that put England ahead. "That made a big difference to come in at half-time 2-1 up instead of 1-1," Eriksson said.

Once Owen had added another two, with a sharp shot and a triumphant run through the heart of the Germany defence, and then Heskey, who deserved reward for his toil, had slid in the fifth when he ran on to Scholes's perfectly threaded pass, England could afford to start ridiculing their opponents. "I wasn't taking the mickey out of him, although it might've looked like that," Gerrard said of his elaborate double dummy of Dietmar Hamann. There was even the chance for Eriksson to give Owen Hargreaves a second cap and, coming in a competitive fixture, he is now officially English. If there was any time to declare his allegiance, this was surely it.

MATCH FACTS

Germany 1	England 5
Jancker 6	*Owen 12 48 66, Gerrard 45+3, Heskey 74*

Germany: O. Khan, C. Worns (sub: G. Asamoah, HT), J. Bohme, T. Kinke, J. Nowotny, D. Hamann, M. Rehmer, M. Ballack (sub: M. Klose, 65), R. Jancker, S. Deisler, O. Neuville (sub: S Kehl, 78)

England: D. Seaman, G. Neville, A. Cole, R. Ferdinand, S. Campbell, D. Beckham, S. Gerrard (sub: O. Hargreaves 78), P. Scholes (sub: J. Carragher, 83), N. Barmby (sub: S. McManaman, 64), M. Owen, E. Heskey

Referee: P. Collina (Italy)

Attendance: 63,000

41

CHELSEA v LIVERPOOL

BARCLAYCARD PREMIERSHIP, 2003

When UEFA decided to give a place in the lucrative Champions League to the top four teams in some leagues it changed the game's dynamic more radically than they might have intended. Instantly, finishing fourth became a higher priority than winning a domestic cup. On the last day of 2002–03 Chelsea met Liverpool with Champions League qualification the prize. The full impact of Chelsea's win was only appreciated several weeks later when the club was bought by Russian billionaire Roman Abramovich. His purchase had been contingent on the club being in the Champions League.

"The impression in the build-up to this fixture was that it was less a football match and more an extended financial transaction"

CHELSEA 2
LIVERPOOL 1

BARCLAYCARD PREMIERSHIP
11 MAY 2003
STAMFORD BRIDGE
....

BY OWEN SLOT
12 May

A £20 million party, you may have heard. The gateway to the Champions League. The most valuable victory in the history of the Premiership. Or ever, depending on which hyperbole you prefer. The view of Ken Bates, the Chelsea chairman, was that this was "the real Cup Final, not next week at the Millennium Stadium."

In which case, you wonder if someone forgot to tell Liverpool. Granted the opportunity of pulling off a rescue mission on a season of woe, they have now contrived to lose their last two games, dying out quietly, barely raising their voices, never raging like giants.

The impression in the build-up to this fixture was that it was less a football match and more an extended financial transaction. But put the cash on the table and dangle a ticket to Europe's high table, and still you don't seem to inspire Liverpool.

The best man in a Liverpool shirt was the man who got sent off. Steven Gerrard played with a determination that matched the occasion, passion and urgency to the fore, but his frustration was reflected in the increasing aggression in his challenges and two yellow cards in the last ten minutes were his undoing. After the second, a high foot left trailing into a late tackle on Graeme Le Saux, he didn't even bother to turn to see the colour of the referee's card.

And he didn't receive a word of criticism from Gerard Houllier. Quite the opposite, in reference to the attitude with which he plays the games, Houllier said: "I sometimes wish I had a couple more like that."

A couple more would maybe have brought Liverpool close. As it was, they didn't even get there. A draw would have taken the rewards to Chelsea, so you might have expected to see Liverpool hammering away at the opposition goal, but Michael Owen was silenced effectively by Marcel Desailly. He produced just one save from Carlo Cudicini in the first minute and thereafter the Chelsea goalkeeper was only required once again and that was from a 30-yard shot from Gerrard.

When it was done, Owen made straight for the tunnel but was pushed back onto the field by Phil Thompson. The travelling fans have been given little else this season, so a vote of thanks was the least they deserved.

Then the stage was left for Chelsea to do their own cup final day cameo. A lap of honour was applauded by an almost-full stadium, the camera lingering repeatedly on their foreign favourite, Gianfranco Zola, a reference perhaps to Bates's programme declaration that "today is tinged with sadness" because "we have seen some familiar faces for the last time". The brilliant Italian has featured regularly and highly in the line-up for Chelsea's supposed great summer sale, but now that their bank accounts look suddenly so considerably less red, gleeful shoppers may instead be disappointed.

After weathering a difficult first quarter of an hour, Chelsea maintained control for the majority of the game. The opening was certainly frantic. Liverpool went ahead from a curling free kick from Danny Murphy that Sami Hyypia nodded in at the far post but, two minutes later, Chelsea emptied any reserves of confidence that the visiting team may have been building by scoring a copycat goal, Desailly heading in a curling cross from Jesper Gronkjaer.

The winner, a splendid individual effort from Gronkjaer, came soon after. The Dane received a pass from Mario Melchiot and drove forward to the edge of the penalty box, brushing off a challenge from John Arne Riise and striking his shot before Djimi Traore could mount a second challenge. The strike was left-footed, low and curling fast round a melee in the box so that Jerzy Dudek was barely sighted until the ball was inside the right side-netting of his goal.

The chances thereafter fell more to Chelsea. Liverpool will not enjoy recalling Owen's miss from eight yards or the time that they did succeed in bundling the ball into the net, but only with the assistance of Milan Baros's right hand. Chelsea, for whom Melchiot hit the post, were more deserving of the huge rewards on offer.

"I wouldn't say it's a disappointing season," Houllier said. The fans would disagree. Houllier cited the Worthington Cup victory as evidence – which is scraping the barrel. He also said that refereeing decisions had let down their campaign – which left the barrel completely dry.

MATCH FACTS

Chelsea 2	Liverpool 1
Desailly 14 Gronkjaer 27	*Hyypia 11*

Chelsea: C. Cudicini, M. Melchiot, W. Gallas, M. Desailly, C. Babayaro, J. Gronkjaer (sub: M. Stanic, 68), E. Petit, F. Lampard, G. Le Saux, E. Gudjohnsen (sub: G. Zola, 73), J.F. Hasselbaink (sub: C. Cole, 80)
Liverpool: J. Dudek, J. Carragher, S. Hyypia, D. Traore, J.A. Riise (sub: B. Cheyrou, 75), E.-H. Diouf, (sub: P. Berger, 63), S. Diao (sub: E. Heskey, HT), S. Gerrard, D. Murphy, M. Baros, M. Owen
Referee: A. Wiley (Staffs)
Attendance: 41,911

ARSENAL'S SWEET HART LANE

RED-LETTER DAY

The Gunners secure the point they need against Tottenham Hotspur to win the Premiership. Matt Dickinson and Alan Davies report **11-14**

A MAN OBSESSED

Exclusive extracts from John Motson's new book of statistics **4-5**

05 MARK POUGATCH
06 THE MONEY GAME
07 TONY CASCARINO
21 GABRIELE MARCOT

EVERY KICK. EVERY PASS. EVERY TACKLE. EVERY SAVE. EVERY GOAL. EVERY BLADE OF GRASS. EVERY MONDAY.

42

TOTTENHAM HOTSPUR v ARSENAL

BARCLAYCARD PREMIERSHIP, 2004

Going through an entire league season unbeaten was a feat that had been achieved just once in England – by Preston North End's 'Invincibles' in 1888–89, the first season of league football. But in 2003–04 Arsenal mounted an unlikely bid to equal that landmark. Tantalisingly, fate gave them a chance to seal the title at the home of bitter rivals Tottenham Hotspur.

"... they have not only come unscathed through 34 matches unbeaten but done so playing some of the most breathtaking football this country has ever seen"

TOTTENHAM HOTSPUR 2
ARSENAL 2

BARCLAYCARD PREMIERSHIP
25 APRIL 2004
WHITE HART LANE

....

BY MATT DICKINSON, FOOTBALL CORRESPONDENT
26 April

Winning the championship at White Hart Lane was not without its complications for Arsenal yesterday, who wanted to stay alive long enough to celebrate their Barclaycard Premiership title. A team jig in front of their fans was brought to an abrupt halt when a scuffle broke out on a nearby terrace. Patrick Vieira led a swift retreat to the dressing-room to ensure that they remained unbeaten in all respects.

Inside, the Arsenal players will have found Sol Campbell, who had made the quickest departure of all to avoid antagonising the Tottenham Hotspur supporters. Jens Lehmann, too, after he gave away the ridiculous late penalty which, Arsene Wenger admitted, had spoilt the finale. As the final whistle signalled that the championship trophy would be returning to Highbury, the Arsenal manager slapped his side in frustration.

"That tarnished it at first," Wenger admitted, but it was not long before the annoyance was swept away by a tidal wave of delight and deep fulfilment.

"I don't want to diminish the other two [championships]," he said, but it was clear that of the three titles he has won in seven full seasons in North London, this was the most special.

Special because his team have pushed back the boundaries of the game, setting records almost every week. Special, too, because they have not only come unscathed through 34 matches unbeaten but have done so playing some of the most breathtaking football this country has ever seen thanks to masters of the game such as Patrick Vieira and Thierry Henry.

A special championship will become an historic one if they can just find the energy to match Birmingham City, Portsmouth, Fulham and Leicester City in the last four games. "No champagne, just water," Wenger said as he entered the press conference clutching a drink, "We are serious."

Even if they slip before the end, the title is all the more impressive because, after surrendering the championship to Manchester United last May, Wenger went out and spent less than £2 million. Most of that was on Lehmann, who will surely be replaced this summer on grounds of suspect temperament. The Frenchman will know that the challenge of Chelsea will be augmented by another £50 million-plus in new signings this summer but there are no reasons to doubt Arsenal's pre-eminence in England this morning. He has even made sense of the defeat to Chelsea

in the European Cup quarter-final, which is the single, significant regret. "You never forget a defeat like that in a big game but what I would say is that the European Cup has become a complete cup," he said. "One game not at your best and you are out. You can't base a season on that."

Yesterday was not the day for wondering why this team of many talents has yet to fulfil its potential in Europe. News of Chelsea's defeat away to Newcastle United found its way into the Arsenal dressing-room ten minutes before kick-off. A draw and the title would be theirs. Their resolve was evident when, with less than three minutes gone, Henry gathered the ball on the edge of his own penalty area and carried it over the halfway line. Henry found Dennis Bergkamp who crossed for Vieira to score. From the Arsenal box to Tottenham's net, the move had taken 115 seconds.

More flowing passing brought the second goal before half-time when Bergkamp saw Vieira's break forward. The France midfield player, who was immense throughout despite Michael Brown's valiant attempts to bring the maestro down to size, cut the ball back for Robert Pires to sidefoot an easy finish. The Arsenal fans were jubilant, taunting their rivals that it had been 43 years since their last title. Victory seemed assured for Arsenal even after Jamie Redknapp beat Lehmann in the

62nd minute with a cracking first-time shot from outside the area.

Although guilty of defending far too deep, Arsenal seemed to have survived Tottenham's second-half rally until Lehmann, overreacting as usual, pushed Robbie Keane after the pair had jostled for a corner. After booking both of them, Mark Halsey, the referee, pointed to the penalty spot. Keane scored and, from White Hart Lane's celebrations, you would have thought that Spurs had just secured the title themselves.

The final whistle went soon after and Lehmann stalked off to the dressing-room. "It has become a game to wind him up," Wenger said but the German goalkeeper has brought most of the trouble on himself. His team-mates must be tiring of his antics because they have been impeccably behaved since the shameful scenes at Old Trafford in September when they mugged Ruud van Nistelrooy after he missed a late penalty. "That was 28 games ago and we are still unbeaten," Wenger said. "That shows you how precarious it all is. The championship was closer than people think."

Retaining the crown for the first time is the task for Wenger and more records. Can his players match the 42-game unbeaten run by Brian Clough's Nottingham Forest spread two seasons? Worryingly for Chelsea and United, Wenger believes that the best is yet to come from this youthful, admirable and special team.

MATCH FACTS

Tottenham Hotspur 2	**Arsenal 2**
Redknapp 62, Keane 90 pen	*Vieira 3, Pires 35*

Tottenham Hotspur: K. Keller, S. Kelly (sub: G. Poyet, 79), A. Gardner, L. King, M. Taricco (sub: G. Bunjevcevic, 90), S. Davies, M. Brown, J. Redknapp, M. Brown, J. Jackson (sub: J. Defoe, HT), F. Kanoute
Arsenal: J. Lehmann, Lauren, K. Toure, S. Campbell, A. Cole, R. Parlour (sub: Edu, 67), P. Vieira, Gilberto Silva, D. Bergkamp (sub: J.A. Reyes, 81), R. Pires, T. Henry
Referee: M. Halsey (Bolton)
Attendance: 36,097

THE TIMES

No. 68397 ■ THURSDAY MAY 26 2005 ■ www.timesonline.co.uk ■ 55p

CHAMPIONS OF EUROPE

NINE-PAGE SPECIAL SPORT

British exports to Uzbek troops

British military equipment was used by the Uzbek troops who killed hundreds of protesters despite government promises that it would block arms exports to tyrannical regimes.
NEWS pages 6, 7

Student murdered

A "caring and creative" A-level student has been found murdered 500 yards from her home in northwest London days after her 18th birthday.
NEWS page 5

Film-maker dies

Ismail Merchant, the film-maker whose co-productions with James Ivory became a byword for lavish period dramas, died yesterday.
NEWS page 11
OBITUARY page 66

Olympic ejections

Beijing residents have been illegally forced to move home as the city prepares to host the Olympic Games, Amnesty International said. Those who complain may be jailed.
WORLD NEWS page 35

CAREER
New jobs section
EVERY THURSDAY

Car giant shake-up

General Motors, the world's biggest car-maker, could be about to sell its $10 billion residential mortgage business.
BUSINESS page 48

Henman beaten

Tim Henman can focus on Wimbledon sooner than he might have hoped after losing in the French Open.
SPORT page 79

'Why are Europeans saying "no"? It's the economy, stupid'
ANATOLE KALETSKY page 21

COMMENT 18	**WEATHER** 75	
BUSINESS 48	**TELEVISION**	
REGISTER 66	**AND RADIO** T2	

Breath testing lottery as death toll soars

By Ben Webster
Transport Correspondent

DRIVERS are up to ten times more likely to be breathalysed in some counties than in others, according to Home Office figures which reveal huge regional differences in police policy on drink-driving.

Road safety groups accused many forces of failing to take drink-driving seriously and encouraging drivers to believe that they can escape detection.

One in six fatal collisions involves a driver who is over the limit and drink-drive deaths rose to 560 in 2003, the highest level for seven years. But the number of breath tests is at its lowest level for a decade.

Many forces now focus on motoring offences that can be detected remotely. Speed camera penalties rose by more than 500,000 to 1.8 million in 2003.

Hertfordshire police carried out only 387 breath tests per 100,000 residents in 2003, compared with 3,384 per 100,000 in Derbyshire. West Midlands, Staffordshire, Northamptonshire, Gwent and Lancashire also carried out relatively few tests, while drivers in North Wales, Hampshire and Lincolnshire were far more likely to be breathalysed.

Hertfordshire has one of the highest road casualty rates, with 600 injuries per 100,000 people against a national average of 500.

The force said that it had failed to follow guidelines from the Association of Chief Police Officers which state that every driver involved in a collision must be breath tested. Only one in five drivers in crashes involving an injury is tested in Hertfordshire, compared with two out of three in Derbyshire.

A Hertfordshire police spokesman initially claimed that drivers in the county were less likely to drink-drive and therefore there was less need to carry out tests. But, after studying the figures obtained by The Times, the force revised its response: "We are holding up our hand to this.

"Over the next year officers will receive training and guidance informing them that breath tests need to be conducted following injury road traffic collisions. In the past, officers have used their discretion at Continued on page 2, col 5

The triumph and glory

MARC ASPLAND

Steven Gerrard, the Liverpool captain, lifts the European Cup after the most remarkable of victories in Istanbul last night. Liverpool, who were 3-0 down at half-time, scored three times after the restart and completed victory over AC Milan by winning a penalty shoot-out PAGE

Good University Guide

T2 pages 8, 9

43

AC MILAN v LIVERPOOL

CHAMPIONS LEAGUE FINAL, 2005

After years of failing to match the achievements of Manchester United, Liverpool began to reassert themselves under the management of the Spaniard Rafael Benitez. In his first season at Anfield he guided them to a first Champions League final for twenty years where they faced an intriguing clash with fellow European heavyweights AC Milan.

*"The engraver must have been tempted to
get to work during the interval"*

**AC MILAN 3
LIVERPOOL 3**

AFTER EXTRA TIME: LIVERPOOL

WIN 3-2 ON PENALTIES

CHAMPIONS LEAGUE FINAL
25 MAY 2005
ATATURK STADIUM, ISTANBUL

BY MATT DICKINSON, CHIEF
FOOTBALL CORRESPONDENT
26 May

Trounced by half-time, triumphant by the end, Liverpool celebrated their fifth European Cup all the more joyously because of the astonishing manner of victory. Alan Hansen and Kenny Dalglish had said that success against AC Milan would surpass any of their achievements and, in coming back from three goals down last night, Steven Gerrard and his team-mates can be sure that they have earned their place in Anfield's hall of fame.

All the arguments about whether the second best team on Merseyside could call themselves the kings of Europe were forgotten in the drama of a remarkable match and a penalty shoot-out that concluded, famously, when Andriy Shevchenko – scorer of the penalty that secured the trophy for Milan two years ago against Juventus – was foiled by Jerzy Dudek, who was almost certainly playing his last game for the club. Last night's performance has certainly made him easier to sell.

The previous time Liverpool won the European Cup, 21 years ago in Rome, Bruce Grobbelaar had staggered around the goal line like a drunk. Dudek did not resort to tricks, but he did break all the rules by bounding yards forward for more than one of the spot-kicks. The saves from Andrea Pirlo and Shevchenko in the shoot-out were not his only heroics – Milan had enjoyed the better of extra time, but Dudek pulled off a miraculous double save from Shevchenko to take the match to penalties.

It is a shame that three of the past five finals have had to be decided on spot-kicks – this more than any other – but Liverpool's ecstasy was unbounded in the most extraordinary denouement since Manchester United's improbable comeback in 1999 to clinch the treble. A spectacularly see-sawing match saw Milan take a three-goal lead by half-time and Liverpool strike back with three in six minutes early in the second half.

When it was all over, Rafael Benitez passed into Anfield legend, his name chiming from the terraces more than any of his players', but it was despite rather than because of the manager that Liverpool overcame the odds. His decision to abandon the system that had worked so well against Juventus and Chelsea, dropping Dietmar Hamann and selecting Harry Kewell, was Ranieri-esque in its perversity. His players saved him.

Fitness was one issue given that Kewell was starting only his second match in three months, but as far as the Liverpool fans were concerned, so was character. "He owes us," one said of a player whose commitment has

been questioned on the terraces and by his manager. His withdrawal after 23 minutes, clutching his groin, was interpreted as desertion and he was jeered off the field.

It was no coincidence that the German's arrival at half-time, replacing Steve Finnan in a switch of formations to a five-man midfield, prompted the fightback that Carlo Ancelotti, the Milan coach, said was impossible to explain.

An unforgettable evening got off to a terrible start for Liverpool when Djimi Traore felled Kaka. Pirlo swung in the free kick that Paolo Maldini was allowed to meet with a hooked, right-foot shot. Dudek was not up to the job of keeping it out and at that stage it seemed clear why he will be replaced this summer by Jose Reina, of Villarreal.

It was a calamitous opening for any team, but particularly one with Liverpool's inexperience. Gerrard and Xabi Alonso worked hard to establish some stability, but in players such as Traore and John Arne Riise, they had team-mates who looked overawed.

Every attack from Milan threatened a goal in the first half and only marginal offside decisions delayed the second until the 39th minute.

Cruelly for Liverpool, it came from their own attack. Running at Alessandro Nesta, Luis Garcia believed that he had a strong case for handball against the Italy defender, but the referee waved play on. Seconds later it was nestling in Dudek's net as

Kaka fed Shevchenko, who crossed to Hernan Crespo at the far post for an easy finish.

Game over, it seemed, and, as if to confirm the fact, Crespo added another before the interval. Kaka's through-pass was superb and, after Crespo had sprinted behind Jamie Carragher and Sami Hyypia, so was the clipped finish. Benitez had been stalking a technical area the size of a tennis court, but by now he was rooted to his seat in the dugout, knowing that his team were in danger of being embarrassed.

The engraver must have been tempted to get to work during the interval. No one, least of all Milan, expected the comeback, which was inspired by Benitez's belated intro-duction of Hamann to add an extra body in midfield and give Gerrard more freedom.

The captain scored Liverpool's first, meeting Riise's cross with a looping header beyond Dida. Gerrard waved his arms manically at the great sea of Liverpool fans and they responded deafeningly. Many of them must still have feared defeat, but when the second goal arrived two minutes later, Vladimir Smicer beating Dida with a crisp shot from outside the area, their faith was fully restored.

Back came Liverpool again and when Gerrard charged into the area, the contact from Gennaro Gattuso was enough to knock the Liverpool captain to the floor. The referee pointed to the spot and Gerrard stepped aside to allow Alonso to take it. Dida saved his shot, but the Spaniard pounced on the rebound. Liverpool were back from the dead, but the game still had to be won. It was, unforgettably.

MATCH FACTS

After extra time

AC Milan 3
Maldini 1, Crespo 39 44

Liverpool 3
Gerrard 54, Smicer 56, Alonso 59

Penalties: AC Milan – Serginho missed, Pirlo saved, Tomasson scored, Kaka scored, Shevchenko saved. Liverpool – Hamann scored, Cisse scored, Riise saved, Smicer scored.

AC Milan: Dida, Cafu, A. Nesta, J. Stam, P. Maldini, G. Gattuso (sub: Rui Costa, 112), A. Pirlo, Kaka, C. Seedorf (sub: Serginho, 86), A. Shevchenko, H. Crespo (sub: J.D. Tomasson, 86)
Liverpool: J. Dudek, S. Finnan (sub: D. Hamann, HT), S. Hyypia, J. Carragher, D. Traore, L. Garcia, X. Alonso, S. Gerrard, J.A. Riise, H. Kewell (sub: V. Smicer, 23), M. Baros (sub: D. Cisse, 84)
Referee: M.E. Mejuto Gonzalez (Spain)
Attendance: 80,000

the game

Monday May 30 2011

Made for each othe

**Messi and Barcelona
prove greatness on
Wembley stage**
Pages 2-10

**Allardyce set
for West Ham**
Page 11

**Final success
for Ferguson**
Page 12

RESPE

44

BARCELONA v MANCHESTER UNITED

CHAMPIONS LEAGUE FINAL, 2011

It is possible that no team in history has had more impact on the way the game is played all over the world than the Barcelona side managed by Pep Guardiola between 2008 and 2012. It was a style defined by brilliant, quick-fire passing, elusive movement and marvellous individual skills from the likes of Lionel Messi. In 2011 they came to Wembley to face Manchester United in the final of the Champions League.

"United found themselves comprehensively outclassed, with no antidote to the precision and pace with which Xavi and Andres Iniesta pass the ball through the middle of the pitch"

BARCELONA 3
MANCHESTER UNITED 1

CHAMPIONS LEAGUE FINAL
28 MAY 2011
WEMBLEY STADIUM

BY OLIVER KAY, FOOTBALL CORRESPONDENT
30 May

The great and the good of European football were at Wembley on Saturday evening. The gulf in class between Barcelona and Manchester United really was that vast.

Barcelona describe themselves as *"mes que un club"*, more than a club,

and this was more than a victory. This, their third Champions League triumph in six seasons, was affirmation of their greatness and, in particular, that of Lionel Messi and Xavi Hernandez.

Henceforth it is only degrees of greatness and historical context that are up for debate.

Barcelona are a great team. United, at present, are not. They were good enough to win the Barclays Premier League once again this season – and by a margin of nine points – but rarely did they scale the heights achieved in previous title-winning campaigns. That is not a reactionary appraisal but one that Sir Alex Ferguson and United's players heard throughout a strange season in which none of their domestic rivals posed a credible title challenge.

This was an altogether different kind of test for United. One consolation is that no team in the world can live with Barcelona right now. Another is that Ferguson's side reached another Champions League final and won a Premier League title in what had appeared to be a season of transition. His players took off their runners-up medals almost as soon as they were given them, but, at a time when Barcelona reign supreme, there is for once some solace to be taken in being the best of the rest.

How do you stop Barcelona? Not like this. This was the teams' second meeting since Pep Guardiola began his glorious tenure three years ago and, as in the 2009 final in Rome, United found themselves comprehensively outclassed, with no antidote to the precision and pace with which Xavi and Andres Iniesta pass the ball through the middle of the pitch and, as Ferguson conceded, no answer to the mesmerising quality of Messi.

It was possible to talk of Barcelona's three goals in terms of three lapses in the United defence – Nemanja Vidic and Patrice Evra losing track of Pedro Rodriguez for the first, the same players giving Messi too much space for the second, Michael Carrick and Nani contriving to assist David Villa for the

wonderfully taken third – but in some ways that would miss the point.

Barcelona do that to teams. Their presence and quality are so unnerving that they make good teams and very good players behave erratically, as was seen when Real Madrid lost 5-0 at the Nou Camp in November. Barcelona, as Ferguson suggested beforehand, appear a better team than the one that beat United in the 2009 final. Few would claim that United look better for the loss of Cristiano Ronaldo or for their failure to address the midfield deficiencies that were exposed in Rome. Once again Carrick, Park Ji-Sung and Ryan Giggs were powerless in their efforts to stem the unrelenting tide of Barcelona attacks. Once again United had no player capable of disrupting the rhythm of Xavi and Iniesta.

Messi's performance will live long in the memory, but Xavi was just as integral to Barcelona's triumph. Over the course of the evening Xavi made 141 successful passes. Between them, Carrick and Giggs made 56. Some like to look at such statistics and ask how many of Xavi's passes amounted to anything, to which an obvious answer is that he laid on the first two clear chances of the game, for Pedro and Villa, before setting up the opening goal in the 27th minute, showing impeccable timing and precision to release Pedro, who rolled the ball inside Edwin van der Sar's near post.

It is to United's credit that they responded and equalised seven minutes later with a goal that was Barcelona-like in its conception and execution, Wayne Rooney creating space by exchanging passes with Carrick and then with Giggs before sweeping a first-time shot past Victor Valdes.

Ferguson said that he "expected us to do better" after Rooney's goal had put them back into the game, but no other United player offered encouragement. Carrick and Giggs are at their most effective when dictating possession, not chasing it.

Park was all perspiration, no inspiration. Antonio Valencia was off the pace all evening. So, too, more damagingly, was Evra, as shown by the number of times that Villa, Pedro and Daniel Alves were picked out in advanced positions on the right-hand side.

Barcelona were insatiable in their desire to win back the ball when they lost it, but there are good reasons why they earn more praise for what they do in possession. Nine minutes into the second half Iniesta slipped a pass to Messi, who, 25 yards from goal, was inexcusably afforded what little time and space he needed to release a fierce left-foot shot that flew past Edwin van der Sar. Fifteen minutes later, after the Carrick-Nani mix-up, Villa curled a spectacular shot into the top corner and it briefly seemed that United could be heading for a humiliation.

In the end, it was not a humiliation, as Barcelona played out the final 20 minutes without so much as taking a shot, but it was humbling nonetheless. Rio Ferdinand suggested that United "gave it a better shot this time than last time", but it was not easy to side with that view. Although they at least scored a goal on Saturday, through a moment of high class from Rooney, that was their only notable attack after the opening six minutes.

From the moment United's early spark fizzled out, it looked a mistake by Ferguson to play with Javier Hernandez up front rather than an extra man in midfield. Perhaps a fit Darren Fletcher – or, stretching the imagination, Owen Hargreaves – would have made a difference, but on reflection it seemed that Ferguson had become hostage to the good form of his team and of Hernandez over the final weeks of the season, leading him to opt for a more cavalier approach when previously the instinct would have been for caution.

Barcelona, though, are a great team – even better than they were two years ago. The terrifying thought for the rest of Europe is that they and Messi threaten to get better still.

MATCH FACTS

Barcelona 3	Manchester United 1
Pedro 27, Messi 54, Villa 69	*Rooney 34*

Barcelona: V. Valdes, D. Alves (sub: C. Puyol, 88), J. Mascherano, G. Pique, A. Abidal, S. Busquets, Xavi, A. Iniesta, D. Villa (sub: S. Keita, 86), L. Messi, Pedro (sub: I. Afellay, 90+2).
Manchester United: E. van der Sar, Fabio (sub: Nani, 69), R. Ferdinand, N. Vidic, P. Evra, A. Valencia, M. Carrick (sub: P. Scholes, 77), R. Giggs, P. Ji-Sung, W. Rooney, J. Hernandez
Referee: V. Kassai (Hungary)
Attendance: 87,695

45

BARCELONA v CHELSEA

CHAMPIONS LEAGUE SEMI-FINAL, 2012

Backed by Roman Abramovich's millions, Chelsea became one of the most consistently successful clubs in England in the second half of the Noughties. But the Champions League that the owner craved remained elusive and that did not seem likely to change when they took a slender 1-0 lead to Barcelona in the second leg of the 2012 semi-final.

"It was a triumph of bloody-minded defiance against truly overwhelming odds"

BARCELONA 2
CHELSEA 2

CHELSEA WIN 3-2 ON AGGREGATE

CHAMPIONS LEAGUE
SEMI-FINAL, SECOND LEG
24 APRIL 2012
NOU CAMP STADIUM

BY OLIVER KAY, FOOTBALL CORRESPONDENT
25 April

Amazing, just amazing. Chelsea did more than reach the Champions League final last night, in the most trying of circumstances, against a Barcelona team widely lauded as the best in a generation, they defied logic, somehow standing firm against wave upon wave of attacks, before Fernando Torres scored the most cathartic of goals in stoppage time.

To progress to the final by any means would be an incredible feat in a turbulent season. To do so at Barcelona's expense, after John Terry's idiotic sending-off left them to play most of the game a man short, was a breathtaking achievement; a triumph of bloody-minded defiance against truly overwhelming odds. And for Torres to score the decisive goal, after 15 wretched months at Chelsea, made the sweetest of triumphs even sweeter.

Victory came at a heavy personal cost, with Branislav Ivanovic, Raul Meireles and Ramires picking up bookings that mean they, like Terry, miss the final. But it was that kind of night, those yellow cards feeling like acts of self-sacrifice for the greater good.

It was truly extraordinary. You could cite all manner of statistics to illustrate the one-sided nature of the contest – for example, Xavi Hernandez completed 161 passes, 67 more than the entire Chelsea team – but only one statistic matters.

Somehow, with a supremely dogged defensive display, Roberto Di Matteo's players had forced themselves into a winning position through an away goal by Ramires even before Torres raced clear to put the matter beyond doubt.

In Barcelona, they will call it anti-football. Well, they can. It was not a victory for pure football, but how else were Chelsea expected to beat Pep Guardiola's multi-talented team than by trying to suffocate them with ten men behind the ball? It has worked before for Jose Mourinho's Real Madrid, but, if anything the blueprint for last night's triumph was the way Inter Milan, coached at the time by Mourinho, overcame Barcelona in almost identical circumstances in the 2010 semi-finals.

Di Matteo deserves huge credit not just for the game plan, but also turning Chelsea into a team again. When they lost 3-1 away to Napoli two months ago, in the dire final weeks of Andre Villas-Boas's tenure, they looked the antithesis of a team.

Last night they were exemplary, from Petr Cech in goal to a makeshift back four in which Ivanovic excelled, to the tireless scrapping of Frank Lampard and his team-mates in midfield to Didier Drogba, who started off as the loneliest of lone strikers and ended up an auxiliary left back before making way for Torres late on.

For Chelsea to produce a performance such as this, you would imagine that Terry would be the central figure, but his actions in the 37th minute were astounding in their stupidity. Chelsea had just fallen behind to a goal by Sergio Busquets and desperately needed to stabilise, not for their captain to take leave of his senses and leave them a man short, inviting a red card by thrusting his knee into Alexis Sanchez's back in an off-the-ball incident.

It was brainless and irresponsible and it left his team with a mountain to climb. With Gary Cahill having already succumbed to injury, Chelsea had Jose Bosingwa, a right back, and Ivanovic in central defence and Ramires, a midfield player, at right back.

When Lionel Messi released Andres Iniesta to score with a sublime finish on 43 minutes, to give Barcelona a 2-1 aggregate lead, you feared for Di Matteo's team.

Yet, incredibly, by half-time they had restored their advantage, leading on away goals after Ramires unexpectedly charged forward to beat Victor Valdes with a wonderful chip from Lampard's pass. Everything else – the two goals, even the opposing captain's red card – had been in the Barcelona script, but the Ramires goal certainly was not.

Barcelona had lost Gerard Pique to injury, concussed in a collision with Valdes, but, if anything, that helped them. To that point their 3-4-3 formation had been a little too narrow, but the introduction of Daniel Alves gave them some of the width they had been lacking.

Alves was in a central position when he seized upon Drogba's header from a Barcelona corner after 35 minutes. Alves passed to Isaac Cuenca, whose low cross was deflected by John Obi Mikel into the path of Busquets, who levelled the tie with a left-foot shot.

Then came Terry's moment of madness and soon it was 2-0 for Barcelona on the night, a crisp move through the middle allowing Messi to stroke a perfectly weighted through-ball for Iniesta to roll a precise right-foot shot beyond Cech. A Barcelona victory now looked inevitable, but the atmosphere changed with Lampard setting up Ramires for that lovely chip.

The second half was like a practice match, Barcelona's 11 men camped on the edge of the Chelsea penalty area with nine white shirts in front of Cech. Drogba's work rate was remarkable, but his rash challenge on Cesc Fabregas gave Barcelona a penalty after 48 minutes. This, seemingly, was Messi's moment, but he struck the crossbar. Was this really going to be Chelsea's night?

And so it went on for the entire second half, Barcelona passing and passing, but Chelsea putting bodies in the way. Clear-cut opportunities were surprisingly scarce, the best of them missed by Cuenca, denied by Cech, and Busquets, who shot over the crossbar.

With eight minutes remaining, Sanchez put the ball in the Chelsea net, but Alves was offside in the build-up and when Cech pushed Messi's shot on to the foot of a post, the belief seemed to disappear from Barcelona.

Torres had just replaced the tiring Drogba when he raced clear in stoppage time, waltzed around Valdes and rolled the ball into the net with a composure that made his previous travails at Chelsea feel like a trick of the mind. To quote a famous soundbite on this very ground: football, bloody hell.

MATCH FACTS

Barcelona 2	Chelsea 2
Busquets 35 Iniesta 43	*Ramires 45+1, Torres 90+2*

Barcelona: V. Valdes, C. Puyol, G. Pique (sub: D. Alves, 26), J. Mascherano, Xavi, S. Busquets, A. Iniesta, I. Cuenca (sub: C. Tello, 58), L. Messi, A. Sanchez, C. Fabregas (sub: S. Keita, 74)

Chelsea: P. Cech, B. Ivanovic, G. Cahill (sub: J. Bosingwa, 12), J. Terry, A. Cole, J.O. Mikel, R. Meireles, J. Mata (sub: S. Kalou, 58), F. Lampard, Ramires, D. Drogba (F. Torres, 80)

Referee: C. Cakir (Turkey)

Attendance: 95,845

46

MANCHESTER CITY v QUEENS PARK RANGERS

FA PREMIER LEAGUE, 2012

Like Chelsea before them, Manchester City suddenly became upwardly mobile after the overnight arrival of vast sums of foreign investment. It took them a while to adjust to their new-found status, but on the final day of 2011–12 they needed one more victory to become champions for the first time since the days of Joe Mercer and Malcolm Allison.

"The Argentinian beat Taiwo with his first touch, then, as history beckoned, smashed a shot past Kenny. Cue bedlam"

**MANCHESTER CITY 3
QUEENS PARK RANGERS 2**

BARCLAYS PREMIER LEAGUE
13 MAY 2012
ETIHAD STADIUM

....

BY OLIVER KAY, CHIEF FOOTBALL CORRESPONDENT
14 May

At 4.51pm yesterday it was all over. Long-suffering Manchester City supporters turned to each other and shook their heads. A few even walked out. They had waited 44 years for their club to be champions of England and, with time and ideas running out on a nerve-shredding afternoon, it seemed that the dream had died.

What happened next defied belief. Truly, it stretched the bounds of even football's credibility. Edin Dzeko's 92nd-minute header gave City a glimmer of hope. Then, in the fourth of five minutes of stoppage time, Sergio Aguero broke free and struck a shot that will reverberate through the ages.

Manchester United's grip on the Barclays Premier League trophy had been relinquished and City, for the first time since 1968, were champions.

An outpouring followed. This was catharsis. Some supporters swarmed on to the pitch to mob their heroes. Others wept or embraced. And even as the trophy was taken on to the pitch by Mike Summerbee and Tony Book, two of the members of City's previous title-winning team, some still looked stunned by a piece of drama that can immediately be elevated alongside Anfield in 1989, the Nou Camp in 1999 and Istanbul in 2005 as epochal moments in the history of this glorious, thrilling sport.

Roberto Mancini, the City manager, called it "a crazy finish for a crazy season". He was not wrong. This Premier League campaign has been a basket-case. If it was a television series, you might wonder whether the scriptwriters had lost the plot. And even before that late flourish, yesterday's plot at the Etihad Stadium included survival and an implausible comeback for Mark Hughes's Queens Park Rangers after Joey Barton, the former City player, was sent off in unedifying circumstances early in the second half.

If you wanted, you could shrug and say that money had prevailed, that City had been transformed by petrodollars from Abu Dhabi. City have indeed bought the title, but the alternative was to say no to Sheikh Mansour and remain mired in mediocrity. In any case, what happened in the closing stages yesterday was not about money. It was about a triumph of will.

At 91 minutes, City looked like a busted flush. They had dominated possession, but, like Barcelona against Chelsea last month, they had been smothered by an opposing team who defended with remarkable spirit and focus after their captain was sent off. QPR's resilience seemed to have denied City the title – and what a remarkable story that would have been, given that Hughes still believes that he should be their manager – but, when all hope seemed to be lost, Mancini's team mustered one final push.

As Vincent Kompany said: "Miracles do happen in Manchester – and this time it's on this side of the road." City had done, not for the first time this season, what United are famous for, snatching victory from the jaws of defeat. Spirit, unity and collective belief, the very attributes that seemed five weeks ago to have cost Mancini's team this league title, had won the day.

And what a day. It began with a mood of quiet optimism – that for once this would not be "typical City" – and turned to discomfort in the stands after half an hour as one patient build-up after another foundered on the edge of the penalty area.

The breakthrough came six minutes before half-time. Pablo Zabaleta had scored only six goals in a ten-year professional career, but his seventh looked set to go down in history as his shot was deflected into the air and over the line by the unconvincing Paddy Kenny.

Even with Yaya Toure lost to a hamstring injury, the second half looked set to be a procession, but three minutes after the restart QPR scored with their first real attack. Shaun Wright-Phillips hit a hopeful ball forward, Joleon Lescott produced a calamitous header and Cisse seized on the opportunity to beat Joe Hart.

Barton's moment of madness came on 54 minutes. He swung an elbow at Carlos Tevez, albeit seemingly in retaliation, but when the red card was shown Barton compounded matters by lunging at Aguero and squaring up to Kompany.

It was even more irresponsible than John Terry's red card in Barcelona, but, as on that occasion, the under-dogs produced a jaw-dropping response, with Armand Traore flying forward from left back and superbly picking out Jamie Mackie for a header to make it 2-1.

City dominated possession thereaf-ter, but as the tension grew they could only create half-chances. Some sup-porters clasped their hands together in prayer. A few walked out, unable to take the anguish any more. Then came the miracle. First Dzeko rose highest to beat Kenny with a header from Silva's corner, then, with one more goal needed, Nigel de Jong carried the ball forward and found Aguero 30 yards from goal. Aguero passed to Mario Balotelli and car-ried on his run. Balotelli turned and, as he stretched, poked the ball back into Aguero's path. The Argentinian beat Taiwo with his first touch, then, as history beckoned, smashed a shot past Kenny. Cue bedlam. Aguero had done for City what his father-in-law, a certain Diego Maradona, did for Napoli in the 1980s: bring uncon-fined joy to a downtrodden club. But before there could be romance yesterday, there was drama on a scale that had to be seen to be believed. Simply incredible.

MATCH FACTS

Manchester City 3	**Queens Park Rangers 2**
Zabaleta 39, Dzeko 90+2,	*Cisse 48, Mackie 56*
Aguero 90+4	

Manchester City: J. Hart, P. Zabaleta, V. Kompany, J. Lescott, G. Clichy, D. Silva, Y. Toure (sub: N. de Jong, 44), G. Barry (sub: E. Dzeko 69), S. Nasri, C. Tevez (sub: M. Balotelli 76), S. Aguero

Queens Park Rangers: P. Kenny, N. Onuoha, A. Ferdinand, C. Hill, T. Taiwo, J. Mackie, J. Barton, S. Derry, S. Wright-Phillips, R. Zamora (sub: J. Bothroyd, 76), D. Cisse (sub: A. Traore, 59)

Referee: M. Dean

Attendance: 46,000

47

BRAZIL v GERMANY

WORLD CUP SEMI-FINAL, 2014

Brazil were widely fancied to win the World Cup for a sixth time on home soil in 2014. But their progress to the last four was far from smooth, and there was something close to a mood of national trepidation before their semi-final with Germany in Belo Horizonte. What followed was one of the most extraordinary matches in the history of the tournament.

"The real effect of the opening goal was to plunge Brazil's players into a period of ragged, wretched defensive indiscipline that Germany punished in quite merciless, devastating fashion"

BRAZIL 1
GERMANY 7

WORLD CUP, SEMI-FINAL
8 JULY 2014
MINEIRAO STADIUM,
BELO HORIZONTE

....

BY OLIVER KAY, CHIEF
FOOTBALL CORRESPONDENT
9 July

It was a masterclass, a thumping, a humiliation. It was an extraordinary result that did not just secure Germany's place in the World Cup final but plunged Brazilian football into darkness as their crowd went from hope, to shock, to deflation, to anger, to derision and then, briefly, to respect for their awe-inspiring conquerors.

When Andre Schurrle struck the magnificent seventh Germany goal with 11 minutes remaining, the Brazilian supporters applauded, as if to say that they, of all fans, can recognise and appreciate the class that abounds through Philipp Lahm, Toni Kroos and the rest of this team. Then the mood darkened again at the final whistle as Luiz Felipe Scolari and his similarly beleaguered players faced the wrath that inevitably followed this pathetic, shambolic capitulation.

Germany were brilliant, breaking intelligently and clinically again and again to rush into a 5-0 lead inside an astonishing first half-hour. As magnificently as Germany played, though, scoring through Thomas

Muller, Miroslav Klose, Kroos, Kroos again and Sami Khedira, their task was facilitated by a complete defensive breakdown from this Brazil team who, following their hearts and losing their heads, suffered the implosion that had never seemed far away during this World Cup.

David Luiz, captain for the night, had held aloft the shirt of the unfortunate, absent Neymar beforehand. It was a nice touch, but what a joke. Luiz evidently has no more self-awareness than positional awareness, because Thiago Silva was a far bigger loss to Brazil. In the absence of their best defender and their star centre forward, Scolari's team were hopeless and Luiz confirmed his popular billing as the symbol of this Brazil team – a symbol of over-exuberant, brainless defending.

Do not let anyone tell you that Muller's 11th-minute goal silenced the home crowd. It did not. Stunned disbelief did not take hold until the third goal arrived from Kroos all of 13 minutes later. The real effect of the opening goal was to plunge Brazil's players into a period of ragged, wretched defensive indiscipline that Germany punished in quite merciless, devastating fashion.

There was less than three minutes – 179 seconds, to be precise – between Germany's second goal, scored by Klose in the 23rd minute, and the fourth, which was Kroos's second. Khedira then made it 5-0 before the half-hour mark. No team had ever scored five goals in the first 29 minutes

of a World Cup match. Not only had Germany made history, but they had done so against Brazil on Brazilian soil.

It was wonderful stuff from Germany, with Kroos, Khedira and Lahm particularly outstanding, but the way they continually broke from midfield, playing their way into goal-scoring positions with one-touch and two-touch passes, it was as if they were playing against mannequins on the training pitch – except, of course, that Luiz will never stay still like a mannequin. He just charged around ineptly, his heart ruling his head, conforming to Gary Neville's description of a player who looks like he is "being controlled by a ten-year-old on a PlayStation."

There might be a small measure of sympathy for Luiz over the first goal, as his run was blocked off cynically by Klose, but what does it say of the Brazil defender and his fellow ball-watchers that they were reliant on their captain to cover that kind of distance to reach Muller, who had merely hung back to the far post, no more than eight yards out? From Kroos's corner, Muller produced a side-foot finish that put Germany 1-0 up and sent Brazil towards turmoil.

When Marcelo galloped forward into the penalty area, he was tackled superbly by Lahm. Marcelo was enraged, as if there had been some wild injustice, and some shoving ensued. Brazil, caught up in the occasion, were about to descend into self-destruction.

Midway through the first half, a crossfield ball from Lahm was missed by Fernandinho. Muller's lay-off sent Klose through and, while the forward's first effort was saved by Julio Cesar, he scored with the rebound to make it 2-0. To compound Brazilian pain, Klose's goal saw him break Ronaldo's record as the all-time highest World Cup goalscorer.

Within six minutes it had gone from 2-0 to 5-0. Lahm's cross was scuffed by Muller into the path of Kroos, who scored with a wonderful left-foot shot; Kroos then got his second, dispossessing Fernandinho and stroking the ball home after an exchange of passes with Khedira; Khedira then got the goal he richly deserved, teed up by Ozil after Luiz, in true PlayStation mode, had conceded possession and then charged 20 yards to be beaten to the ball by Mats Hummels.

It took until half-time for the Brazil supporters to express their disapproval, but they booed their team back onto the pitch for the second half.

By the hour mark, the locals had turned – horribly – on Fred. An immobile, unrefined centre forward, unbefitting the Brazil No 9 shirt. Scolari has chosen to build a team around brute strength and physical and emotional intensity. Fred's clunky touch is one symptom – not a cause – of their failings.

Luiz continued to defend as if ... well, defending really is not the word. He was dozing or absent again when Schurrle made it 6-0 on 69 minutes after a patient build-up down the right side, with Kroos and Ozil combining to play Lahm into the crossing position. Schurrle got his second ten minutes later, lashing the ball in off the crossbar, with again among those culpable, and it was then that the applause came.

Brazil somehow had the audacity to claim the last word, but Oscar's 90th-minute goal cannot possibly be called a consolation. The humiliation and Germany's superiority was far, far too great for that.

MATCH REPORT

Brazil 1	**Germany 7**
Oscar 90	*Mueller 11, Klose 23, Kroos 24 26,*
	Khedira 29, Schurrle 69 79

Brazil: J. Cesar, Maicon, D. Luiz, Dante, Marcelo, L. Gustavo, Fernandinho (sub: Paulinho, HT) Bernard, Oscar, Hulk (sub: Ramires, HT), Fred (sub: Willian, 69)
Germany: M. Neuer, P. Lamm, J. Boateng, M. Hummels (sub: P. Mertesacker, HT), B. Howedes, B. Schweinsteiger, T. Kroos, S. Khedira (sub: J. Draxler, 76), M. Ozil, T. Muller, M. Klose (sub: Schurrle, 58)
Referee: M. Rodriguez (Mexico)
Attendance: 58,141

48

MANCHESTER CITY v LEICESTER CITY

FA PREMIER LEAGUE, 2016

The conventional wisdom was that romance was dead in football, killed off by the super-rich clubs who annexed the top prizes. Then along came Leicester City – managed by the endearingly dotty Claudio Ranieri – and a gloriously unlikely title challenge. Almost everyone expected them to implode at some point but there was no sign of nerves by early February when they faced title rivals Manchester City in what was expected to be a pivotal 90 minutes.

"Manchester City looked like the championship chasing novices, Leicester the seasoned pros at this sort of thing"

MANCHESTER CITY 1
LEICESTER CITY 3

BARCLAYS PREMIER LEAGUE
6 FEBRUARY 2016
ETIHAD STADIUM

BY JAMES DUCKER
8 February

For a club that are climbing a mountain most imagined would be impossible to scale, Claudio Ranieri's analogy after watching his wonderfully fast and furious Leicester City crush their closest title challengers was as apt as it was evocative.

"It's important for us to concentrate and keep our feet on the ground," the Leicester manager said. "It's the first time in their lives that they are doing something special. So it's important not to look down or behind you. Like a climber, you need to look up. If you look down, you go, 'Ooof! My God, look where we are!' But how do you keep their feet on the ground? "I know how," Ranieri added. "Because we made a lot of mistakes and when we come back to the training ground I tell them the mistakes they made."

If Leicester made "a lot of mistakes" at the Etihad Stadium on Saturday, it is hard to know where that leaves Manchester City. Leicester were supposed to be feeling queasy by now in the rarefied air at the summit of the Barclays Premier League, but if anyone was buckling under the stresses and strains of the title race, it was Manuel Pellegrini's dysfunctional team. Manchester City looked like the championship chasing novices, Leicester the seasoned pros at this sort of thing.

Ranieri acknowledged that the pressure could become a factor the closer to the finishing line his team get. "It could be a problem but it's important for us to maintain our calm," he said. Yet, for the moment at least, it is Leicester's more gilded rivals who are stumbling. "Of course they're nervous but it doesn't matter to me, it's not my problem," the Italian said, with a cheery shrug of the shoulders.

It is interesting to note that Ranieri believes that the experience of last season, when Leicester won seven of their last nine league games under Nigel Pearson to avert what had seemed near certain relegation in late March, has helped his players to cope with their extraordinary exploits at the opposite end of the table. The pressure at that time, Ranieri says, was greater than what they face now.

"Yes, because last season was a big, big pressure for them," he said. "Now they can remember the pressure they faced, they can smell how it was and stay calm this season. I don't know exactly if the pressure was bigger last season but I would think 'yes' because if you don't survive and go down it's difficult to come back. That is helping the spirit now.

"The pressure was when we started out because our goal was to maintain our position in the Premier League but now the pressure is on the other teams who have spent a lot of money to win the Premier League, the Champions League."

Leicester were better in every department at the Etihad. Their movement was faster, sharper, they were quicker and stronger in the tackles, their passing brisker and more penetrative, they were better organised, more composed and concentrated and, crucially, they simply wanted it more. Nowhere were those contrasting levels of desire better illustrated than in the duels between Robert Huth and Martin Demichelis for the first and third goals.

Actually, it was not so much a duel as a mismatch, a metaphor really for the game as a whole. Huth's determination to get to the ball first to turn home Riyad Mahrez's free kick, albeit with the help of a deflection, after just three minutes shamed Demichelis.

And by the time Christian Fuchs whipped over a corner on the hour that Huth rose above the stationary Demichelis to head home, the Manchester City defender seemed to have concluded that it was a battle he would not win.

Individually and collectively, are Manchester City unable or simply unwilling to do the ugly, defensive basics? The back four, embodied by the hapless Demichelis and Nicolas Otamendi, were risible, but Fernandinho spent the afternoon chasing shadows and Yaya Toure looked in need of an extended leave of absence before the captain was mercifully withdrawn just seven minutes into the second half.

The sight of the Ivory Coast midfielder trotting back, while Fernandinho and Fabian Delph at least tried to race back as Mahrez spearheaded one of Leicester's many high speed counter-attacks in the first half, warranted an inquest of its own.

There would be no place for that in Pep Guardiola's Manchester City.

Watching Manchester City get picked off time and again on the break, one would have thought that Pellegrini had no idea of Leicester's strengths. The home team never got close to cutting off the source of Leicester's counterattacks. All afternoon, the outstanding Danny Drinkwater, Marc Albrighton and Mahrez played balls in behind Demichelis for Jamie Vardy, who signed a new three-and-a-half-year contract with the club yesterday, to chase with characteristic relish.

As for Otamendi, has no one at Manchester City pulled him aside yet to ask why he repeatedly commits one of the cardinal sins of defending by needlessly going to ground, although should that really need stating to a centre back who cost £32 million? Leicester's brilliant second goal was a catalogue of errors from Manchester City's perspective but amateur defenders across the country winced when Otamendi dived in at the feet of Mahrez, who scooped the ball over his witless opponent before sidestepping another Argentinian, Demichelis, to fire in.

It was Manchester City's sixth defeat in the league this season. Blackburn Rovers are the only team in the Premier League era to have won the title after losing seven matches so it underlines how slim the margins have become for Pellegrini's side. Moreover, they have taken just three points from a possible 21 against opponents in the top six this term, which does not augur well ahead of the visit of Tottenham Hotspur on Sunday. There is quality in this City squad but do they come close to mirroring the appetite and application that infuses Leicester?

MATCH FACTS

Manchester City 1	**Leicester City 3**
Aguero 87	*Huth 3 60, Mahrez 48*

Manchester City: J. Hart, P. Zabaleta, N. Otamendi, M. Demichelis, A. Kolarov, F. Delph (sub: K. Iheanacho, 52), Fernandinho, Y. Toure (sub: Fernando, 52), R. Sterling, S. Aguero, D. Silva (sub: B. Celina, 77)
Leicester City: K. Schmeichel, D. Simpson, W. Morgan, R. Huth, C. Fuchs, R. Mahrez (sub: D. Gray, 77), N. Kante, D. Drinkwater, M. Albrighton (sub: N. Dyer, 86), S. Okazaki (sub: L. Ulloa, 81), J. Vardy
Referee: M. Atkinson (Yorkshire)
Attendance: 54,693

In association with

THE TIMES

All the action from the Euros

EURO 2016 SPECIAL

the game

Tuesday June 28 20

Lowest of the low

Henry Winter, Matt Dickinson,
Oliver Kay and Tony Cascarino on
England's most shameful defeat P2–8

49

ENGLAND v ICELAND

EUROPEAN CHAMPIONSHIP ROUND OF 16, 2016

The build-up to major tournaments was no longer accompanied by overheated predictions about England's prospects but, with a young team, there was justifiable expectation that England could make an impact at the 2016 European Championship in France. Their group displays were unconvincing, but a last 16 tie with minnows Iceland seemed to offer a comfortable passage to the quarter-finals.

"Maybe England were intoxicated by taking the lead. Maybe they are just not very good. Maybe they had not been paying attention in team meetings."

ENGLAND 1
ICELAND 2

EUROPEAN CHAMPIONSHIP
ROUND OF 16
27 JUNE 2016
ALLIANZ RIVIERA, NICE

BY HENRY WINTER,
CHIEF FOOTBALL WRITER
28 June

Nothing in England's 144-year history compares to this ignominy. Nothing. Not even losing to the United States in Belo Horizonte in 1950. Not even the Wembley draw with Poland in 1973. Not even the defeats by Norway in 1981 and 1993. Not even that wretched night at Windsor Park in 2005. England's 959th game was the nadir. This was a disgrace.

This was the worst because of the huge investment in resources the FA had put into preparing England for these Euros at a time when they were laying off staff. This was the worst because England do have talented players, like Harry Kane, who under-performed here. They were shadows of their strong club selves.

This was the worst because of the immense support who managed to find tickets, sort travel and plead with loved ones, employers and probably bank managers to make it to Nice's

Allianz Riviera in time and then be treated to a display lacking organisation, belief and commitment.

At the final whistle, as the Icelandic hordes were singing "England's going home", the patience of the England supporters finally snapped. Jeers and boos poured forth like bile from a broken sewer. "You're not fit to wear the shirt," came the chant, time and again. Incipient revolution filled the Riviera air. After showing restraint at the World Cup in Brazil, they finally let rip here and those players fully deserved the catcalls.

England were so predictable, playing similar passes time and again, playing into Iceland's hands time and again. They were so profligate in possession, finding an opponent or a ball-boy rather than a team-mate. They lacked the leadership, ideas, composure and guile to break down the massed ranks of the Icelandic defence. They lacked a decent Plan A, let alone a Plan B. They lacked shape. It was all wearyingly familiar to seasoned England watchers. *Plus ça change*, as they say in these parts. Déjà vu. Encore.

The players deserved the chorus of disapproval. They will go back to their clubs, to their comfort zones. Roy Hodgson, their manager until he resigned, humiliated after the final whistle, was also deeply culpable. It was his decision to rest Wayne Rooney against Slovakia that so backfired on England. It was his failure to organise and inspire the players that proved so expensive. The Lions were lambs to the slaughter.

Departing the scene deeply chastened, England had arrived actually looking calm with Rooney hugging a laughing Jack Wilshere, Raheem Sterling and Daniel Sturridge walking together, smiling, sharing a joke, while Hodgson sauntered in, his jacket slung over his shoulder, like a City exec returning from an agreeable lunch in the sun.

"Roy Hodgson – he's taking us to Paris" sang the thousands of England fans. Optimism ruled. The Free Lions' fanzine even devoted a couple of pages, "Looking ahead to Paris, our quarter-final venue, if England win in Nice." Iceland had other ideas. More ideas. More hunger. More sharpness.

Yet England actually took an early lead. Sturridge floated the ball above Birkir Saevarsson, for Sterling, who had timed his run perfectly. Hannes Halldorsson, the Iceland goalkeeper, came flying out, rashly, ploughing into Sterling, presenting Damir Skomina, the referee, with the most straightforward of decisions.

The Slovenian pointed to the spot and Rooney accepted the responsibility. England have been practising penalties with greater frequency since reaching the knockout rounds. Even though Halldorsson guessed the right way in every sense, Rooney's penalty was too quick, too well-placed and it hurtled past the diving keeper for his 53rd England goal on the day he equalled David Beckham's outfield record of 115.

All seemed well. The supporters had enjoyed their day by the sea or in it. They were in good heart and voice, unleashing an almighty roar when Rooney struck. The autoroute to Paris seemed to be opening up nicely, invitingly. But they had forgotten that England's defence is weak, that the centre back pairing of Gary Cahill and Chris Smalling lacks conviction and concentration.

England themselves had forgotten about one of Iceland's weapons, the long throw of their captain, Aron Gunnarsson, whose popularity at Cardiff City will have grown even more. Maybe England were intoxicated by taking the lead. Maybe they are just not very good. Maybe they had not been paying attention in team meetings.

Hodgson had warned of Gunnarsson's threat, comparing the Icelandic captain's long throw to Rory Delap's. He'd explained it in terms that his players would understand. The ball came speeding through the warm Mediterranean air, demanding that a defender showed some strength of character, and attack it.

Kari Arnason simply wanted the ball more than Rooney, reaching it and flicking it on for the onrushing Ragnar Sigurdsson, outpacing Kyle Walker, to slide the ball past Joe Hart. Rooney lost his man. Walker lost his man. Smalling and Cahill lost their bearings. Iceland's supporters almost lost their voices such was their ecstatic reaction.

England were rocked back, their famously brittle confidence rattled again. Where was the leadership, the tactics, the organisation – even a semblance of it. Iceland were more of a team, well drilled in their 4-4-2 shape, each player knowing his task and working over-time. They kept closing down England players, drowning them in a sea of blue.

Walker ran into traffic. Sturridge saw a pass was picked off. Kane's shot was blocked by Gylfi Sigurdsson. Danny Rose had a pass intercepted. Kane tried to work the ball but Ari Skulason was too defiant.

England were creating chances but not taking them, a theme of the group stage. Dele Alli chested the ball down and sent a half-volley just over. Kane powered a drive over. England's radar was askew. Iceland's wasn't. Their fairy tale was a horror story for England. After 18 minutes, Iceland seized the lead. Sigurdsson's lay-off was judged neatly for Jon Dadi Bodvarsson, who controlled the ball calmly and played it across for Kolbeinn Sigthorsson. Again England were too sluggish, too anaemic. There were more holes in the England defence than in the shadow cabinet.

Smalling and Cahill belatedly slid in but Sigthorsson was too quick. He shot low and with reasonable power but Hart should have done so much better. Occasionally vulnerable down to his left, Hart was caught out badly. His left hand reached the ball but was not strong enough and the ball carried on over the line. "Iceland 2, Poundland 1" as some wit tweeted. England were being outwitted by 4-4-2 and occasional set-pieces.

England were staring into the abyss. Kane met the delivery with a right-foot volley that Halldorsson pushed over. Hodgson sent on Wilshere for Eric Dier. At the break, those watching at home were treated to a particularly ill-timed dandruff ad featuring Hart when England were at risk from having their heads separated from their shoulders in the land of the guillotine.

England hunted an equaliser but Iceland still threatened a third on the counter. Ragnar Sigurdsson almost scored with an overhead kick. The magnificent Iceland fans

loved it, never stopping singing. Outnumbered, Iceland were never out sung.

Iceland were so mature, so determined. Hodgson acted again, removing Sterling for Jamie Vardy on the hour mark. England fans hoped the cocky cavalry was arriving. Vardy did sprint through, charging down the inside-left channel but Ragnar Sigurdsson, the man of the match, put in a marvellous saving challenge, sliding in to steer the ball away from under the forward's feet.

Iceland broke again, Saeversson powering down the right, turning into the Cafu of the North Atlantic, and shooting just over. Gunnarsson muscled his way past Wilshere but Hart managed to save. Hodgson's last card was Marcus Rashford, the teenager replacing Rooney, but Iceland were too determined, too disciplined and England too abject. This was truly the worst.

MATCH FACTS

England 1	**Iceland 2**
Rooney 4 pen	*R. Sigurdsson 6, Sigthorsson 18*

England: J. Hart, K. Walker, G. Cahill, C. Smalling, D. Rose, D. Alli, E. Dier (sub: J. Wilshere, HT), W. Rooney (sub: M. Rashford, 87), D. Sturridge, H. Kane, W. Sterling (sub: J. Vardy, 60)
Iceland: H. Halldorsson, B. Saevarsson, K. Arnason, R. Sigurdsson, A. Skulason, J. Gudmundsson, G. Sigurdsson, A. Gunnarsson, B. Bjarnason, K. Sigthorsson (sub: E. Bjarnason, 76), J.D. Bodvarsson (sub: A. Traustason, 89)
Referee: D. Skomina (Slovenia)
Attendance: 33,901

50

LIVERPOOL v ROMA

CHAMPIONS LEAGUE SEMI-FINAL FIRST LEG, 2018

Liverpool's special relationship with the European Cup was revived again in 2018–19 when, under their charismatic German manager Jurgen Klopp, they reached the last four. Their opponents were Roma and the question was whether Liverpool's remarkable attacking skills could compensate for their defensive frailties.

"If Roma had done their homework on Liverpool, the dog must have eaten it because there was no evidence at Anfield"

LIVERPOOL 5
ROMA 2

CHAMPIONS LEAGUE
SEMI-FINAL FIRST LEG
24 APRIL 2018
ANFIELD
....

BY HENRY WINTER,
CHIEF FOOTBALL WRITER
25 April

Three hours before kick-off, hundreds of Liverpool fans, eventually more than a thousand, gathered on the roads leading to Anfield to await the team coaches. They held their flares high, sending plumes of red smoke into the sky and sung their new song about Mo Salah, running down the wing, Salah, Salah, Egyptian king.

They sang of Kenny Dalglish, Ian Rush, Steven Gerrard and Luis Suarez, beloved former players, but the loudest salute was for Salah to the tune of James' *Sit Down*. It was heard again and again before kick-off and with even greater passion when Liverpool's No 11 took control of this game.

Even an Italian back line could not live with him. Juan Jesus, a defender who has played for Brazil, was reduced to a nervous wreck. Salah kept running at Jesus, twisting him this way and that, wrong-footing him, exhausting him mentally and physically until the left-sided centre back looked broken. If Roma had done their homework on Liverpool, the dog must have eaten it because there was no evidence at Anfield. Roma seemed ill-prepared for what Liverpool, and Salah, would do. Jesus and Kostas Manolas seemed to have no inkling that he liked to cut in on to his left foot, his signature move. It brought his 42nd goal of the season.

Roma played a high line which was duly punished by Liverpool's pacey attackers. Salah's 43rd goal duly followed. Sadio Mane could easily have had a hat-trick in the first half-hour, while Roberto Firmino scored twice and had two assists, and would have been comfortably man of the match but for the majesty of Salah's contribution.

Only when Salah went off to a standing ovation with 15 minutes left did Roma believe and score two late goals. Jurgen Klopp can hardly be blamed for making the substitution as Salah had run himself into the ground and he could have risked injury in his 47th game of the season. It made sense, even if there had been a warning last weekend when West Bromwich Albion scored an equaliser after Salah went off.

Maybe Liverpool tire late on, drained by their pressing and sprinting, but there is a psychological boost for the opposition at the sight of Salah, the PFA player of the year, heading to the bench. Liverpool were frustrated to ship two away goals but will travel to the Stadio Olimpico with hope. Roma will point to the three-goal deficit they overturned against Barcelona in the quarter-finals, but Klopp will ensure there is no complacency with Liverpool, who showed against Manchester City that they can score in high-stakes away games.

The concern will be off the field, too, with a group of Roma fans showing their ugly side last night with a vicious attack on a Liverpool supporter after emerging from a side street.

Liverpool play in Rome next Wednesday but first face Stoke City in a Premier League game with important points at stake for a top-four finish. Klopp has to juggle his shrinking resources, especially in midfield. Emre Can is already out and Alex Oxlade-Chamberlain departed early on a stretcher here with a knee injury after challenging Aleksandar Kolarov. It was wretched luck for the Englishman, who has been in vibrant form of late, and the prognosis will be nervously awaited by Gareth Southgate as well as Klopp.

Georginio Wijnaldum stepped in and was outstanding with his ball-winning, and refusal to give the ball away. Jordan Henderson was again immense in Europe and James Milner excelled in midfield. Firmino was fabulous but this was the Salah show. It was one of the great, raucous nights at Anfield shaped by the Egyptian's brilliance.

His first goal was rooted in the determination of Henderson to turn the ball over in midfield, being too strong for Edin Dzeko and Kevin Strootman. Wijnaldum and Mane combined to work the ball forward to Firmino, who picked out Salah. Rather than advance to challenge him, Manolas stood his ground, clutching his privates. Roman statues were everywhere. Daniele De Rossi stood with his hands behind his back, fearing a handball.

Given a yard of space, Salah took full advantage and that wonderful left foot swept down and into the ball, sending it curling over Alisson, the Roma goalkeeper, and in via the crossbar. Out of respect to his former club, Salah kept his celebrations to a minimum.

A party raged through everybody else of a Liverpool persuasion. The Kop sang Salah's name with even greater gusto. Klopp turned away with a look of complete joy. Up in the smart seats, Dalglish high-fived Marina, his wife.

Liverpool were so devastating on transition. The move for their second on the cusp of half-time was started by Virgil van Dijk's clearance. Salah elegantly flicked the ball into the path of Firmino and hared down the inside-right channel before moving inside as Firmino returned the ball. Salah was too fast for the hapless Jesus, too sharp for Federico Fazio and too clinical for Alisson, dinking the ball over him. Salah's aim has been true so often.

Anfield was absolutely shaking with glee, and the half-time whistle was lost in a blizzard of roars. The poacher then turned goal-maker in the second period. Released by Trent Alexander-Arnold, Salah ran into the box and squared for Mane to score. Another pass from Alexander-Arnold, this time a clever flick highlighting the teenager's huge potential, sent Salah down the right. A drop of the shoulder sent Jesus the wrong way and a low ball was turned in by Firmino.

Salah did a pirouette to guide the ball around De Rossi and shifted it past Strootman. Liverpool added a fifth after Firmino headed in Milner's corner. Salah left to a standing ovation and Roma finally came alive. Dejan Lovren badly misjudged Radja Nainggolan's long pass, Dzeko chested the ball down and placed his shot past Loris Karius. Nainggolan's shot then caught Milner's hand and Roma screamed for a penalty.

Felix Brych, the referee, pointed to the spot and Diego Perotti was composure personified with his spot kick, sending Karius the wrong way. Salah looked on, knowing that Liverpool still have work to do in Rome. But they remain on course for the final in Kiev.

MATCH FACTS

Liverpool 5
Salah 36 45+1, Mane 56,
Firminio 61 69

Roma 2
Dzeko 81, Perotti 85 pen

Liverpool: L. Karius, T. Alexander-Arnold, D. Lovren, V. van Dijk, A. Robertson, A. Oxlade-Chamberlain (sub: G. Wijnaldum, 18), J. Henderson, J. Milner, M. Salah (sub: D. Ings, 75), R. Firmino (sub: R. Klavan, 90+3), S. Mane
Roma: Alisson, F. Fazio, K. Manolas, J. Jesus (sub: D. Perotti, 67), A. Florenzi, D. De Rossi (sub: M. Gonalons, 67), K. Strootman, A. Kolarov, C. Under (sub: P. Schick, HT), R. Nainggolan, E. Dzeko
Referee: F. Byrch (Germany)
Attendance: 51,236

ACKNOWLEDGEMENTS

A NUMBER OF people contributed to the compilation of this book and all deserve my sincere thanks. Bill Edgar, the inimitable *Times* football numbers man (statistician does not begin to cover it) was a brilliant sounding board and suggested matches I may otherwise have overlooked. Head of Sport Tim Hallissey was also always on call when I needed an answer to a question or a second opinion.

At The History Press Mark Beynon was always full of enthusiasm for the idea and in the syndication department at News UK I was grateful for the help of Robin Ashton and Rosie Grabowski.

Alan Miller and Sam Feast helped to source more recent photographs and, when I needed to go further back in time, I was assisted by Steve Baker and Mark Barnes and the picture services team.

Nick Mayes and Anne Jensen from the fabulous *Times* archive again proved absolutely vital to the success of the project.

I would also like to thank Henry Winter for providing the foreword and, of course, to all the *Times* football writers who were such a pleasure to work with over the years.

Finally, special thanks must go to my wife Marion Brinton and son Alex who have put up with me being even less sociable than usual.

ABOUT THE EDITOR

RICHARD WHITEHEAD WORKED for *The Times* for twenty-one years after joining the newspaper in 1995. He held senior roles in a number of departments, including obituaries and books, as well as spending ten years on the sports desk. He is the editor of *The Times on the Ashes* (The History Press, 2015) and *The Times England's World Cup* (The History Press, 2019). He is now an assistant editor on *Wisden Cricketers' Almanack*.